Strategic Pricing and Management Accounting

Management accountants should have a key role to play in developing and executing pricing strategy and policy. However, their historical focus on costing and operations means that their potential as business partners with marketing and sales professionals is easily overlooked. This book focuses on how management accountants can help key stakeholders in the formulation and execution of pricing policy and, conversely, on showing managers responsible for pricing decisions how they could be helped by management accountants. It equips management accountants with a unique overview of pricing theory, the practical, quantitative techniques they should know and the value they can bring to the pricing function.

The book analyses segmentation, value to customer, price-value maps, segmental pricing, product differentiation and dynamic pricing, with traditional economic theory, showing how these ideas have implications for management accountants and the value that they can bring to the business. Differences in customer value have been integral to economic theory for decades and price discrimination, the technique of charging different prices to different customers for the same or similar goods, is well-established. This observation provides the central core of this book. The methods of price discrimination are set out in detail, showing how management accountants can bring their analytical skills to bear in helping executives and pricing professionals take advantage of differences in customer valuation to improve profits.

The book provides a thorough overview of the field and offers a good introduction for researchers and students. Equally, the book shows managers, marketers and pricing professionals how management accountants can assist them in delivering better pricing practice.

David Dugdale is Emeritus Professor of Management Accounting at the University of Bristol, UK. He was awarded the CIMA Shield for services to the Institute in 2002 and a Lifetime Achievement Award by the British Accounting and Finance Association in 2014.

Routledge Studies in Accounting

5. **Auditor Going Concern Reporting**
   A Review of Global Research and Future Research Opportunities
   Marshall A. Geiger, Anna Gold and Philip Wallage

6. **Accounting Ethics Education**
   Making Ethics Real
   Edited by Alberto J. Costa and Margarida M. Pinheiro

7. **Business Models and Corporate Reporting**
   Defining the Platform to Illustrate Value Creation
   Lorenzo Simoni

8. **Accounting and Auditing Standards for Islamic Financial Institutions**
   Mohd Ma'Sum Billah

9. **Quality Management and Accounting in Service Industries**
   A New Model of Quality Cost Calculation
   Wojciech Sadkowski and Piotr Jedynak

10. **Artificial Intelligence in Accounting**
    Organisational and Ethical Implications
    Othmar Lehner and Carina Knoll

11. **The Financial Reporting Quality of Public Companies**
    The Cultural Dimension
    Katarzyna Mokrzycka-Kogut

12. **Strategic Pricing and Management Accounting**
    David Dugdale

For more information about this series, please visit www.routledge.com/Routledge-Studies-in-Accounting/book-series/SE0715

Strategic Pricing and Management Accounting

David Dugdale

Routledge
Taylor & Francis Group
LONDON AND NEW YORK

First published 2023
by Routledge
4 Park Square, Milton Park, Abingdon, Oxon OX14 4RN

and by Routledge
605 Third Avenue, New York, NY 10158

Routledge is an imprint of the Taylor & Francis Group, an informa business

British Library Cataloguing-in-Publication Data
A catalogue record for this book is available from the British Library

Library of Congress Cataloging-in-Publication Data
Names: Dugdale, David, author.
Title: Strategic Pricing and Management Accounting/David Dugdale.
Description: Milton Park, Abingdon, Oxon ; New York, NY : Routledge, 2023. | Includes bibliographical references and index.
Identifiers: LCCN 2022024752 (print) | LCCN 2022024753 (ebook) | ISBN 9781032224824 (hardback) | ISBN 9781032224848 (paperback) | ISBN 9781003272731 (ebook)
Subjects: LCSH: Managerial accounting.
Classification: LCC HF5657.4.D84 2023 (print) | LCC HF5657.4 (ebook) | DDC 658.15/11—dc23/eng/20220609
LC record available at https://lccn.loc.gov/2022024752
LC ebook record available at https://lccn.loc.gov/2022024753

ISBN: 978-1-032-22482-4 (hbk)
ISBN: 978-1-032-22484-8 (pbk)
ISBN: 978-1-003-27273-1 (ebk)

DOI: 10.4324/9781003272731

Typeset in Times New Roman
by Apex CoVantage, LLC

Dedicated to our grandchildren:
Isabella
Daisy
Daniel
Orla

Contents

Acknowledgements

The author expresses grateful thanks for the support of the Chartered Institute of Management Accountants for providing a grant to support the research that underpinned the publication of this book.

Thanks also to Alison Kennedy, who checked the manuscript with great care. Any remaining errors or omissions are, of course, the responsibility of the author.

Figures and Tables

Figures

Tables

Preface

This book has two aims. Firstly, to show how management accountants should have a vital role in supporting marketing, sales, HR and product development throughout the pricing process. This will also be valuable to marketing and pricing professionals: highlighting the contribution that management accounting and financial analysis can make to the pricing function. References to high-quality practitioner-oriented publications such as the *Harvard Business Review* and the *McKinsey Quarterly* will help those wishing to pursue specific ideas.

Secondly, the book aims to integrate traditional and behavioural economics with recent developments in pricing theory and practice. This will make the book helpful to academics, students and researchers needing an overview of price theory. Relevant ideas and concepts are supported by references to the literature that point to important sources for further, more specialised, reading.

Brief treatments of relevant economic models such as perfect and monopoly competition and the Cournot and Bertrand pricing models of duopoly competition are included where appropriate and aside their intrinsic interest, these models demonstrate the difficulty of pricing in even simple situations.

The reader interested only in practical pricing advice might reasonably skip Chapters 1, 2, 6 and 16. Such a reader is likely to find Chapters 13, 14 and 15 dealing with competitor and customer-related issues especially important.

The book requires limited mathematical ability and, where possible, examples are used to illustrate concepts and techniques. It is assumed, however, that the reader has a basic knowledge of management accounting, especially the ideas of contribution, break-even analysis and discounting to present value. Knowledge of activity-based costing would also be helpful although an example is included to illustrate the technique.

If this book helps management accountants, marketing professionals and students to see the potential of management accounting and financial analysis in the practice of pricing it will have achieved its aim.

David Dugdale
Bristol, May 2022

1 Introduction

1.1 Why another book about pricing?

There are many excellent books on pricing, so why do we need another one? Because a book that takes an overview of economic theory, pricing practice and managerial "how-to-do-it" advice is needed. This book focuses on how management accounting and financial analysis can help sales and marketing professionals in formulating and executing pricing policy. Management accountants should become business partners working with marketers and salespeople to understand markets, identify target market segments, set prices and last, but not least, ensure that pricing policy is implemented.

1.2 Limitations of traditional economic theory

When I studied economics, I naively assumed that there would be advice about how to set prices. Much later I realised that traditional economic theory does not *prescribe* how to set prices. Instead, it *presumes* that firms set profit maximising prices. The foundation of economic price theory is marginalism: prices will be set at the volume where marginal revenue (MR), the incremental revenue from another unit, is equal to marginal cost (MC), the incremental cost of another unit. A moment's reflection explains why profits are maximised where MR = MC. If MR is greater than MC, an extra unit should be produced, but if MR is less than MC, the output should be reduced, the profit maximising firm will therefore set MR = MC.

Traditional economic theory does not trouble itself with exactly how businesspeople will work out the volume and price that sets MR = MC. Instead, it is assumed that MR = MC and then economic theory derives a series of results relating to perfect and imperfect competition, oligopoly, monopoly, and other forms of industrial organisation. The underlying presumption is well-stated by Joan Robinson (1969, p. 56):

> if the conditions of demand and supply remain constant over a fairly long period, the monopolist will be able to hit upon the exact monopoly output merely by balancing marginal receipts against marginal cost . . . he can see

DOI: 10.4324/9781003272731-1

> whether selling a little more of his product . . . will increase or decrease his net gains.

For the moment it is sufficient to say that the explosion of practical pricing advice since the late twentieth century would hardly have been necessary if businesspeople did, in fact, set profit maximising prices.

1.3 Limitations of management accounting theory

Management accounting texts have a heavy focus on cost ascertainment and analysis, and this can be seen in the typical treatment of pricing. Variable product cost provides the minimum short-run price while a full cost, including product and facility-sustaining costs, is recommended for long-run pricing decisions. Most texts show how a cost-plus price can be calculated with the "plus" depending on the desired profit. If the markup is on variable cost, it must cover all the organisation's fixed costs as well as profit; if the markup is on production cost it must cover selling, administration and general costs as well as profit. However, no matter how calculated, cost-plus pricing is flawed, it fails to recognise the circular link between price and quantity. A volume assumption is needed to calculate the price, but the price affects the volume sold.

The "economist's model" overcomes this problem by taking account of both costs and demand. The demand curve allows calculation of marginal revenue (MR) and some management accounting texts show how optimal price and volume can be derived by setting MR equal to MC. This might be achieved by differentiating the demand and cost functions or by enumeration of profit at different levels of price and volume.

Of course, in both economic and management accounting theory, the derivation of profit-maximising price and volume is straightforward *if demand and cost functions are known*. Then simple examples can be used to demonstrate the technique. It is a different story in practice where firms may produce thousands of products and, even if demand functions can be estimated, they may quickly become out of date as economic conditions and fashions change.

Management accounting texts may mention target costing and pricing and there may be a reference to market segmentation and revenue management. However, there is scope for management accountants to do much more. My dissatisfaction is driven by the commonplace observation that prices vary dramatically for essentially the same or similar products and services. Everyday experience of airline, rail, supermarket, broadband and many more prices suggest that pricing practice has outrun typical management accounting treatments. My observation of everyday prices is complemented by supervision of countless MSc dissertations dealing with pricing in industries as varied as theme parks, bottled water, fashion shoes, cosmetics, coffee shops and Airbnb.

1.4 Developments in theory and practice

While traditional economic theory does not prescribe how prices should be set, since the late twentieth century pricing consultants have provided pricing prescriptions in abundance. The central advice is to *exploit differences in customer value*. Differences in customer value have always been central to economic analysis as in the "law of diminishing marginal utility" (each successive unit has less utility than the one before) and the downward-sloping demand curve (some customers will buy at a high price, but others have a lower "reservation price"). However, now customer value becomes vital not to *understand* demand curves, but to *exploit* differences in customer valuation so that companies generate profitable sales and, as consultants say, do not "leave money on the table".

McKinsey consultants were central to the development of **value-based price theory**. They developed the ideas of "economic value to the customer," price-value maps, the "pocket-price-waterfall" and the "pocket-price band". These techniques have significant implications for pricing in practice and for the role of management accountants. They form the core of Chapters 4, 5 and 14.

At the same time, in the late twentieth century, **behavioural economics** emerged as a reaction against the unrealistic assumptions of traditional economic theory. Instead of presuming utility-maximising, rational economic agents, behavioural economics is devoted to understanding how *real* human beings behave. Despite the objections of traditional theorists, behavioural economics has become an accepted and important branch of economics with implications for understanding customer behaviour and for price-setting. Chapter 7 provides an overview of developments in behavioural economics with specific reference to its implications for pricing.

As these theoretical ideas were developed, there was an important practical development: **"revenue management"**. Phillips (2005) traces this to the deregulation of the US airline industry in 1978 and the emergence of the low-cost carrier, People Express. If the dominant player, American Airlines, cut prices to compete, costs would not be covered, but, if it did not, market share would be lost. The solution was to meet the competition with low prices *but only if passengers stayed over Saturday*. At the same time, the number of seats sold at low prices was limited to ensure availability for full fare passengers just before departure. This was the genesis of dynamic pricing, varying prices over time to ensure something close to full utilisation, a technique subsequently adopted by hotels, cruise lines and car rental operators.

Two more important concepts must be mentioned: market segmentation and product differentiation. **Market segmentation** is a crucial stage in the value-based pricing project because, only by segmenting the market into groups of customers with different price sensitivities, can different prices be charged to different customers in accordance with their differing valuations. Chapter 3 provides examples of market segmentation in several consumer markets and Chapters 8 to 12 deal with the various techniques in detail. These chapters are the core of the book, providing managers and management accountants with the techniques needed to implement value-based pricing.

Product differentiation has become increasingly important for several reasons. *First*, the "value-based revolution" implies that customers' needs, desires and preferences should be identified so as to provide products and services that will appeal to different customers and exploit differences in their valuations. *Second*, Porter's (1980) seminal work, *Competitive Strategy*, identified "three generic strategies" that companies might adopt, and differentiation is one of them. *Third*, the internet and growth of information products have forced companies to differentiate their services. Failure to do so would see prices driven toward marginal cost which, in the case of some information products, would be close to zero.[1] *Fourth*, the rapid developments of behavioural economics and pricing theory led to concepts such as "extreme aversion" (the tendency to avoid the lowest and highest priced versions of the product) and the advantages of product differentiation through "good-better-best" pricing.

1.5 Structure of this book

This book combines the ideas set out earlier: segmentation, value to customer, price-value maps, segmental pricing, product differentiation and dynamic pricing, with traditional and behavioural economic theory. The aim, throughout, is to show how these ideas have implications for management accountants and the value that management accountants can bring to the business. Differences in customer value have been integral to economic theory for decades, and the theory of *price discrimination*, the technique of charging different prices to different customers for the same or similar goods, is well-established. This observation provides a framework for the book. The methods of segmentation and price discrimination are set out in detail in Chapters 8–12, showing how management accountants can use their analytical skills to help executives and pricing professionals take advantage of differences in customer valuation to improve profits.

Chapter 2 reviews surveys of pricing in practice. There is a consistent theme that emphasises cost-based pricing although careful reading reveals a more nuanced picture with costs, market demand and competition all important in price setting. However, there are two important limitations in many of the surveys. First, even recent surveys sometimes miss the important developments in pricing practice by failing to ask about price discrimination, and second, industrial pricing is disproportionately represented in survey research.

The focus on business-to-business (B2B) pricing is redressed in Chapter 3, which switches the emphasis to business-to-consumer (B2C) pricing. The prevalence of market segmentation and price discrimination is demonstrated with examples from the transport, consumer goods and service industries. The aim is to show how segmentation permeates consumer markets and to demonstrate how *price fences* are used to separate market segments.

In Chapter 4, value-based pricing techniques are introduced. While surveys suggest that cost-plus pricing methods are prevalent, since the late twentieth century, the idea of pricing based on "value-to-customer" has been increasingly advocated. The calculation is based on the differential value between a reference product and the target product with "economic value to the customer" for the target product calculated as the reference price plus the differential value. The technique is especially relevant in B2B pricing, and the DEC case study shows how economic value to the customer can be combined with the principles of segmentation to meet a competitive threat.

McKinsey consultants developed the idea of "value to the customer" and quickly extended it to the construction of "price-value" maps. Chapter 5 shows how price-value maps can be created by plotting perceived value on one axis versus perceived price on the other axis. The technique is a vital tool in analysing product position relative to competitors and it can be extended to provide a graphical representation of customer demand. Examples show how price-value analysis can help companies diagnose problems and the technique also has important implications for the management of industry prices.

Chapter 6 reviews basic economic ideas of perfect competition, monopoly and price discrimination. Confusion can arise because some authors refer to price differentiation and segmentation instead of "price discrimination" and this semantic confusion is unhelpful. "Price discrimination," the standard economic term, is used in this book and direct and indirect price discrimination provides the underlying themes in Chapters 8–12.

Chapter 7 reviews developments in behavioural economics, a branch of economics that studies how, in practice, behaviour differs dramatically from that assumed in traditional economics. Concepts such as loss aversion, the endowment effect, the (mis)use of sunk and opportunity costs, price anchors, decoys and extreme aversion have important implications for pricing policies in consumer goods industries. This chapter concludes by considering when management accountants should employ tried and trusted methods and when behavioural effects come into play.

Chapters 8–12 are the core of the book, dealing with pricing strategies, direct methods of price discrimination based on buyer identity and geography, and indirect methods based on quantity, product and time.

Chapter 13 deals with competitors, bidding and the regulatory framework. Pricing consultants emphasise the avoidance of price wars and, instead, the importance of managing industry prices (upwards). This can suggest collusion with competitors, a practice that must be avoided. Regulatory bodies are introducing increasingly draconian penalties that can see individuals that contravene regulations go to prison.

Chapters 14 and 15 focus on customer and transaction profitability, the "pocket-price waterfall" and how to negotiate with different types of customers. Marn and Rosiello (1992) and Marn et al. (2004) are indispensable to a discussion of the pocket-price-waterfall while Holden (2012) and Nagle and Müller (2018) provide excellent advice on how to deal with different types of customers.

Chapter 16 deals with the economic theory of price discrimination. The techniques of price discrimination can be employed to increase profit. However, whether price discrimination *in the economic sense* exists is not always easy to determine as it hinges on the method used to determine the relationship between prices and costs, an issue discussed by Clerides (2004). Finally, how a price-discriminating monopolist "should" set prices is an important theoretical question for regulators and the theoretical recommendation, Ramsey pricing, is discussed.

Chapter 17, the Conclusion, recaps the contribution that management accountants can and should be making, leveraging their analytical expertise to increase profitable sales. Some businesses have adopted a "culture of profit" where sales personnel have access to cost data and can see the additional profit that can be made by improving product mix, upselling to higher margin products and adding higher margin accessories and services. This culture must be supported by strategies and policies throughout the company, not least the sales incentive scheme which should be oriented to *profitable* sales, not volume or market share.

Note

1 Shapiro and Varian (1998) point to the "dangerous economics" of information products with high development costs, very low variable costs and ability to operate at enormous scale; they argue that "versioning" is necessary to avoid commoditisation that drives prices lower and lower.

References

Clerides S. K. (2004) Price discrimination with differentiated products: definition and identification, *Economic Enquiry*, 42(3), 402–412

Holden R. K. (2012) *Negotiating With Backbone*, FT Press, Upper Saddle River, NJ

Marn M. V., Roegner E. V. and Zawada C. C. (2004) *The Price Advantage*, Wiley & Sons, Hoboken, NJ

Marn M. V. and Rosiello R. L. (1992) Managing price, gaining profit, *Harvard Business Review*, Sep–Oct, 84–94

Nagle T. T. and Müller G. (2018) *The Strategy and Tactics of Pricing*, 6th edition, Routledge, New York and Abingdon, Oxon

Phillips R. L. (2005) *Pricing and Revenue Optimization*, Stanford University Press, Stanford, CA

Porter M. E. (1980) *Competitive Strategy*, Free Press, New York

Robinson J. (1969) *The Economics of Imperfect Competition*, 2nd edition, MacMillan Press Ltd., London and Basingstoke

Shapiro C. and Varian H. R. (1998) Versioning: the smart way to sell information, *Harvard Business Review*, Nov–Dec, 106–114

2 Surveys of pricing practice

2.1 The marginalist controversy

Hall and Hitch (1939) caused consternation by casting doubt on the presumption, in economic theory, that firms maximise their profits by equating marginal cost and marginal revenue. Instead, their 38 business interviewees reported that they based prices on average costs (variable plus fixed) and a profit markup. Economists reacted by arguing that, no matter what interviewees say, they still base prices on marginal principles. Blinder et al. (1998, p. 40) wryly comment: "It appears that this was both the first and the last interview study of pricing to have a major impact on the thinking of economists."

Hall and Hitch's findings led to the "marginalist controversy" hinging on whether businesses did or did not follow marginal principles in setting prices. Economists pointed to the many adjustments to cost-plus prices which might lead to "implicit marginalism" and noted that the test of economic theory was not what interviewees say, but what they do. Nevertheless, in the twenty-first century, Lucas (2003) concluded that the controversy remained unresolved, especially as some econometric studies reached different conclusions even based on analysis of the *same dataset*.

Lucas called for more case studies of pricing practice to resolve the issue. However, if cases reveal that companies use cost-plus prices, mainstream economists will claim that they still, implicitly, use marginalist methods. At the same time, sceptics (such as the author) will argue that, just because they make many adjustments before finalising prices, this does not prove that they are using marginalist methods.

2.2 Prevalence of (modified) cost-plus pricing

There was interest in UK pricing practice by academic accountants in the 1970s and 1980s. Skinner (1970) found that 70% of respondents used cost-plus pricing but concluded: "The picture that emerges fairly clearly is of considerable sensitivity to the effects of competition and demand, as well as to cost and price, in setting prices" (p. 206).[1] Further surveys were undertaken by Atkin and Skinner (1975) and Mills and Sweeting (1988). Both surveys reported that cost-based

DOI: 10.4324/9781003272731-2

methods dominated, and, for most firms, the basis was full costs although a significant minority preferred direct/marginal costs. However, both surveys reported that cost-plus prices were often adjusted. For example, Mills and Sweeting found that "76 per cent of companies considered factors other than cost when determining selling price" (p. 27).

Drury et al. (1993) surveyed UK manufacturing firms and found that, although 84% of respondents used cost-plus pricing, they were 'vitally important' for only 10% of respondents. Once again, most companies undertook cost-based calculations, but these did not determine the final price. Consistent with prior surveys, they also found that most respondents (52%) used total manufacturing cost "often" or "always" while a significant minority (41%) used variable manufacturing cost "often" or "always".

Guilding et al. (2005) specifically investigated the importance of cost-plus pricing and surveyed firms across the manufacturing, retail, finance and service sectors in the UK and Australia. Once again manufacturing companies usually calculated cost-plus prices, more than 60% rated their importance in price-setting 4 or above on a 7-point scale. However, a large percentage of these firms reported that cost-plus prices were important for only a minority of their sales. In the retail, financial and service sectors cost-plus methods were *both* important (average score almost 5 on the 7-point scale) *and* widely used.

Noble and Gruca (1999) investigated pricing practice in industrial markets. Given the choice of 10 strategies: "A full 56% of the 270 managers mentioned cost-plus pricing . . . even after all the research on market- and competitive-oriented pricing, cost-based methods remain prevalent" (p. 451).

Indounas (2009) investigated the pricing methods used by industrial service firms. A mail survey of 129 transportation and 48 information technology companies was supplemented by 20 in-depth interviews. The most important pricing *objectives* were related to satisfying customers. However, the most important pricing *methods* were cost-plus pricing and pricing similar to competitors, 3.72 and 3.65, respectively, on a 5-point scale (1: not important at all, 5: very important).

Since the 1990s the most important surveys have been undertaken by central bank economists. They have taken an interest in price setting and, especially, price stickiness, because of the implications for economic policy. Hall et al. (1997) surveyed UK companies and found market level to be the most important determinant of prices (39% of respondents), markup on direct cost[2] was most important for 37% of respondents and competitor prices were most important for 25% of respondents. If respondents are asked for the *most important* method of pricing, the cost-plus method is important but no more than other methods.

A second Bank of England survey was undertaken by Greenslade and Parker (2010). They allowed multiple responses and, for most respondents, direct cost-plus percentage markup was important or very important. At the same time, 68% of respondents identified competitors' prices and 27% the principal customer as the *primary* determinant of prices. Inconsistency in the way questions were asked makes it difficult to interpret the results.

Fabiani et al. (2005) drew together the results of surveys conducted in 2003 and 2004 by nine Eurosystem national central banks, covering more than 11,000 firms. The overall study is large and authoritative but:

> There is some over-representation of the industrial sector in most of the national samples, which explains why the majority of companies (75% on average) sell their main product predominantly to other firms. Thus, the conclusions we draw are mainly related to producer prices rather than to consumer prices.
>
> (pp. 7–8)

A key result was the finding that 54% of firms in the Euro area employ markup prices, 27% refer to competitors' prices in price setting and 18% use "other" methods. The results are consistent across seven Eurozone countries although German firms (74%) make more use of markup prices.[3] However, 69% of these German firms also said that the markups were variable. The authors conclude: *Stylised fact 4 – mark-up (constant or variable) pricing is the dominant price setting practice adopted by firms in the euro area. The lower the level of competition, the more frequently used this method is* (p. 15) [emphasis as original].

All the European surveys investigated the factors driving price changes and confirmed an asymmetry originally observed by Hall and Hitch (1939). Price increases tend to be driven by cost increases that usually affect all firms in the industry. However, price decreases are primarily driven by the state of the market and, especially, competitor prices. This led Hall and Hitch to postulate the "kinked demand curve" where firms resist price cutting because it might start a price war and only increase prices when confident that other firms will follow. There is therefore a tendency for prices to be "sticky" at the current price.

2.3 Price stickiness

Central bank economists have studied price-setting because of its implications for monetary policy. If prices are "sticky" (slow to respond to economic shocks) then central banks can influence the real economy because a change in the money supply influences the level of economic activity rather than feeding immediately into inflation.[4]

Interest in price setting by central banks was stimulated by Blinder (1991, 1994) and Blinder et al. (1998) in the US. Blinder and his assistants asked interviewees how important various theories of price stickiness were in practice. Respondents were asked to rate theories on a 4-point scale and the most important reasons for price stickiness were: (1) coordination failure (competitors not following a price increase and/or matching a price cut); (2) cost-based pricing (because cost changes take time to move through the production cycle); (3) non-price competition (thus avoiding price changes as the size or quality of the product or service is amended instead); (4) implicit contracts with customers; and (5) explicit contracts with customers that restrain price changes.

Blinder's template was followed in the European surveys and rankings for the Eurozone could therefore be compared with those for other countries. There are some differences, in particular "change in non-price factors" is important in North America but less so elsewhere. However, overall, the results are remarkably consistent with an emphasis on customer relations (implicit and explicit contracts), cost-based inertia and concern for competitor reactions (coordination failure) the main reasons for price stickiness.

2.4 Price discrimination

Relatively few surveys have investigated price discrimination (charging different prices for the same or similar products) but, where they have, it has been found to be prevalent. Atkin and Skinner (1975) highlighted the extensive use of discounting both by quantity and by type of customer and, similarly, Greenslade and Parker (2010) found that 57% of firms determined prices on a case-by-case basis while, in 22% of firms, prices depended on the quantity sold.

Several of the national surveys reported by Fabiani et al. (2005) investigated price discrimination, described as "selling each unit of the same product at different prices either to the same customer or to different customers" (p. 10). Approximately 42% of Eurozone companies employ quantity-based pricing, 40% price "case-by-case" and only 18% charge the same prices to all customers (source: figure 2, p. 10). In addition, in the surveys for Belgium, Spain and Luxembourg, about 50% of firms reported that pricing was different across Eurozone countries. The highest-rated reasons were competitor prices in foreign markets and transportation costs. The authors conclude that uniform pricing schemes are strongly rejected and the results: ". . . robust across countries, show that firms operate in monopolistically competitive markets, where prices are mostly set following markup rules and where price discrimination is common" (p. 4).

Indounas (2009) investigated the pricing policies adopted in their sample of transport and IT firms. The most important policies based on a 5-point scale were negotiated pricing (3.64), differentiated pricing (3.55) and list pricing (3.44). Negotiated pricing can be interpreted as setting prices case by case and differentiated pricing refers to varying prices according to the customer's size, importance, location etc. Comparing high- and low-performing firms, Indounas found that the high performers put more emphasis on competitors and customers and tended to price: "according to the value that customers attach to the service and differentiating prices across different target segments" (p. 93).

A consistent picture emerges of industrial companies varying their prices across customers. They might negotiate, setting prices on a case-by-case basis; they might offer quantity discounts; and they may vary prices by location. While cost-plus prices might be important, they can hardly be applied rigidly!

2.5 Summary

Hall and Hitch's (1939) finding that many companies use cost-plus methods had considerable influence because it appeared to undermine a fundamental assumption of microeconomics, that companies employ marginalist methods, aiming to set prices that maximise their profits. Lucas (2003) concluded that the "marginalist controversy" remained unresolved.

Generally, surveys of pricing reveal a consistent picture. Most companies see cost-plus pricing as important or very important and confirm Hall and Hitch's (1939) finding. The most recent surveys to reaffirm this were the central bank surveys throughout the Eurozone. However, surveys also indicate that companies consider market conditions and competitor reaction, and most companies adjust cost-based prices to take these factors into account.

Surveys motivated by investigation into price stickiness confirm the importance of possible customer reaction: explicit contracts or informal "implicit contracts" that restrain price changes. Competition is also a key factor, referred to euphemistically as "coordination failure" (competitors fail to move their prices together). Also important is the prevalence of cost-plus pricing because of delay as price changes move through the supply chain. The importance of customers, competitors and costs in pricing is reaffirmed.

There has been only limited investigation of price discrimination, charging different prices for the same or similar products. However, where investigated, companies indicate that they do not usually charge the same price to all customers. Prices might be charged on a "case-by-case" basis or there may be quantity discounts. There were also different prices charged across the Eurozone, significant because these (geographical) differences are obviously not driven by currency fluctuations.

Overall, surveys of practice lead to the unsurprising conclusion that companies take account of costs, customers and competition in setting prices. There has been only limited investigation into the practice of price discrimination but, where investigated, it was found to be important. Most of the surveys have concentrated on price setting by manufacturing companies and therefore, implicitly, on business-to-business (B2B) pricing. In the next chapter examples of pricing in consumer goods markets are considered.

Notes

1 Nevertheless, Skinner's findings did not provide direct evidence of implicit marginalism as firms reviewed prices relatively infrequently and did not consciously attempt to maximise profits.
2 Central bank economists usually assume that if companies use cost-plus methods, they will be based on variable costs, there are no questions referring to total costs.
3 Where respondents were asked whether markups were fixed or variable (in Belgium, Germany and the Netherlands) most used a variable markup.
4 This follows from the identity, MV = PT, where M is the money supply, V the velocity of money circulation, P the general price level and T the volume of transactions. If M,

the money supply, is changed by monetary policy while P remains more-or-less constant (because prices are "sticky") and velocity of money circulation is also more-or-less stable, a change in M will lead to an increase or a decrease in the volume of transactions: the level of economic activity will change.

References

Atkin B. and Skinner R. (1975) *How British Industry Prices*, Industrial Market Research Limited, London

Blinder A. S. (1991) Why are prices sticky? Preliminary results from an interview study, *Working Paper Number 3646*, National Bureau of Economic Research, downloaded from: www.nber.org/system/files/working_papers/w3646/w3646.pdf

Blinder A. S. (1994) On sticky prices: academic theories meet the real world, in: *Monetary Policy*, pp. 117–154, National Bureau of Economic Research, Inc., Cambridge, MA

Blinder A. S., Canetti E. D., Lebow D. E. and Rudd J. B. (1998) *Asking About Prices: A New Approach to Understanding Price Stickiness*, Russell Sage Foundation, New York

Drury C., Braund S., Osborne P. and Tayles M. (1993) *A Survey of Management Accounting Practices in UK Manufacturing Companies*, The Chartered Association of Certified Accountants, London

Fabiani S., Druant M., Hernando I., Kwapil C., Landau B., Loupias C., Martins F., Mathä T. Y., Sabbatini R., Stahl H. and Stokman C. J. (2005) The pricing behaviour of firms in the Euro area: new survey evidence, *Working Paper Number 535*, European Central Bank, downloaded from: www.ecb.int or http://ssrn.com/abstract_id=825628

Greenslade J. and Parker M. (2010) Price setting behaviour in the United Kingdom, *Bank of England Quarterly Bulletin*, Q4, 404–415

Guilding C., Drury C. and Tayles M. (2005) An empirical investigation of the importance of cost-plus pricing, *Managerial Auditing Journal*, 20(2), 125–137

Hall R. L. and Hitch C. J. (1939) Price theory and business behaviour, *Oxford Economic Papers*, 2, 12–45

Hall S., Walsh M. and Yates A. (1997) How do U.K. companies set prices? *Bank of England Working Paper No 67*, downloaded from SSRN: https://ssrn.com/abstract=114948 or http://doi.org/10.2139/ssrn.11948

Indounas K. (2009) Successful industrial service pricing, *Journal of Business and Industrial Marketing*, 24(2), 86–97

Lucas M. R. (2003) Pricing decisions and the neoclassical theory of the firm, *Management Accounting Research*, 14(3), 201–217

Mills R. W. and Sweeting C. (1988) *Pricing Decisions in Practice*, Chartered Institute of Management Accountants, London

Noble P. M. and Gruca T. S. (1999) Industrial pricing: theory and managerial practice, *Marketing Science*, 18(3), 435–454

Skinner R. C. (1970) The determination of selling prices, *The Journal of Industrial Economics*, 18(3), 201–217

3 Market segmentation and price fences

3.1 Introduction

Surveys of pricing practice were reviewed in the previous chapter and, unsurprisingly, showed that firms take account of either full or variable costs while also being sensitive to potential reaction by both customers and competitors. There is a heavy focus on business-to-business pricing in the surveys and, in this chapter, by contrast, the focus is on pricing for services and consumer goods. Examples are drawn from a wide range of industries: transport, coffee chains, hearing care, drugs, roadside assistance, internet conferencing, mobile phone contracts and fantasy-gaming. The aim is twofold: first, to show how widespread is market segmentation and segmentation-based pricing; and second, to illustrate the variety of methods (fences) used to segment consumer goods markets.

3.2 Train fares: segmentation strategies in transport services

Train fares are a good place to start because they provide examples of several methods of market segmentation: buyer identity, location, time of use/purchase, product differentiation and quantity purchased. Buyer identity and location are *direct* methods of segmentation: the seller *directly* identifies purchasers by their identity or location and offers them different prices. The remaining methods are *indirect* methods of segmentation: the seller offers a range of options and buyers self-select their segment by their choice.[1]

The following analysis is based on the methods used by CrossCountry Trains and, where specific fares are quoted, these refer to journeys from Bristol Temple Meads to Manchester Piccadilly and from Bristol Temple Meads to Birmingham New Street. The following sections are based mainly on data collected in 2018 before the COVID-19 pandemic disrupted train travel and pricing.

Demographic and geographic segmentation

In 2018, CrossCountry Trains provided 11 separate railcards. Some related to demographic characteristics such as age (16–25, 26–30, senior), occupation (HM Forces, Jobcentre Plus) and geographical region (Devon and Cornwall, Highland, New Deal

DOI: 10.4324/9781003272731-3

Scotland). There were also railcards for the registered disabled, Family and Friends and Two-Together. In 2021, the number of railcards had been reduced to eight: four relating to age: 16–17, 16–25, 26–30 and seniors; two for groups: family-and-friends and two-together; a veterans' railcard and a disabled persons railcard.[2]

These cards typically cost £30 for one year (with a discount for a 3-year card) and holders save 1/3rd off most rail fares (although the 16–17 railcard can save 50%). No doubt the aim is to generate increased revenue and contribution by encouraging increased take-up of rail services by price-sensitive customers.

The railcards offered by CrossCountry Trains in 2021 were also available on the National Railcard website[3] together with a Network Railcard, available for travel in 16 counties in the Southeast of England and Greater London. Fares are reduced by 1/3 for the cardholder, up to 3 other adults and 4 children.

Method of purchase

There may be a difference between purchasing through the CrossCountry website (also accessible through the National Rail website) and purchasing on the Trainline website. The tickets are identical, but a service fee may be charged for purchases through the Trainline.

Time of travel

There are significant price differences depending on time of travel; see Table 3.1.

This is peak-load pricing with a high price for price-insensitive passengers or those who simply must take an early train. Lower prices are charged to passengers who have the flexibility to take advantage of travelling off-peak. The aim is to increase demand when there is spare capacity as off-peak fares both attract new passengers and shift demand from the peak to the off-peak period.

A further review was undertaken in April 2021 but there was no clear pattern in the price structure and this was likely due to the influence of the COVID-19 pandemic.

Time of purchase

There are significant price differences depending on the time of purchase; see Table 3.2. Booking more than two weeks in advance ensured a significantly lower fare. Passengers having flexibility to book in advance are likely to be more price

Table 3.1 Bristol Temple Meads – Manchester Piccadilly, 2 February 2018 (booked 26 January) accessed at: www.crosscountrytrains.co.uk/

Time of travel	*Single fare (£)*
Peak trains: 8.00 am and 9.00 am	89.40
Off-peak trains: 10.00 am and 11.00 am	43.40

Table 3.2 Bristol Temple Meads – Manchester Piccadilly, departing 9.00 am, booked 26 January 2018

Date of travel	*Single fare (£)*
Within two weeks: Jan 27, Feb 3	70.80
Two weeks or later: Feb 10 and thereafter	43.40

sensitive and are offered lower prices. Passengers that delay booking are likely to be limited in their travel options, are therefore less price sensitive, and pay a higher fare.

A further review in April 2021 failed to reveal the expected pattern of significantly cheaper fares if booked in advance. Again, the COVID-19 pandemic made data collection problematic.

Product design

Rail companies differentiate their product by offering first class as well as standard class travel; see Table 3.3. Price-insensitive passengers who would like more space (and "free" drinks and biscuits) paid 86% more at peak time and 164% more off-peak.

For weekend travel fares were lower and interestingly, it was also possible to buy a standard ticket but upgrade to first class for an additional charge of £15. Thus, at weekends, CrossCountry Trains offered three price points to travellers, a standard class fare, an upgrade to first class (if available) and a first-class fare. The fares are lower than weekday fares to appeal to leisure travellers who are assumed to be more price sensitive than weekday, business travellers.

Quantity

Finally, rail fares also provide an example of quantity discounting. CrossCountry Rail offers a range of season tickets. For the journey Bristol Temple Meads to Birmingham New Street, the prices for standard travel, accessed 27 January 2018 are shown in Table 3.4.

The National Rail website indicated that, if it is intended to take more than three journeys in a seven-day period, a season ticket is likely to be cheaper than the standard fares. Heavy users of rail travel are likely to benefit by purchasing a season ticket.

Rail fare segmentation is easy to implement in the UK because the rail companies have significant monopoly power: many rail users would not consider an alternative mode of transport and only a single company has the franchise for a particular route. Fixed capacity, a "perishable" product and low variable costs (at off-peak times) are the key characteristics that lead to such a range of segmentation strategies. Other industries that share these characteristics, such as live entertainment, package holidays, cruise liners and hotels, use similar techniques: peak-load pricing, early purchase discounts and product differentiation.

Table 3.3 Bristol Temple Meads – Manchester Piccadilly, standard and first-class single fares (booked more than 2 weeks in advance)

	Standard fare (£)	*First class fare (£)*
Peak times (2/3/2018)	89.40	166.40
Off-peak times (2/3/2018)	43.40	114.40
Weekend (3/3/2018)	35.00	88.80

Table 3.4 Bristol Temple Meads to Birmingham New Street, season ticket prices

Season ticket	*Price (£)*	*Average price per day (£)*
7 day	158.30	22.61
1 month	607.90	20.00
3 months	1,823.70	20.00
6 months	3,647.30	20.00
12 months	6,332.00	17.35

3.3 Starbucks: segmentation strategies for a consumer product

Geography

Starbucks provides several examples of segmented pricing. First, prices vary across the world. On 25 May 2020, Finders reported that the lowest prices were charged in Turkey, Egypt and Colombia, £1.44, £1.58 and £1.66, respectively. The highest prices were charged in Denmark, Switzerland and Finland, £4.91, £4.81 and £4.38, respectively.[4] Of course, this is partly a reflection of lower incomes and spending power in the low-price countries and, in addition, running costs are much lower in these countries.

Buyer identity

In 2021 Starbucks did not offer discounts to students or seniors but customers could register a loyalty card which accumulated three stars for each £1 spent. At green level 150 stars could be exchanged for a free drink, while at gold level, 450 stars, the customer qualified for various extras and a free birthday drink.

Product differentiation and quantity discrimination

Starbucks offers its drinks in different sizes and flavours; see Table 3.5. The larger sizes cost less per oz: a quantity discount. For a flavoured drink the price is significantly higher: an example of product differentiation.

Time of purchase/use

In the US Starbucks also runs a happy hour (2.00pm– 7.00pm) on some Thursdays, customers can purchase one drink and receive a second drink free.

Table 3.5 Starbucks caffe latte prices 2021, accessed 23 April 2021 at www.fastfoodmenuprices.com/uk/starbucks-menu-prices-uk/

	Caffe latte		*Vanilla spice latte*	
	Price	*Price per oz*	*Price*	*Price per oz*
Tall (12 oz)	£2.25	18.75p	£3.25	27.08p
Grande (16 oz)	£2.60	16.25p	£3.55	22.19p
Venti (20 oz)	£2.85	14.25p	£3.75	18.75p

Table 3.6 Amplifon hearing care packages, May 2021 Source: Amplifon Retail Centre

Advanced	*Premium*	*Elite*
Streaming music or calls, rechargeable, outdoor and noisy environments, 2-year warranty	Streaming music or calls, rechargeable, outdoor and noisy environments App to control volume and settings, high fidelity sound, 3-year warranty	Streaming music or calls, rechargeable, outdoor and noisy environments App to control volume and settings, high fidelity sound Group conversations in complex noise environments, 4-year warranty
£2,395 per pair Discount price £2,195 per pair	£3,095 per pair	£3,795 per pair Discount price £2,995 per pair

3.4 Hearing aids: product differentiation for a consumer durable

In May 2021 Amplifon offered two "essential" care packages, an advanced care package, a premium care package and an elite care package. The highest-level packages, advanced, premium and elite, are compared in Table 3.6. The author needs hearing aids and is a customer of Amplifon. As the UK emerged from the first wave of the COVID-19 pandemic in May 2021 he received a call from Amplifon explaining that a pair of hearing aids could be purchased at a discounted price. Not having had a hearing test for 18 months he booked an appointment.

The audiologist fitted the "elite" hearing aids and persuaded the author to try them for two weeks. We can see that Amplifon has adopted "good-better-best" pricing (there was no mention of the "essential" options). The initial call made an offer sufficiently attractive to interest the author and the discount on the elite package was designed to make this seem a good deal (cheaper than the advanced package). As the author hesitated the audiologist said that interest-free credit could be arranged.

This example illustrates several pricing techniques. First, there was a cold call that avoided technicalities but suggested that an attractive offer was available. Second, there was a range of product options with a heavy discount on the expensive option. Third, the "free trial" might lead to the "endowment effect": having experienced the product there is unhappiness at the prospect of giving it up. Fourth, the "easy payment" terms were probably intended to soften the pain of purchase by spreading the payments and making them less visible by using direct debit.[5]

3.5 Drugs: the power of branding

The drug manufacturers are often criticised for charging high prices for drugs that, once in production, cost very little to manufacture. However, drug manufacturers need to recover heavy research and development costs and patent laws typically protect the pricing of new drugs for 20 years or more. After the patent expires there is no restriction on manufacture, drugs can be offered by companies that have not suffered heavy R&D costs and prices fall. Some very common drugs such as aspirin, paracetamol and ibuprofen have long been "out-of-patent" and there is competition in the market. However, it is common experience that a drug such as aspirin can be purchased at widely differing prices.

Generic drugs are essentially the same as the branded drugs marketed by the original developer. All drugs must be approved by the appropriate regulatory authority, the Medicines and Healthcare Products Regulatory Agency in the UK, and both branded and generic drugs must meet the same regulations: the active ingredients must be the same by law.

Given the medical equivalence of branded and generic drugs, one might expect customers to purchase the cheaper alternative. However, in practice, many customers trust the branded drug and are prepared to purchase it at a higher price. The difference in price can be significant; see Table 3.7.

The power of branding is further illustrated by the Anadin brand name. Anadin was the brand name used by Wyeth and was continued by Pfizer after taking over Wyeth in 2009. No doubt part of the reason for the takeover was the Anadin brand and Pfizer provides a range of "Anadin" products.

Table 3.8 presents the prices for Anadin branded drugs in April 2021. Inspection of Tables 3.7 and 3.8 makes it obvious that there is a very wide range of prices for essentially the same drug. To take one example, 16 tablets of ibuprofen (200 mg active ingredient per tablet) can be purchased as a generic drug at £0.55, as Anadin Ibuprofen at £2.29 and as Anadin Ultra at £3.19. (Anadin ultra is in liquid form and is claimed to be quick acting.) The point is that some customers are prepared to pay several times as much for a branded product compared to the generic

Table 3.7 Prices of branded drugs and generic equivalents accessed at www.boots.com/, 12 April 2021

Brand	*Price*	*Generic version*	*Price*
Disprin (300 mg)	£3.59 (32 tablets)	Aspirin	£0.65 (32 tablets)
Panadol (500 mg)	£1.69 (16 tablets)	Paracetamol	£0.80 (32 tablets)
Nurofen (200 mg)	£2.29 (16 tablets)	Ibuprofen	£0.55 (16 tablets)
Lemsip	£4.79 (10 sachets)	Boots Cold & Flu relief powder	£2.99 (10 sachets)

Table 3.8 Examples of drugs marketed under the "Anadin" brand name accessed at www.boots.com/ 12 April 2021

Brand name	*Description*	*Price*
Anadin Original (325 mg)	aspirin and caffeine	£1.69 (16 tablets)*
Anadin Extra (545 mg)	aspirin, caffeine and paracetamol	£1.69 (12 tablets)*
Anadin Paracetamol (500 mg)	Paracetamol	£1.69 (12 tablets)*
Anadin Ibuprofen (200 mg)	Ibuprofen	£2.29 (16 tablets)*
Anadin Ultra (200 mg)	Ibuprofen in liquid form	3.19 (16 tablets)

*Note: there was an offer on these products at the time; they could be purchased at up to 20% off the normal prices shown in the table

Table 3.9 Illustrative roadside assistance packages offered by major UK providers, accessed at AA, RAC and Green Flag internet sites, 28 January 2018

AA	*RAC*	*Green Flag*
Basic breakdown cover: limited to 1 call out per year **£37 per year**		
Roadside assistance: 1 vehicle whoever is driving **£89 per year**	Rescue essential: personal cover (any vehicle) **£96 per year** (advertised as £8 per month)	Rescue: **£25 per year**
Roadside assistance and "At home" (assistance within ¼ mile of home) **£99 per year**	Rescue anywhere: (includes assistance within ¼ mile of home) **£120 per year**	Rescue plus (includes cover at home) **£40 per year**
Roadside assistance, At home and national recovery **£119 per year**	Rescue plus: includes national recovery to destination **£144 per year**	Roadside assistance, home cover and national recovery **£60 per year**
	Winter complete: replacement car hire, hotel accommodation or alternative transport **£162 per year**	

version despite both being certified as having the same active ingredient. Clearly, a trusted brand is worth a lot to the supplier and a significant price premium can be charged to those customers prepared to pay for the brand they trust.

3.6 Roadside assistance: product versions for a service provider

In the UK there are three major providers of roadside assistance to motorists that break down, the AA, the RAC and Green Flag. The packages of assistance offered in 2018 are set out in Table 3.9.

In 2018 the three providers adopted similar strategies. They provided basic roadside assistance together with a series of options, offering better service but at higher prices. Their aim was to offer a competitive entry-level price to attract price sensitive buyers together with packages designed to attract relatively price insensitive buyers prepared to pay for enhanced breakdown and recovery. The AA and RAC are "premium" brands that charge more, while Green Flag competes on price.

In this case the products are not identical, there is a series of product "versions" in ascending levels of "quality" at increasing prices. No doubt the supplier would prefer the customer to purchase a "better" version of the service, the better versions will undoubtedly generate higher contribution than the entry-level versions. For example, the inclusion of home recovery service is unlikely to cost much more than the provision of roadside assistance, but the price charged can be significantly higher.

In April 2021 the AA offered its packages at reduced, sale prices: "1/3 off breakdown cover when you add At Home, National Recovery or Onward Travel". The discounted monthly prices advertised were £8 (Roadside assistance and At Home), £9 (add National Recovery) and £11 (add Onward Travel). Note that the AA has changed its "price metric" to *per month* rather than per year (presumably because the monthly price seems cheaper), "basic" roadside assistance was not prominently advertised, and the discount offer applied only to the more expensive options.[6]

In April 2021 RAC advertised the "standard" package including roadside and home rescue and alternative transport at £10 per month with the claim that this was simpler and more comprehensive (including assistance at home and other benefits) than the AA's basic roadside assistance package. The "advanced" and "ultimate" packages at £14 and £19 per month respectively did not limit number of call outs or towing and, for the ultimate package, included 7 days alternative transport and "ultimate" garage support. The more expensive options are obviously more profitable, and, for the advanced package, RAC offered one month free and, for the ultimate package, three months free to new customers[7]

If the reader is finding it difficult to compare the various options and prices offered by the AA and RAC that is probably because these providers are trying to differentiate their (essentially similar) products. Some investigation would be needed to establish which option offered the best combination of product features and price and some customers will not bother. The policy adopted by the AA and RAC in 2021 contrasts with that of Green Flag, the provider that competes on price. Green Flag explicitly compares its prices with those offered by AA and RAC for similar services, see Table 3.10.

In April 2021 Green Flag's prices were not neatly tabulated and some vehicle and personal details were needed to obtain quotations. Green Flag make comparisons with AA and RAC to show how much cheaper is their cover and they also advertise "up to 40% off booked online compared with telephone prices." (The prices quoted were for online booking.)

There are several points to make:

(1) AA and RAC show monthly rather than annual prices, the "price metric" is chosen to make the price seem cheaper. Green Flag, on the other hand, quotes annual prices and shows AA and RAC equivalents to emphasise their price advantage.

Table 3.10 Quoted prices by Green Flag in April 2021 for the author's vehicle. Green Flag provide AA and RAC rates for comparison, accessed 12 April 2021 at www.greenflag.com/breakdown-cover

Service	*Prices (AA and RAC prices were provided by Green Flag) (£ per year)*		
	Green Flag	AA	RAC
Basic roadside assistance (1 vehicle)	23.52	59	
Add: cover at home	36.96	119	90
Add: national recovery	44.80	169	140
Add: personal cover (any vehicle)	78.40	179	170

(2) The AA's reduced-price sale is designed to encourage purchase of one of the more expensive options, there is no reduction for basic roadside assistance.
(3) The RAC has tried to differentiate its product by offering a more complete package as "standard" but with additional more expensive "advanced" and "ultimate" options.
(4) The AA was offering a discount (1/3 off) when accessed in April 2021 while the RAC was making introductory offers for its more expensive packages.
(5) Green Flag majors on its low price and encourages online booking (up to 40% cheaper than booking by telephone).

3.7 Video conferencing: versioning information products

The COVID-19 pandemic in 2020 and 2021 saw vastly increased demand for videoconferencing, and the company that most obviously benefited was Zoom. The versions of Zoom's videoconferencing service provide an excellent example of the way that information services can be differentiated; see Table 3.11.

As a regular user of Zoom I received an offer to upgrade to Zoom Pro on 15 April 2021, with a 25% discount for an annual license, valid until the end of April 2021.

Zoom provides a typical example of product versions with each higher version incorporating all the features of the lower versions and adding more. Zoom also provides an example of a free product, the basic version, limited to either two people or 40 minutes duration. In this case, the aim of the "freemium" product is obvious, to encourage a wide group of users to use the product. They may encourage others to use the service thus generating "network effects," the value of the service increases as more people connect to it and some will be encouraged to move up to higher, subscription-based, levels of service.

3.8 Mobile phone data plans: quantity-related pricing

Sky Mobile had an offer on its mobile phone data plans in June 2021. All plans were available at a 25% discount, and the following plans were available to invited users. The prices quoted are after deducting the 25% discount (see Table 3.12):

Table 3.11 Zoom video-conferencing and phone plans, accessed 16 April 2021 at https://zoom.us/pricing

	Basic Free	*Pro £119.90 per year per license*	*Business £159.90 per year per license*	*Zoom United £240 per year per license*
Maximum participants	100	100	300	300
Groups, maximum duration	40 minutes	30 hours	30 hours	30 hours
Social media streaming		✓	✓	✓
Cloud recording		✓	✓	✓
Recording transcripts			✓	✓
Managed domains			✓	✓
Company branding			✓	✓
Phone facilities				✓

Table 3.12 Discounted prices offered by Sky to invited users, received by post, June 2021 (Offer ends 17 June 2021)

Data per month	*2GB*	*8GB*	*12GB*	*25GB*	*40GB*
Price per month (£)	4.50	6.00	9.00	11.25	18.00
£ per GB per month	2.25	0.75	0.75	0.45	0.45

As might be expected the price per GB falls if the contract is for more GBs. The aim seems to be to attract customers that have a minimal need for data with the £4.50 per month contract but to tempt them to move up to the 8GB plan which provides four times as much data but is only £1.50 per month more expensive. Heavy users of data are offered contracts at a significantly lower rate per GB.

There is probably no difference in the cost to Sky of the different plans and the price structure is intended to generate as much revenue as possible from the customer base. Heavy users of data are likely to be price sensitive and might shop around for a good deal. These customers are offered a competitive monthly rate. Low users of data are offered a low rate per month in absolute terms but pay significantly more per GB.

Interestingly, hardly had these words been written, and another offer was received from Sky. This time the focus was on deals available for iPhone12, but the flyer also included prices for data plans; see Table 3.13.

If the reader finds it difficult to make sense of these offers, so does the author. Where direct comparisons can be made, the 12GB plan is offered at £10 per month (discounted offer, £9 per month) and the 25GB plan is offered at £15 per

Table 3.13 Data plans offered by Sky Mobile, received by post, June 2021 (Offer ends 25 September 2021)

Data per month	*6GB*	*12GB*	*25GB*	*50GB*	*60GB*
Price per month (£)	8.00	10.00	15.00	25.00	30.00
£ per GB per month	1.33	0.83	0.60	0.5	0.5

month (discounted offer, £11.25 per month). While the 25GB plan was, indeed, offered at a 25% discount, the 12GB plan was at a 10% discount compared with the later price.

3.9 Collectable card games: the power of value to customer

The final example is drawn from the world of collectable card games. In the game, "Magic the Gathering," two players take turns to play cards that attack the opponent or ward off attacks. The impact of an attack depends on the power of the card played as does the likelihood of successful defence. Aficionados purchase packs of cards and, in June/July 2021, two booster packs of 15 cards became available.

Although the packs seem very similar to the uninitiated, both containing 15 magic cards, one pack is priced at £2.95 and the other at £5.95. The reason? The more expensive pack contains more powerful cards: a near-perfect example of product differentiation by the seller and difference in "value-to-the-customer" from the buyer's perspective. The idea of value-to-the-customer is the subject of the next chapter.

3.10 Price fences

As can be seen, segmenting the market makes it possible to charge different prices for the same or similar products and services. The more price-sensitive customers are targeted with a lower price while the relatively price-insensitive customers are encouraged to pay more. The seller needs monopoly power and must also be able to prevent (or minimise) arbitrage. Arbitrage occurs when a buyer purchases at the lower price and resells at the higher price: price fences are needed to separate the market segments. If a direct approach is used, segmenting by demography or geography, the price fence is obvious. Students, seniors and others might be required to show proof of identity or their railcard to take advantage of lower prices while geographical price differences can mean that it is impractical to purchase in one location and resell in another.

Indirect segmentation does not employ "hard" price fences based on demography or geography. However, in some cases, the method of segmentation has the same effect, for example, it may be practically impossible for some passengers to travel at off-peak times or to take advantage of advance-purchase fares. It is usually assumed that businesspeople travel at peak times or delay purchase because of their flexible schedules. Leisure travellers, on the other hand, can travel off peak and can plan their journeys. Business travellers are assumed to be relatively price insensitive while leisure travellers are assumed to be relatively price sensitive.

If segmentation is achieved by branding or by differentiating the product the customer has a choice and "self-segments" by their choice of product. Price-sensitive customers tend to purchase the lower-priced "value" products and services while price-insensitive customers might value the extra service or benefits sufficiently to purchase the higher priced product. It is the *perception* of benefits that is important. For example, as we have seen, the customer may be prepared to pay more for the extra security felt by purchasing a well-known brand.

The examples highlight a range of methods that might be used to segment the market:

(1) buyer identification (railcards),
(2) customer loyalty (Starbucks reward card),
(3) geography (network rail card relates to the Southeast of England),
(4) method of purchase (an extra fee may be charged if the Trainline is used or if Green Flag assistance is purchased by telephone instead of online),
(5) time of use (peak and off-peak rail fares, Starbucks happy hours),
(6) time of purchase (advance rail tickets),
(7) random discounting ("sale" by the AA, reduced prices for Anadin products, offer by Zoom, large discount on the "best" product by Amplifon, 25% discount on mobile phone data plans by Sky),
(8) quantity purchased (season tickets for rail travel, size of drink at Starbucks, contract for mobile phone data),
(9) product versions (standard and first-class rail travel, roadside assistance options, Zoom options, Amplifon hearing care options, booster packs in fantasy gaming).

A final point is worth making. In some cases, one has the impression that the seller deliberately makes it difficult to compare products, either with the competition or with different/later versions. This may lead the buyer to purchase an inferior choice and/or it may make a price increase more difficult to spot. Caldwell (2012), writing about the price of a two-litre bottle of Pepsi or Diet Coke, recounts that "my local prices have shifted between £1.40 and £1.99 including variations such as two bottles for £2.99, a promotional discount from £1.89 to £1.50 and a variety of labelling strategies". He goes on to note that: "This inconsistency has the effect of blurring the consumer's memory of the standard price of the product" (p. 59).

3.11 Implications for management accounting

The first implication for management accountants, a recurring theme in this book, is that profitability is not all about cost. A company that successfully segments its markets can generate multiple revenue streams and cost-plus pricing is likely to be inadequate. The point of segmentation is the ability to set different prices for customer groups with different price sensitivities and this implies that, even if cost-plus methods are a starting point, the percentage add-on will differ across customer segments.

The second implication is that profitability analysis must take account of all related customer segments and products. To take the example of Anadin products described earlier, the analysis could proceed as in Table 3.14.

Some products might provide higher absolute and/or percentage contributions than others but viability is to be judged by whether individual products cover their directly attributable costs and whether the whole family of products makes sufficient contribution after covering all attributable costs. The contribution from generic products might be low but, so long as they do not reduce sales of the high-margin branded goods, there is extra contribution to be made. It is likely that, in addition to their branded products, Pfizer also supply unbranded, generic drugs because, if they do not, other companies will. Companies like Pfizer that supply branded drugs rely on the strength of the brand to protect their market share and this justifies significant advertising expenditure.

A third implication is the likelihood, in consumer goods markets, that prices will be varied over time. Management accountants should work with marketing professionals to report the volume, revenue and contribution by product and product line over time as prices change. Consider a product that retails at a "standard" price of £1.00 per unit and is subject to frequent price promotions so that the price is regularly discounted to 75p (buy second half price) and 50p (half price). The manufacturer sells to the retailer at 80p, 60p and 40p per unit depending on whether the regular price or one of the promotions is in force. The manufacturer's variable cost, including materials, labour, packaging and distribution costs is estimated at 30p per unit. Sales volume increases significantly during promotions and contribution based on typical volumes over a period are calculated in Table 3.15.

Table 3.14 Analysis of the profitability of a related group of products

	Anadin original	*Anadin extra*	*Anadin Paracetamol*	.....	*Total Anadin products*	*Generic related products*	*Total Anadin and related products*
Revenue	XXX	XXXX	XXX		XXXXX	XX	
Direct costs	(X)	(X)	(X)		(XX)	(X)	
Product contribution	XX	XXX	XX		XXX		
Sales, marketing and advertising costs attributable to the Anadin brand					(XX)		
Contribution from Anadin and related products					X	X	XX
Manufacturing and facility costs attributable to Anadin and related products							(XX)
Contribution from Anadin and related products							X

Table 3.15 Contribution generated by a promotional strategy

				Total
Price per unit	£0.80	£0.60	£0.40	
Volume (millions of units)	100	120	150	370
Revenue (£m)	80	72	60	212
Variable cost (£m)	30	36	45	111
Contribution (£m)	50	36	15	101

Table 3.16 Tesco revenue and net income, impact of 1% increase in prices

	Financial year 2020/21 *£ millions*	*1% price increase* *£ millions*
Revenue	57,887	58,466
Net income before taxes	825	1,404

Table 3.15 shows the contribution generated by the strategy of regular promotions. Further analysis could employ a sales analysis to compare the contribution generated with budget and break it into volume, price and mix elements.

The use of regular prices together with regular promotions is known as a "HiLo" strategy designed to capture sales to different customers, those that buy regularly and are prepared to pay higher prices, and those that are prepared to wait for a reduced price or simply purchase because they see a bargain.

3.12 The power of price

Pricing texts usually make the point that price adjustments can have a hugely significant impact on contribution and profit. The "HiLo" marketing strategy in the previous section leads to an average price of 57.3p generating a contribution of 27.3p per unit. However, assuming no change in volume, and keeping the same promotional strategy and mix of sales, a price increase of 10% would generate £21.2 million more contribution, a 21% increase. If a complex pricing policy can hide a price increase the result can be dramatic. Table 3.16 shows the impact of a 1% price increase on the net income generated by Tesco. A 1% price increase can translate into a 70% increase in net income.

3.13 Conclusions

This chapter shows how essentially the same products (such as generic and branded drugs) and similar products (such as train journeys at different times) sell at very different prices. Once attention is drawn to these practices it is obvious that they are commonplace and management accountants should be aware of these practices and the opportunities they offer. A vital step in taking advantage of the range of customer price sensitivity is segmenting the market and we have seen how this can be achieved.

Segmentation with multiple prices immediately casts doubt on the value of cost-plus prices because, while establishing cost is no doubt important, prices are related to the range of customer price sensitivities across market segments. A technique that has been gaining increasing popularity is the estimation of "economic value to customer," a method of estimating the price that a customer (or customer segment) might rationally be prepared to pay. This is the topic of the next chapter.

Notes

1 It may be difficult to classify time-based discrimination as direct or indirect. If the buyer *must* travel at peak time, it becomes direct, and if the buyer can choose time of travel, then it is indirect.
2 Downloaded from www.crosscountrytrains.co.uk/tickets/railcards, 11/04/2021
3 www.railcard.co.uk/about-railcards/#network_railcard_anchor downloaded 12/04/2021
4 www.finder.com/uk/starbucks-index downloaded 23/04/2021
5 The deal was closed when the audiologist agreed to adapt the "old" hearing aids for use by the author's wife.
6 www.theaa.com/breakdown-cover downloaded 12/04/2021
7 www.rac.co.uk/breakdown-cover downloaded 12/04/2021

Reference

Caldwell L. (2012) *The Psychology of Price*, Crimson Publishing Limited, Richmond

4 Value-based pricing

4.1 The idea

Surveys reveal that pricing usually takes account of costs, customers and competitors and, in the previous chapter, we saw that consumer-led companies segment their markets and charge different prices in different market segments. But how are these prices set? Since the late twentieth century a customer-focused technique has been increasingly advocated: economic value to the customer. The idea was set out by McKinsey consultants, Forbis and Mehta (1979, 1981). The most succinct definition appears in the 1979 McKinsey staff paper: "The goal of EVC (economic value to the customer) is to quantify the additional value a product brings to customers above what they already receive from their present suppliers."

Economic value to the customer is calculated by comparison to a similar, "reference product," and estimating differences in value *from the customer's point of view*. Then the differential value is added to the price of the reference product in order to determine "economic value to the customer" (EVC). The economic value to the customer is the *maximum* the customer might be expected to pay given the price of the reference product and the differentiation value of the new product.

4.2 A simple example

A fuel-efficient car is more economical than a similar specification car that sells at £15,000.

Reference product	*New product*
Price: £15,000	Price: ?
Fuel efficiency: 40 miles per gallon	Fuel efficiency: 60 miles per gallon

Assume that a typical driver covers 12,000 miles per year and petrol costs £1.50 per litre, what price could be charged for the new product? There are 4.55 litres in a gallon.

In this example there is no indication of additional functionality but there is a significant saving to the customer in fuel costs.[1] The savings due to greater fuel efficiency:

DOI: 10.4324/9781003272731-4

Saving in fuel: (12,000/40–12,000/60) × 4.55 = 455 litres per year
Value of savings: 455 litres per year × £1.50 per litre = £682.5 per year

This is the annual value of savings versus the reference product and the savings will accrue every year throughout the car's life. If the customer keeps the car for five years after a credit purchase at 12% APR (annual percentage rate) the net present value of the savings can be calculated:

Year	*Cash flow (£)*	*Discount factor*	*Present value (£)*
1	682.5	0.893	609.5
2	682.5	0.797	544.0
3	682.5	0.712	485.9
4	682.5	0.636	434.1
5	682.5	0.568	387.5
Total			2461.0

Finally, when the car is sold, it will be worth more than the reference product because, other things being equal, it is still more fuel efficient. Assume that the new product could be sold for £500 more than the reference product, then there is an additional present value of £500 × 0.568 = £284.

Economic value to the customer is therefore the price of the reference product plus the cost savings the customer can expect to make: £15,000 + £2,461 + £284 = £17,745

Does this mean that the firm can go ahead and charge a price of £17,745? No, because, at a price of £17,745, the customer would be indifferent between reference and target products. The economic value to the customer of £17,745 is the *maximum* price a rational customer would pay based on the assumptions in the calculation. To persuade the customer to switch it will probably be necessary to offer a price that is sufficiently advantageous to overcome the uncertainty of purchasing a new product.

The calculation depends on several assumptions, and, in practice, there are likely to be several dimensions in the comparison to the reference product. For example, cars might be compared on performance, safety, style, space, ride and so on. These factors may involve trade-offs so that, for example, space and safety might be traded against performance. The attributes will be evaluated subjectively by different potential customers so that economic value to the customer can vary considerably across customers and market segments.

4.3 Case study: DEC and minicomputers

The technique of economic value to the customer is based on a simple idea. However, the results of EVC analysis can be highly illuminating as the following case study demonstrates. Shank (2006) set out the problem faced by Digital Equipment Corporation (DEC) from lower-priced minicomputers offered by Data General. When the case study was developed DEC was dominant in the minicomputer market with an excellent product, the micromini computer (MMC) at a premium price. However, Data General (GDS) was gaining market share. Economic Value to Customer (EVC) calculations, based on heavily disguised data, are shown in Table 4.1.

Table 4.1 shows the calculation of EVC for the micromini computer (MMC) taking the Data General product, GDS as the reference product. The market is divided into three segments, each requiring a different level of minicomputer. The price of the reference product, GDS, is $3600 in all segments. In the Hi Speed segment, the MMC has a positive *differential value* because reprogramming, installation and post-purchase costs ($2,450) are lower than for GDS ($4,450). The advantages of the MMC are worth $2,000 so economic value to customer is the price of the reference product, $3,600, plus $2,000: $5,600. As the MMC was priced at $4,200 in all three segments, EVC in the Hi Speed segment was significantly higher than the price charged. Similar calculations for the Medium- and Lo-speed market segments yield EVC of $4,510 for the Medium segment, $310 more than the MMC purchase price of $4,200; and $3,900 for the Lo speed segment, $300 *less* than the MMC purchase price of $4,200.

Management considered two options: (1) cut price to match GDS and so maintain market share; (2) invest heavily to develop a new-generation MMC to serve the whole market. Neither was a good idea. Cutting price would significantly reduce profit and may lead to loss, especially as the reduction would do no more than maintain market share. The alternative, a new-generation MMC, would be expensive to develop with no reason to believe that customers would prefer this premium-priced alternative to the GDS.

The case illustrates the importance of segmenting the market and calculating the economic value to customer for each market segment. DEC was already missing out by failing to recognise the considerable value the MMC offered in the Hi Speed segment. Customers received a bargain, and, to a lesser extent, so did

Table 4.1 MMC versus GDS adapted from Shank (2006) Exhibit 1, p. 13

DEC and minicomputers

$	*Segmentation by computing speed*					
	Hi Speed (20%)		*Medium speed (20%)*		*Lo Speed (20%)*	
	MMC	*GDS*	*MMC*	*GDS*	*MMC*	*GDS*
Purchase cost		3600		3600		3600
Start up:						
Reprogramming	800	2500	500	1210	300	500
Installation	1050	1050	1050	1050	1050	1050
Post purchase (PV)	600	900	500	700	400	500
EVC	5600		4510		3900	

Source: In: Cases in Cost management: a Strategic Emphasis 3rd Ed. Cengage Learning Inc. Reproduced by permission.www.cengage.com/permissions

customers in the Medium Speed segment. The situation was different in the Lo Speed segment where the Data General product had the advantage, a sophisticated machine was not needed and the lower GDS price was attractive.

In both Hi and Medium segments the aim should have been to persuade customers that *it was in their interest* to purchase MMC in preference to GDS. Their life-cycle costs would be lower, significantly so in the Hi speed segment. The Lo speed segment presented a problem because the customers in this segment, 60% of the market, saw the GDS as better value than MMC. The answer was not to cut prices or introduce a new, more technologically advanced, MMC. Instead, a *lower* specification machine, priced to compete with GDS, was needed, perhaps by disabling some of the functionality of the MMC. The low-price product would not be attractive to Hi and Medium speed customers and MMC could maintain its dominance in these segments while fighting for market share in the Lo Speed segment.

4.4 The rise of value-based pricing

The Glacier Metal Company quantified "value" in the 1960s adding the value of "special features" to direct costs to calculate "standard value" of its products (Gabor, 1977). However, economic value to customer is different. It deals exclusively with price and value: the emphasis is *on what a customer (or group of customers)* will pay for the product and the starting point is the price of a reference product. *The cost of the product is irrelevant.*

McKinsey consultants have been central in the development of value-based pricing. Following the seminal work of Forbis and Mehta (1979, 1981), Lanning and Michaels (1988) described the firm as a "value delivery system": identifying, creating and communicating value to customers. Their examples included a tender chicken with a more consistent colour that transformed the chicken business and Canon's quality 35mm camera that targeted an unexploited market segment: neither a "professional" nor a cheap "snapshot" camera.

Another McKinsey consultant, Ohmae (1988), analysed the problem faced by Japanese manufacturers, caught between low-cost South Korean and high-end European competitors. He advocated greater attention to customer needs and described the problem faced by Yamaha, struggling to maintain a 40% share of a shrinking piano market. The solution was to target the 40 million existing pianos by developing a retrofit to increase the quality of play using digital and optical technology.

Academics and consultants quickly joined McKinsey in advocating value-based pricing. Nagle (1987) published the first edition of *The Strategy and Tactics of Pricing* emphasising the importance of customer needs and value rather than cost in price setting.[2] *The Strategy and Tactics of Pricing* has been translated into nine languages and, now in its sixth edition, has been restructured by Nagle and Müller (2018) so that economic value provides an underlying theme. Nagle and Müller developed their own version of economic value to the customer, economic value estimation, trademarked EVE™.

4.5 Integration of value-based pricing with economic and management accounting theory

Confusion can arise because economic value is also defined, in economic theory, as consumer surplus, the difference between what the customer is prepared to pay, and the actual price paid. In Figure 4.1 the consumer surplus, the difference between the demand curve and price paid, is shaded.

In this book economic value to the customer is defined as the maximum amount the customer would pay.

The ideas underpinning consumer surplus and economic value to the customer can be integrated with the important management accounting idea of contribution. Assume that value-based analysis based on a reference product, price £15,000, establishes that a customer would pay £20,000 for a new product that has a variable cost of £7,000. Based on an actual price of £18,000 Figure 4.2 sets out the relationships between economic value to the customer, consumer surplus, differential value and contribution.

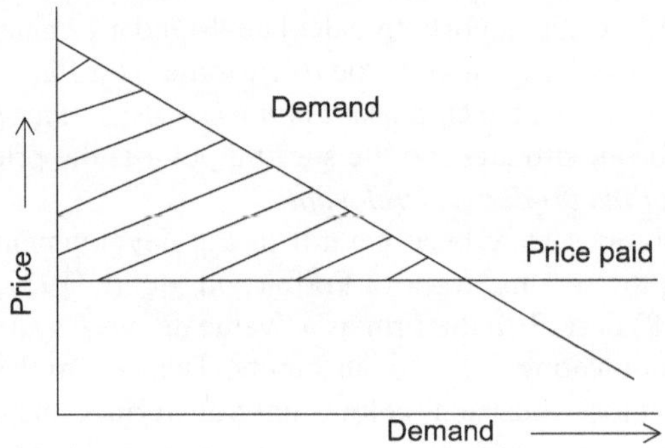

Figure 4.1 Consumer surplus: shaded

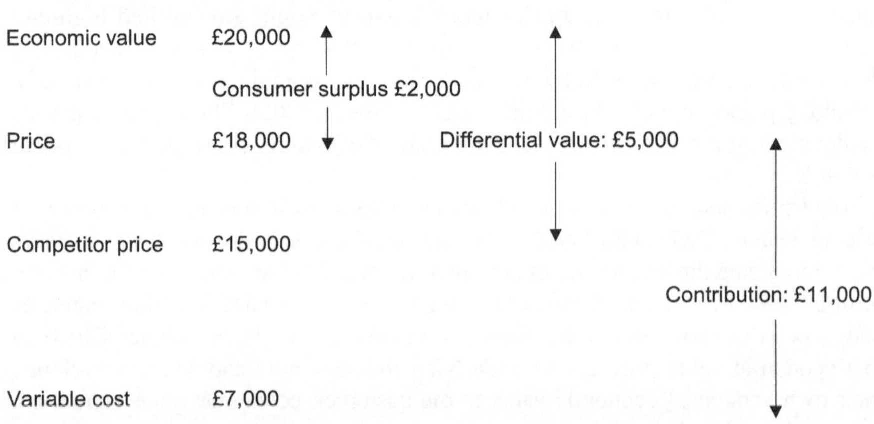

Figure 4.2 Relationships between consumer surplus, differential value and contribution

4.6 Obstacles to implementation

The essence of value-based pricing is simple enough and Hinterhuber (2008) referred to Ingenbleek et al. (2003) for evidence that the method is effective. A survey of 77 marketing managers found a positive correlation between the use of value-based pricing and new product success. There was no such correlation when other pricing methods were used.

However, the implementation of value-based pricing is not easy. Hinterhuber's (2008) survey of B2B industries led to the identification of five main reasons for resistance: value assessment, value communication, market segmentation, sales force management and top management support: there could be obstacles at every stage of the process!

Management accountants have a key role to play in addressing these obstacles, as noted by pricing guru, Thomas Nagle: "One of the missing skills is management accounting, which is usually different from the arbitrary "cost accounting" that companies use to value inventories for tax purposes . . ." (Forth, 2018).[3] We shall see that management accounting skills, identifying relevant cash flows, and evaluating the incremental impact of purchase, are crucial to effective "value management" especially in B2B markets. The following sections consider each step in the value-based pricing process, identifying the key issues in each step and the important role that management accountants should play.

4.7 Value creation

Establishing the extra value that a product or service might deliver *for the customer* is the crux of value-based pricing. In B2B transactions the main source of enhanced value is likely to be revenue gains or cost reductions and management accountants, experienced in identifying *relevant cash flows* and undertaking present value calculations, should have a key role. The management accountant must switch from an internal orientation to considering an investment (purchase) *by the customer*. If the purchase represents an investment, such as a machine, then the discount rate should reflect the *risk associated with the investment*: a risky investment should be evaluated using a relatively high discount rate.

The focus, in B2B pricing, is likely to be on incremental cash flows but, even in B2B markets, a significant part of "value" cannot be objectively quantified. In consumer goods markets the customer may value many aspects of the product other than its function, including emotional and status value. In business markets the emphasis is different, but still the product "package" may include commitments on issues such as reliability, service, support, delivery, inventory availability, priority of supply, warranty, insurance, financing arrangements, etc.

Putting a value on services associated with the product means research, listening carefully to the customer and perhaps offering a range of options: the customer's choice provides valuable insight as to what is really valued. For example, reliability might be especially important if the product's contribution to the "end-benefit" is small while some customers might place considerable value on the supplier's reputation.[4] The management accountant should assess the cost of the various elements of the package, *but it is the incremental value to the customer* that must be estimated and integrated into an overall spreadsheet analysis.

4.8 Value communication: B2B markets

If the management accountant has been involved in the analysis of value to the customer, then there is also a role in communicating that value through spreadsheets and presentations. The key is to show how the product or service benefits the customer. This is not the same as selling "features" such as 256GB memory or 5G connectivity. Nagle and Müller (2018) illustrate value communication with a detailed spreadsheet to identify revenue gains and cost reductions. They also emphasise the importance of price metrics in communicating value. For example, GE rent aircraft engines *per hour flown* so emphasising the performance delivered.

An impressive example of value communication in B2B markets is described by Snelgrove (2017). Snelgrove, Global Vice President of Value at SKF, a manufacturer of industrial bearings, notes that what matters is not the "unique selling proposition" as seen by the SKF engineers but the importance of what *customers* value. This puts the emphasis on engagement with customers to identify (the customer's) total costs and total benefits of ownership. The aim is to "demonstrate in numbers how you can affect and measure the impact of your offering" (p. 79). In the early 2000s SKF developed the "Documented Solutions Program"™ to demonstrate the cash advantages of choosing the SKF product. "At the end of 2015 we had over 66,301 accepted or verified cases" (p. 80).

The management accountant should, again, have a key role to play, creating worksheets that systematically set out the costs, revenues and benefits and communicating the value proposition to the customer. Snelgrove refers to extensive documentation of previous cases that has become a vital sales tool at SKF allowing customers to see the impact of potential savings in financial terms through key metrics such as ROI (return on investment), net present value and cash flow break-even as well as cash savings.

4.9 Value communication: consumer goods markets

In consumer markets the communication of value must include both economic and psychological aspects. Once again, the emphasis must be on what the customer values. For example, Vauxhall draws attention to the practical value of the Crossland X: "Muddy rugby boots. Fizzy-drink spills. Scattered popcorn from the cinema. Luckily, the life-ready Crossland X is ready for it all".[5] Similarly, Nectar focuses on customer needs in advertising the "premium" mattress that "hugs your body and keeps you cool for the best of both worlds."[6]

The communication of value in consumer markets is less about economic benefits and more about the customer's subjective perception of the value of the product. Pricing strategies may focus on tangible benefits such as the practical nature of an SUV or the comfort of a good mattress but, equally, the customer's perception may be influenced by other factors. Insights from the developing field of behavioural economics have been integrated into pricing theory with concepts such as anchoring, extreme aversion, decoys and the endowment effect, topics to be considered in Chapter 7.

We have already seen how companies manipulate price metrics to persuade the customer that they are receiving a good deal. For example, monthly, weekly or daily prices can seem cheaper than an annual fee and it can sometimes be difficult to estimate the "price" because the customer is offered "easy" payment terms or different pack sizes.

4.10 Setting the price: price elasticity

"Economic value to the customer" is the *maximum* that a rational customer would pay, and the actual price needs to take account of company strategy and likely competitor reaction. In theory price setting might be based on the elasticity of demand, ε:

$$\varepsilon = \frac{\text{percentage change in quantity}}{\text{percentage change in price}}$$

Elasticity provides a measure of customers' sensitivity to price changes. If a price change leads to a more than proportionate change in quantity demanded, then demand is elastic; if a price change leads to a less than proportionate change in quantity demanded then demand is inelastic. In the former case revenue can be increased by reducing price, whereas, in the latter case, reducing price leads to a fall in revenue.

However, Nagle and Müller (2018) caution that: "Sensitivity to price depends . . . on ever-changing purchase contexts and perceptions" (p. 7) and Smith (2011) gives an indication of the problems in estimating demand sensitivity: "Disentangling the impact of market environmental factors and industry practices from the relationship of prices and volumes requires carefully collecting the relevant data from numerous sources . . . and repeatedly running a multivariate regression analysis under different assumptions" (p. 32). He adds that attempts to derive economically optimal prices "suffers from a challenge in identifying the relevant elasticity of demand and variable costs . . . neither of these challenges can be overcome appropriately using historic metrics".

4.11 Setting the price: the use of break-even analysis

Recognising the problems in directly identifying demand elasticity, several authors recommend a technique very familiar to management accountants: break-even analysis. The key idea is that sales and marketing managers can be presented with break-even volumes and asked for the probability that they will be achieved.

Nagle and Müller (2018) derive a "simple formula" to calculate the percentage change in sales needed to achieve break-even contribution following a change in price, ΔP:

$$\% \text{ change in unit sales} = (-\Delta P \times 100)/(CM + \Delta P)$$

CM is the existing contribution margin and CM + ΔP is the new contribution margin after the price change. Dividing the change in price by the new contribution margin and multiplying by 100 gives the percentage change in sales needed for break-even.

Changes in price have a disproportionate impact on volume needed to break-even. For example, a product priced at £100 generates a contribution of £30. Volume needed to break-even after a 5% price reduction?

$$\% \text{ change in unit sales} = (5 \times 100)/(30\text{–}5) = 20\%$$

In using the formula, care is needed with the sign of ΔP.

A 20% increase in quantity is needed to compensate a 5% reduction in price. In this case elasticity of demand would be calculated as:

$$\varepsilon = \% \text{ change in quantity}/\% \text{ change in price} = 20/{-5} = -4$$

A very elastic demand response is required to justify a price decrease (the percentage change in volume is four times the percentage change in price).

Break-even volume is a much simpler idea than demand elasticity and, by taking changes in contribution margin into account, immediately provides executives with a benchmark volume. If elasticity of demand were estimated at, say, -3, it would not be immediately obvious whether a price decrease would be compensated by increased demand.

The formula is easily extended to take account of changes in both price and variable cost and Smith's (2011) version is the "volume hurdle formula":

$$\%\Delta Q \geq -\Delta CM/(\Delta CM + CM_i) \qquad \text{(Eqn 2–13 p. 37)}$$

ΔCM replaces ΔP in the numerator while the denominator is still the new contribution margin (the change in contribution margin, ΔCM, added to the initial contribution margin, CM_i)

For example, a product might be improved expecting that this will allow a higher price to be charged. Taking the previous example of a product with price £100 and variable cost of £70, assume that variable cost is increased to £80 and price for the improved product is set at £120:

$$\%\Delta Q \geq -\Delta CM/(\Delta CM + CM_i)$$
$$\%\Delta Q \geq -10/(10 + 30)$$
$$\%\Delta Q \geq -25\%$$

In this example replacing a product with an improved version at a higher price and cost could sustain a sales reduction of 25% without losing contribution.

Schindler (2012) makes extensive use of break-even analysis, taking the ideas step-by-step. He first refers to the simple breakeven formula: BE = ΔFC/CM, where BE is the increase in volume required to cover an increase in fixed costs, ΔFC and CM is the contribution margin. He then extends the formula to deal with incremental fixed costs and/or changes in variable costs:

$$\text{BE} = \frac{\Delta\text{FC} - (\Delta\text{CM} \times \text{Base sales})}{\text{CM}}$$

In this "generalized break-even formula" BE is break-even volume, ΔFC is the change in fixed costs, ΔCM is the change in contribution and CM is the ***new*** contribution after the proposed change. This is essentially the same as Smith's formula but a change in fixed costs is included in the numerator and the formula gives the absolute break-even quantity rather than a percentage change in quantity.

The management accountant is well placed to guide pricing and marketing executives through break-even calculations. "Contribution margin" is fundamental to the analysis and variable cost needs to be carefully considered in the calculation. In addition to direct product and distribution costs, promotion and other expenses might also be important. The role of management accountants in supporting marketing and sales executives is both obvious and important.

4.12 Managing the sales force: incentive schemes

If value has been created, a strategy for communication agreed and a target price set there remains the important step of implementing the value-based strategy and Nagle and Müller (2018) note that incentive schemes can stimulate the wrong behaviour. A scheme that rewards increased volume, market share or plant utilisation may stimulate volume but at low prices while a scheme based on target margins might limit sales volume unnecessarily. Incentive schemes throughout the company need to be aligned with the value-based strategy if it is to succeed.

Nagle and Müller suggest a simple adjustment to the usual volume-based sales goal. Sales reps are to be rewarded based on sales volume but based on *target prices*. The sales credit they receive is adjusted downward if they sell below the target price and upward if they sell above the target price:

"Sales Credit = [Target Price – k (Target Price – Actual Price)] × Units Sold" (p. 278)

k is a profitability factor and could be set to adjust sales credits proportionately to profitability by making it: ". . . equal 1 divided by the product's percentage contribution margin at the target price" (p. 278).

Management accountants can work with senior managers to develop incentive schemes in line with a value-based focus and the management accountant's first task is to agree with a target price that would generate the desired contribution and profit targets.

> To take our now familiar example, if the target price is £100 with 30% contribution margin, to ensure that there is no financial incentive to lose contribution by offering a discount, k would be set at 3.33 (1/0.3). This has the effect of reducing the "sales credit". For example, a sale of one unit at £90 generates £66.67 of "sales credit" rather than £90 (the actual sale) or, even worse, £100 (the price before discount):
>
> Sales Credit = [Target Price – k(Target Price – Actual Price)] × Units Sold
> Sales Credit = [100–3.33(100–90)] × 1 = £66.7

If the sale had been at the target price of £100 contribution, then £30 of sales credit would have been generated but, by offering a 10% discount, the contribution has been reduced to £20 per unit. The discounted sale generates 33.3% less contribution than expected so the sales credit is reduced by 33.3% from £100 to £66.7. In this case, if k is set higher than 3.33 then the adjustment is more than proportional to the contribution lost, an even greater disincentive to giving discounts. Of course, if a sale is made at a higher price than the target then the sales rep benefits from an increased sales credit.

4.13 Take-up of value-based pricing

Despite the advantages of value-based pricing, take-up is slow. A study by Liozu (2017) revealed a similar picture to Hinterhuber (2008). Questionnaires to 2,500 companies resulted in 144 usable replies and respondents reported that the most popular primary pricing method was competition-based (44%), the second was cost-based pricing (31%) and just 25% for value-based pricing.[7]

There was confusion over whether value-based pricing was a strategy (39%), a method (22%), a framework (13%), an orientation (13%) or an approach (9%). The main problems were identification of proper drivers of value; segmentation of the customer base; and a reference value based on identification of prices of competitors: technical obstacles, similar to those discovered by Hinterhuber (2008). In addition, there was agreement that multifunctional collaboration was key to successful implementation but, in practice, there was insufficient collaboration between the innovation and product development teams and the pricing organisation. Liozu concluded that successful value-based-pricing required resources to drive customer intimacy, customer segmentation, competitive analysis and managed differentiation.

4.14 Summary

Value-based pricing has been strongly recommended by high-profile consultants and authors and, in principle, it provides an important counter to cost-based pricing by emphasising what the *customer* values. While consideration of cost can provide an indication of the *minimum* price, a value-based price indicates the *maximum* price that might be charged. The third element in the decision is the competitive situation. Consideration of competitor prices and the value they offer will be a major consideration in pitching the price between a cost-based minimum and a value-based maximum.

Value-based pricing requires estimation of a product's incremental value to a customer or group of customers and management accountants should have a key role to play both in the calculation of economic value to the customer and in communicating that value. *Relevant* cash flows are key in both calculating and demonstrating quantitative aspects of value and should ensure a vital role for management accountants in the team. Equally the numerical skills of management accountants should see them play an important role in assessing the consequences of a price change, particularly in the calculation of the volume change needed to break even. Finally, management accountants should have a role in the development of incentive schemes that support value-based pricing. Numerical and technical expertise should be invaluable in setting target prices and in considering the consequences of various formulas that might be used to incentivise value-based pricing.

In sum, value-based pricing should see management accountants become active business partners working with marketing, product development and HR in developing value-based management. Value-based pricing needs an integrated multifunctional team although, as Liozu found, this is not easy to achieve.

This chapter has emphasised the relation between customer perceived value and price and this relationship is fundamental to understanding a company's position in relation to its competitors and the broader market. Price-value maps are the basis for this analysis and are considered in the next chapter.

Notes

1 It can be argued that there is additional functionality because higher milage per gallon means less time spent filling up with petrol, but this has been ignored.
2 Nagle established the Strategic Pricing Group Inc. in 1987, which subsequently became part of Monitor Group and, in 2013, Monitor Deloitte.
3 Steven Forth (2018) is a representative of Ibbaka, a technology consultancy specialising in market segmentation, customer targeting and pricing design.
4 Global accounting companies such as KPMG and Deloitte can charge a premium for their accounting services. The importance of reputation was demonstrated when, following its perceived role in the Enron disaster, the major accounting firm, Arthur Andersen, went out of business.
5 www.edenmotorgroup.com/vauxhall/new-cars/new-crossland/
6 www.nectarsleep.co.uk/pages/bed-and-mattress
7 This despite the population based on a database of past and current customers provided by Leverage Point Innovation, a supplier of value-based pricing software.

References

Forbis J. L. and Mehta N. T. (1979) Economic value to the customer, *McKinsey Staff Paper*, in: Golub H., Henry J., Forbis J. L., Mehhta N. T., Lanning M. J., Michaels E. G. and Ohmae K. (2000) Delivering value to customers, *McKinsey Quarterly*, June, downloaded 23/12/2019 from: www.mckinsey.com/business-functions/strategy-and-corporate-finance/our-insights/delivering-value-to-customers

Forbis J. L. and Mehta N. T. (1981) Value-based strategies for industrial products, *Business Horizons*, 24(3), May–June, 32–42

Forth S. (2018) *Value-Based Pricing's Senior Statesman Tom Nagle on the Skills Needed for Pricing Expertise*, downloaded 29/12/2019 from: www.ibbaka.com/ibbaka-market-blog/value-based-pricings-senior-statesman-tom-nagle-on-the-skills-needed-for-pricing-expertise

Gabor A. (1977) *Pricing: Principles and Practices*, Heinemann Educational Books, London

Hinterhuber A. (2008) Customer value-based pricing strategies: why companies resist, *Journal of Business Strategy*, 29(4), 41–50

Ingenbleek P., Debruyne M., Frambach R. and Verhallen T. (2003) Successful new product pricing practices: a contingency approach, *Marketing Letters*, 14(4), 289–305

Lanning M. J. and Michaels E. G. (1988) A business is a value delivery system, *McKinsey Quarterly*, June 2000, downloaded 7/3/2018 from: www.mckinsey.com/business-functions/strategy-and-corporate-finance/our-insights/delivering-value-to-customers

Liozu S. M. (2017) State of value-based-pricing survey: perceptions, challenges and impact, *Journal of Revenue and Pricing Management*, 16, 18–29

Nagle T. T. (1987) *The Strategy and Tactics of Pricing*, Prentice-Hall Inc., Englewood Cliffs, NJ

Nagle T. T. and Müller G. (2018) *The Strategy and Tactics of Pricing*, 6th edition, Routledge, New York and Abingdon, Oxon

Ohmae K. (1988) Getting back to strategy, *Harvard Business Review*, 66(6), 149–156

Schindler R. M. (2012) *Pricing Strategies: A Marketing Approach*, Sage Publications Inc., Thousand Oaks, CA

Shank J. K. (2006) DEC and minicomputers, in: *Cases in Cost management: A Strategic Emphasis*, 3rd edition, pp. 131–136, Thomson South Western, Mason, OH

Smith T. J. (2011) *Pricing Strategy: Setting Price Levels, Managing Price Discounts, & Establishing Price Structures*, Cengage Learning, Boston, MA

Snelgrove T. C. (2017) Quantifying your value so customers are willing and able to pay for it, in: Hinterhuber A. and Snelgrove T. C. (eds) *Value First Then Price*, pp. 75–90, Routledge, Abingdon, Oxon

5 Price-value maps

5.1 The idea

McKinsey consultants, Forbis and Mehta (1979) developed the idea of economic value to the customer and the idea was extended by Golub and Henry (1981). They suggested a price-value graph such as that shown in Figure 5.1. In the original paper value was shown on the y-axis and price on the x-axis. However, Figure 5.1 follows more recent practice with price on the y-axis and value on the x-axis (for example, see Marn et al. (2004) Chapters 4 and 6 or Smith (2011) p. 62.)

In Figure 5.1 product A lies on the value-price indifference curve while product B lies to the left and product C to the right. The size of the circles is intended to show market share and product B, offering lower value, has the smallest market share. Product C, offering good value at a competitive price, dominates the market. Golub and Henry acknowledge that constructing a price-value map is tricky because it requires an estimate of a product's value as perceived by an average customer. Nevertheless, they suggest that, with industry knowledge and some analysis, the map can be constructed with sufficient accuracy to inform strategic analysis.

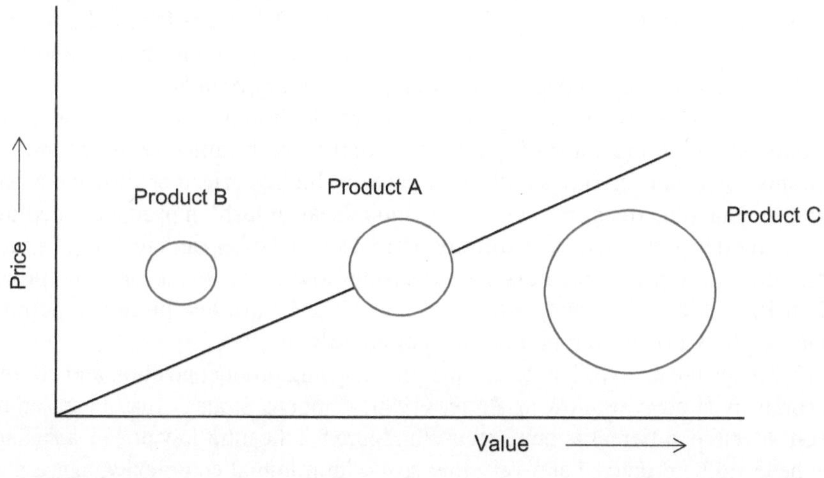

Figure 5.1 Price-value map

DOI: 10.4324/9781003272731-5

5.2 The value-equivalence line

Price-value maps have become a staple of price and marketing theory and Smith (2011) provides a thorough treatment of the basic ideas. The indifference curve is renamed the "value equivalence line" (VEL) and lines running parallel to the VEL delineate the "zone of indifference". Products that lie outside the zone of indifference are considered value advantaged or value disadvantaged so that Product B in Figure 5.1 is value disadvantaged while Product C is value advantaged. Texts now refer to "perceived price" on the Y axis and "perceived benefits" on the X axis. The reference to "perceived" benefits is easy to understand because what matters is *customer perception.* We saw in Chapter 3 that some customers prefer to purchase branded goods rather than functionally equivalent generic products. More difficult to grasp is perceived price, as, apparently, price can be readily observed. However, *perceived* price takes account of the influence of factors such as the price metric. For example, some customers will think that the AA's discounted price of £11 per month for roadside and home assistance plus national recovery is cheaper than the 2018 price of £119 per year.

5.3 Product positioning

A price-value map for cars available in the UK in 2021 is shown in Figure 5.2 based on the lowest price advertised for the models selected. The parallel lines on the diagram reflect the "zone of indifference," models within these lines are judged to lie on the value-equivalence line.

Simon and Fassnacht (2019) provide an in-depth discussion of the characteristics of each of the performance/price positions ranging from ultra-low through low, medium, premium to the luxury price position. Their examples include Tata Nano and Dacia Logan small cars for ultra-low price examples; the discount supermarkets Aldi and Lidl and the low-cost airlines Ryanair and EasyJet for the low-price position; Cadbury chocolate and the VW Passat for medium price examples; BMW 7 series and Ralph Lauren T-shirt for premium brands and Ferrari 458 Italia and Burj Al Arab (Royal Suite) for luxury brands.

They summarise pricing strategies: luxury brands should have a very high price (to some extent an indicator of quality and luxury) with limited editions and no discounts; premium brands should be relatively highly priced with discounting only in special circumstances such as for end of season fashion products; medium prices should be consistent with differentiation, special offers and techniques such as bundling; low-price operators should sustain low prices (everyday low prices or EDLP) with no complexity and no discounts; and ultra-low price competitors sell at very low prices with no discounts or complexity.

Value maps are an excellent technique for analysing product position and clarifying company strategy. Following Porter (1980) company strategy may be based on price-leadership, differentiation or focus. In Figure 5.2 the ultra-low price Dacia Sandero needs to be produced at a very low cost with minimal complexity, aggressive value engineering and tight cost control. For cost leadership, Shank (1989, 1996)

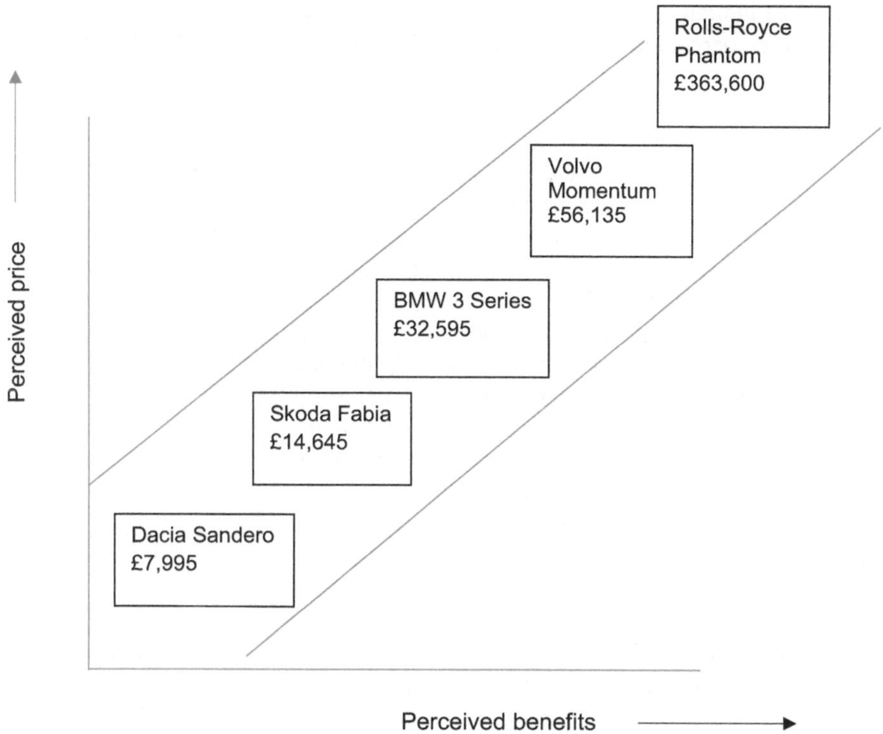

Figure 5.2 Price-value map: examples of UK automobiles April 2021

identifies standard costs, budgets, minimisation of discretionary costs, economies of scale, learning curve effects and competitor cost analysis as important.

In the middle ranges the emphasis moves away from cost minimisation as product differentiation becomes important. Differentiated products can deliver higher margins as in the RAC's "advanced" and "ultimate" versions. For differentiated products Shank emphasises brand loyalty, customer service, dealer network and product features as possible sources of uniqueness.

Finally, there is the luxury product where the cost of production is less important than maintaining the brand image. Effective marketing and advertising become vital and building a loyal customer base that values the luxury offering is crucial, anything that detracts from reputation must be avoided.

5.4 Using the value map

McKinsey consultants Leszinski and Marn (1997) show how the value map can be used to analyse product position. They describe the Alpha Computer Company where the company believed that high processing speed and data access together with a lower price would lead to a value advantage, but, inexplicably, the product was losing market share. Alpha's problem was its focus on technical features while investigation revealed that, instead, customers valued software/hardware compatibility, perceived reliability, technical support and the quality of user documents. From the *customer's point of view*, the product was value disadvantaged. Price-value analysis was the first step to remedial action.

McKinsey consultants continue to disseminate impressive examples. Doucette et al. (2014) discussed the use of market maps in analysing product attributes for consumer-packaged-goods markets. A beverage company discovered that brand and flavour were not the key drivers of customer value: portability and a convenient size were more important. A consumer healthcare company discovered that consumers were broadly indifferent between medications in tablet, capsule or liquid form and was able to reduce its product range. A manufacturer of mattresses discovered that customers were not particularly interested in technological claims and focused product development and advertising on comfort and restfulness. A pharmaceutical company discovered that customers preferred to see products grouped according to their uses, for example in relieving headaches or back pain rather than in categories such as aspirin, ibuprofen etc.

5.5 The dynamic value map

Price value maps can also be used to analyse how changes occur over time. Baker et al. (2010) refer to Gild-tech, the leading supplier in high volume blood diagnostic equipment, about to introduce an improved blood testing machine. The improvements were judged to be worth a price increase of 10% but more market share might be captured by holding the price steady. A compromise, 4% price increase, was agreed. Initially, customers responded by purchasing a product with improved benefits (more accurate and faster cycle times) for a fairly small increase in price. Increased productivity was probably worth much more than the 4% price increase. However, after initial success and increased market share, competitors reacted in the only way they could, by reducing prices. The dynamic value map is shown in Figure 5.3. The dotted line represents the new VEL after competitors reduced their prices to compete with the new Gild-tech product. The consequence was that *the whole industry* became less profitable, consumers benefited by receiving either more value for a modest price increase (the Gild-tech product) or the same value at lower price (the competitors).

Marn et al. (2004) provide more examples. "Sure Motors" developed a more durable model line with a better warranty but held prices steady. As in the Gild-tech example, the new product was value-advantaged and gained market share. However, with no model upgrade readily available, competitors were forced to compete on price, moving the VEL *for the industry* to the right and all firms lost profit. The Mazda Miata, a well-built small sports car was popular but underpriced at a suggested retail price of $13,800 when launched in the US. In this case the VEL did not move but only because dealers saw an opportunity and simply sold the new model at a higher price and "eagerly pocketed the surplus for themselves" (p. 96).

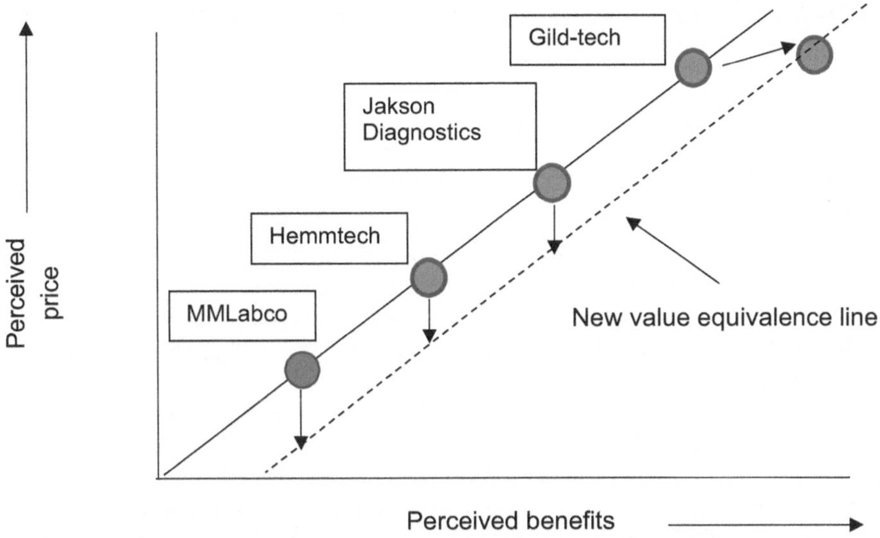

Figure 5.3 Blood Diagnostics Machines Company: Price War Effect

Source: Copyright (2010) Wiley. Used with permission from (Baker, Marn and Zawada, Exhibit 8–3 Blood Diagnostics Machines Company: Price War Effect, *The Price Advantage*, John Wiley & Sons, Inc.)

These examples show the importance of understanding the market and the usefulness of value maps in providing insights when considering price and product strategy and in anticipating the consequences of competitive actions. We return to this topic in Chapter 13 in the discussion of competition and avoidance of price wars.

5.6 Product attributes that customers value

Probably the most difficult step in using value maps is identifying and analysing the product attributes that are valued by customers. However, in some cases, a relatively simple approach can lead to important insights. In the Alpha Computers case, interviews with just 60 buyers established that hardware and software compatibility, reliability and technical support were more important than processor speed. A relatively unsophisticated exercise was sufficient to provide vital insight into customer priorities.

Advances in both theory and data processing have led to more sophisticated methods in evaluating the attributes that customers value, particularly conjoint analysis and discrete choice experiments. Conjoint analysis, typically, has consumers rank the various attributes of the product or service, computes "partial utilities" (the utility provided by each attribute) and aggregates these into the total utility provided by the product. Discrete choice experiments, instead, present consumers with options or scenarios and ask them to state their preferred option.

This allows the weight attached to different product or service attributes to be inferred. Expert advice should be sought if sophisticated methods such as these are considered.

5.7 Implications for management accounting

Company strategy

If the strategy is cost-leadership then the management accountant can bring to bear the full array of cost reduction and cost control techniques. Value analysis and value engineering might reduce direct costs, "operational" activity-based management might reveal opportunities to eliminate or reduce non-value-adding activities and tight budgeting to control discretionary costs together with standard costing will be important.

If a differentiation strategy is adopted then, when selling a durable product, such as an automobile or a washing machine, the aim will be to provide the customer with a choice and, wherever possible, to demonstrate that there is value to the customer in purchasing an upgraded model or version. The management accountant should be part of the multidisciplinary team that establishes product options and the contribution generated by each option.

Incentive schemes

The incentive for sales reps should be to generate the highest contribution possible from each sale. The incentive scheme must be carefully designed taking account of the nature of the product sold. The last chapter emphasised the need to reward *profitable* sales rather than sales volume. This chapter introduces some of the nuances that can arise. For low-price, value products, the "target price" will be the list price, sales reps should be dissuaded from discounting. For relatively higher priced variants it might be judicious to set a target price *below* list price to encourage sales reps to promote higher margin products.

Constructing value maps

The management accountant's quantitative and spreadsheet skills may be valuable in constructing value maps. For example, the value map of automobiles considered earlier is not drawn to scale with the Rolls Royce Phantom some 45 times more expensive than the Dacia Sandero. In this case a logarithmic scale for price would be sensible so that the price-value graph appears as in Figure 5.4.

An analysis such as this would lead immediately to the question whether a model should be developed to tap the market above the Volvo but below the Rolls Royce. However, it is important to remember that the price-value map is only a starting point for analysis. There may be an opportunity to reach a market that is not currently served, but only market research can determine whether such a market exists.

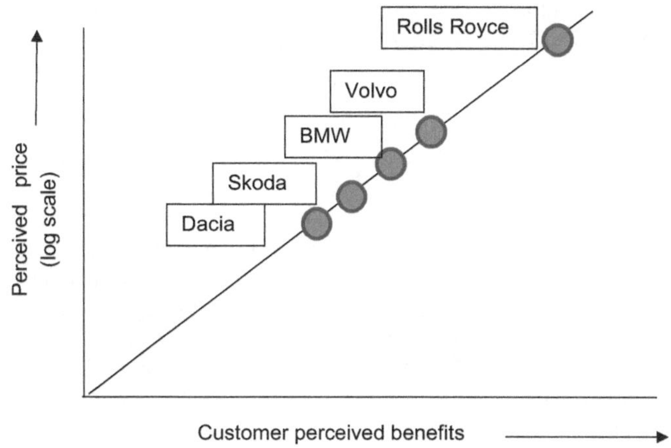

Figure 5.4 Price-value map for automobiles, log scale for price

5.8 Conclusions

This chapter has shown how company strategies can be understood by developing a price-value map.[1] There are a range of possible product positions, and the value map identifies the positions that both the company and its competitors hold. From the company's point of view the value map clarifies an explicit strategy or reveals an implicit strategy and, importantly, clarifies the company's segmentation strategy. A company may attack different segments or market niches in different industries or, more likely, it may attack more than one segment in a particular industry. For example, car manufacturers typically segment the market with models aimed at the low, medium and premium sectors; supermarkets have value, standard and premium versions of their own-brand products; providers of roadside assistance offer basic support supplemented by enhanced packages that sell at premium prices; drug manufacturers target both price-insensitive customers with high priced premium brands and price-sensitive customers with generic alternatives. These examples show how segmentation and price-value analysis can help a company to determine its pricing strategy and can facilitate price discrimination, charging different prices for the same or similar goods.

Note

1 McKinsey consultants have been central to the development of value-based ideas and their seminal papers are available at: www.mckinsey.com/business-functions/strategy-and-corporate-finance/our-insights/delivering-value-to-customers

References

Baker W. L., Marn M. V. and Zawada C. C. (2010) *The Price Advantage*, 2nd edition, Wiley & Sons, Hoboken, NJ

Doucette J., Holsztejn F. and Kuijpers D. (2014) *Market Map: Finding Pockets of Growth in Mature Markets*, downloaded 17/04/2021 from: www.mckinsey.com/~/media/mckinsey/dotcom/client_service/Retail/Articles/Perspectives

Forbis J. L. and Mehta N. T. (1979) Economic value to the customer, *McKinsey Staff Paper*, in: Golub H., Henry J., Forbis J. L., Mehhta N. T., Lanning M. J., Michaels E. G. and Ohmae K. (2000) Delivering value to customers, *McKinsey Quarterly*, June, downloaded 23/12/2019 from: www.mckinsey.com/business-functions/strategy-and-corporate-finance/our-insights/delivering-value-to-customers

Golub H. and Henry J. (1981) Market strategy and the price – value model, *McKinsey Staff Paper*, in: Golub H., Henry J., Forbis J. L., Mehta N. T., Lanning M. J., Michaels E. G. and Ohmae K. (2000) Delivering value to customers, *McKinsey Quarterly*, June, downloaded 6/3/2018 from: www.mckinsey.com/business-functions/strategy-and-corporate-finance/our-insights/delivering-value-to-customers

Leszinski R. and Marn M. V. (1997) Setting value, not price, *McKinsey Quarterly*, Feb, 1–27 downloaded 15/04/2021 from: www.mckinsey.com/business-functions/marketing-and-sales/our-insights/setting-value-not-price

Marn M. V., Roegner E. V. and Zawada C. C. (2004) *The Price Advantage*, Wiley & Sons, Hoboken, NJ

Porter M. E. (1980) *Competitive Strategy*, Free Press, New York

Shank J. K. (1989) Strategic cost management: new wine, or just new bottles? *Journal of Management Accounting Research*, 1, Fall, 47–65

Shank J. K. (1996) Analysing technology investments – from NPV to strategic cost management, *Management Accounting Research*, 7, 185–197

Simon H. and Fassnacht M. (2019) *Price Management: Strategy, Analysis, Decision, Implementation*, Springer, Cham, Switzerland

Smith T. J. (2011) *Pricing Strategy: Setting Price Levels, Managing Price Discounts, & Establishing Price Structures*, Cengage Learning, Boston, MA

6 Basic economics

6.1 Introduction

This chapter introduces (or revises) some basic economic ideas. Price theory is based on the interaction of supply and demand, and, for individual firms, profit is maximised where marginal revenue is equal to marginal cost. The firm's marginal revenue curve is derived from the firm's demand curve which depends upon the firm's market power. The firm may be one of several firms in a very competitive market, or, at the other extreme, the firm might be a monopolist, dominating the market. This chapter begins by considering these extreme cases, then shows how the profit-maximising formula for a company with monopoly power can be derived in terms of the elasticity of demand. The rationale for price discrimination is then introduced.

6.2 "Perfect" and monopoly markets

Basic economics considers two "ideal" types of market: perfect markets and pure monopoly. A perfect market presumes many sellers supplying a single commodity product to many buyers who have a perfect understanding of the market. Individual firms are too small to influence the market price and all firms are "price takers". They must accept the market price no matter how many units they sell, and each firm faces a horizontal demand curve, see Figure 6.1.

In economic theory firms have U-shaped cost curves. Initially, as more units are produced, the cost per unit falls due to economies of scale. (A management accountant would see this as spreading the fixed costs of production over an

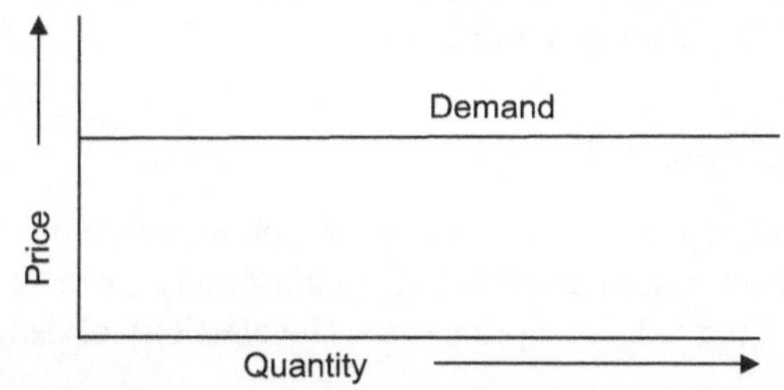

Figure 6.1 Demand curve faced by a firm in perfect competition

DOI: 10.4324/9781003272731-6

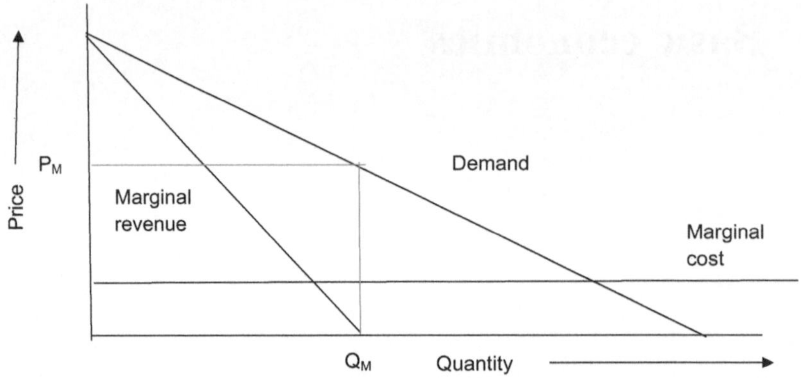

Figure 6.2 Price and quantity set by a profit-maximising monopolist

increasing volume of units produced.) Eventually, however, the firm's cost curve starts to increase as diseconomies set in: it becomes more and more difficult to produce an extra unit from a given arrangement of the factors of production. In perfect competition all firms produce at a scale that minimises cost. Any firm that failed to do this would be driven out of the market because its costs would exceed its revenue. The industry operates at maximum efficiency with each firm just covering its costs and making a "normal profit". In economic theory *normal profit* is a *cost of production*. It is the minimum return needed to attract entrepreneurs to the industry.

At the other extreme a monopoly arises when a single firm supplies all the output in an industry. Now customers must purchase at the price set by the monopolist. The demand curve for a monopolist is the demand curve for the industry and will be downward sloping for two reasons. First, as price falls individuals are tempted to purchase more units: in economic terms the utility received from each unit declines as more are purchased (the law of diminishing marginal utility). Second, some customers will not purchase at high prices but, as the price falls, they are persuaded to purchase.

To maximise profit the monopolist will choose an increased price and reduced output compared to price and output in a competitive market. To demonstrate this, assume the monopolist has a linear, downward sloping demand curve and, to keep things simple, has a constant variable/marginal cost. Then profit will be maximised where marginal revenue, the revenue from another unit, and marginal cost, the cost of producing another unit, are equal; see Figure 6.2. The monopolist restricts output to Q_M and sets a price of P_M.

6.3 Elasticity of demand

If a firm in a perfect market were to reduce price, in theory, it would capture the entire market as customers, buying a commodity product and with perfect knowledge, switch to the lowest price firm. The elasticity of demand is defined as:

$$\varepsilon = \frac{(\%\,\text{change in quantity demanded})}{(\%\,\text{change in price})}$$

And, for a firm operating in a perfect market, elasticity of demand would approach infinity as a very small price reduction would capture the whole market.

For a monopolist the situation is different, if the monopolist reduces price demand will increase, the increase depending on the elasticity of demand at the existing price and quantity. If a change in price has little effect on quantity demanded, then elasticity of demand will be small. For example, if a 20% reduction in price leads to only a 5% increase in demand:

$$\varepsilon = \frac{(\%\,\text{change in quantity demanded})}{(\%\,\text{change in price})} = \frac{5}{-20} = -0.25$$

Elasticity of demand is –0.25.

The steeper the demand curve the less is the elasticity of demand, ε (in absolute terms). Elasticity is negative because a percentage *increase* in price ($\Delta P/P$) will result in a percentage *decrease* in volume ($\Delta Q/Q$). However, in economic theory the reference is usually to the *absolute* value of elasticity (0.25 in the above example). Elasticity greater than 1 is referred to as elastic (percentage change in volume greater than percentage change in price) while elasticity less than 1 is referred to as inelastic (percentage change in volume less than percentage change in price).

6.4 Profit maximising formula for a monopolist

One more unit sold means more revenue: the price, P, of the unit. However, revenue is also lost because, to sell an extra unit, price must be reduced and existing sales, Q, sell at a lower price. There are two effects, an increase from the price P and a decrease from loss of revenue on existing units. Mathematically:

Extra (marginal) revenue $MR = P - Q\,(\Delta P / \Delta Q)$
And as elasticity of demand $\varepsilon = (\Delta Q/Q) \times (P/\Delta P)$
We can write $Q\,(\Delta P / \Delta Q) = P/\varepsilon$
So, marginal revenue $MR = P - P/|\varepsilon|$
And $MR = P\,(1 - 1/|\varepsilon|)$

In this formula we need the absolute value of ε because MR is *reduced* by the lower price from existing sales.

To maximise profit the monopolist sets marginal revenue equal to marginal cost, MC, so:

$$MC = P(1 - 1/|\varepsilon|)$$

$$\text{And } P = MC\,\frac{|\varepsilon|}{|\varepsilon| - 1}$$

This formula, the Amoroso-Robinson equation, restates the profit maximising condition MR = MC in terms of the elasticity of demand and shows that maximum profit is achieved by marking up marginal cost, MC,[1] by a factor dependent on ε, the elasticity of demand.

It is important to be careful with signs in this formula. We noted that ε is negative because a reduction in price leads to an increase in volume and the equation may also be written:

$$P = MC \frac{\varepsilon}{(1+\varepsilon)}$$

In this formulation, there is no need to show ε as an absolute number but now, when inserting a value for ε into the formula, it will be a negative figure.

The formula shows that the optimal price for a monopolist can be derived as an elasticity-based markup on marginal cost and shows that, as one would expect, the more monopoly power, the higher the profit maximising price. For a monopolist with a steep demand curve and demand elasticity of, say, –1.5, the profit maximising price would be:

$P = MC\ -1.5/-0.5$ a 300% markup over marginal cost

Conversely, the greater the elasticity of demand, the lower the markup over marginal cost. For example, if demand elasticity were large, say –10 (a 10% decrease in price results in a 100% increase in volume), the markup over marginal cost would be just 11% and, if elasticity were very large (as in a perfect market where all firms are price-takers), the markup over marginal cost approaches zero: in a perfect market the market price is equal to marginal cost.

The optimum price, P*, is always in the elastic section of the demand curve. It can be seen from the formulas that, if elasticity is less than 1 (in absolute terms), the markup on marginal cost would be negative.

6.5 Segmentation and price discrimination

As we saw in Chapter 3, companies often charge different prices to different customer groups, in different places and for essentially similar products. If a company can divide its market into separate segments and charge different prices in each segment, we have a "discriminating monopolist" where the monopolist sets a profit maximising price in each separate market segment. Naturally, the company charges a higher price in segments that have less price sensitivity and, conversely, a lower price in price-sensitive segments. As noted in Section 6.4, the profit maximising price is related to elasticity of demand and, the lower the elasticity, the higher the markup on marginal cost.

6.6 Definitions

Price discrimination and market segmentation are closely linked. If a market can be segmented then there is the potential to charge different prices for the same or similar goods and, when this happens, if price difference cannot be explained by cost difference, there is price discrimination. Not all authors agree on this definition, and some restrict price discrimination to different prices for only the *same* goods. However, as Phlips (1983) points out, this would limit the term "price discrimination" to only cases such as different prices for adults and children entering Disneyland. Phlips argues that most people would see the very different prices charged for first, business and standard class flights as discriminatory and he, therefore, opts for the wider definition that includes *similar* goods. Most authors adopt the wider definition although it does, of course, raise the question of what is meant by "similar" products.

The more one thinks about price discrimination, the more difficult it is to pin down and the reader should be warned that some authors, notably Phillips (2005) and Simon and Fassnacht (2019), prefer the term *price differentiation*, possibly because of the connotation of discriminating *against* an individual or group. However, this is confusing because the term price differentiation is also used to describe variation in prices *between competitors*. Price discrimination refers to charging two or more prices for the same (or similar) goods *by the same supplier*.

Smith (2011) uses the term "price segmentation" as synonymous with price discrimination: "Price segmentation, also known as price discrimination in economics, is charging different customers different prices for an otherwise identical or similar product" (p. 103). Segmentation and price discrimination are closely linked but Smith over-simplifies because segmenting the market does not necessarily lead to price discrimination. For example, a company might choose to concentrate on a specific market segment, charging a single price in that segment of the market: Porter's "focus" strategy.

Finally, Schindler (2012) avoids the term "price discrimination," referring instead to price-segmentation fences.

These differences should be noted but need not concern us, the main point is that, if a seller can successfully segment the market, different prices may be charged in different market segments to increase profit.

6.7 Classification of types of price discrimination

Pigou (1932)[2] developed three "degrees" of price discrimination. The first degree is perfect discrimination where each individual customer pays the maximum they are prepared to pay. In principle each customer is charged a different price and the seller captures the entire consumer surplus. The second degree "would obtain if a monopolist were able to make n separate prices, in such wise that all units with a demand price greater than x were sold at price x, all with a demand price less than x and greater than y at a price y, and so on" (p. 279). The third degree refers to distinguishing separate groups and charging each group a different price.

Pigou sees first-degree price discrimination as of "academic interest only" and both first- and second-degree price discrimination as applicable only in "extraordinary circumstances" so it is third-degree price discrimination that is of "chief practical importance" (pp. 280–281). Pigou's description of second-degree price discrimination suggests that it is intermediate between the first and third degrees.

However, whatever Pigou intended, modern texts, while agreeing with his description of first-degree discrimination as an "ideal," often treat second-degree as referring to quantity-based price discrimination.

It is much simpler to classify price discrimination as either *direct* or *indirect*. First-degree price discrimination can be seen as a special case of third-degree discrimination where each separate individual constitutes a "group". Both first and third degrees are methods of *direct* price discrimination because the *seller* knows enough to specify a separate price for each individual or group. *Indirect* price discrimination arises when the seller presents the buyer with a range of options and the buyer *self-selects* their market segment by their purchase. For example, faced with a low-price "value" product and a high-price "premium" product the price-sensitive buyer will likely take the value item while the price-insensitive buyer is more likely to purchase the premium item.

There are some clear-cut examples of direct and indirect price discrimination. Demographic and geographic discrimination are direct methods and, on the other hand, branded and generic drugs and versions of roadside assistance or Zoom are examples of indirect price discrimination. More difficult is the classification of peak and off-peak rail fares. If a commuter *must* travel at a certain time, one could say that the method is direct, but, if the traveller has some choice, by delaying a journey, it is indirect.

Although Pigou and many other authors have treated first-degree price discrimination as an impractical "ideal type," long ago Cassady (1946) provided examples that might approximate to first-degree price discrimination. Doctors might charge different prices to different patients; lawyers charged according to the size of the estate and some newspaper content was priced according to the periodical's circulation. Today some sellers employ the internet to estimate the individual's willingness to pay and Woodcock (2017) sees the use of "big data" in this way as a challenge for regulators.

As examples of groups that might be offered preferential prices Cassady referred to discounts for "impecunious" professors and for military personnel; "invitation rates" for new purchasers and different prices depending on product use. Today there are often discounts for students, seniors and occupational groups; special offers for new customers (for example, by broadband providers) and, in the UK, "red diesel" for agricultural use at about half the price of regular diesel fuel (about 70p vs. about 170p per litre in 2022).

In discussing indirect methods of price discrimination Cassady refers to discrimination based on quantity, size, product design, branded versus generic alternatives, format (for example hardback vs. paperback books), "quality" as in differential prices depending on location at theatres and sporting events, the timing of purchase and distribution channel. All these methods have become increasingly important and are the essence of value-based pricing as products are differentiated by design, function, brand, time of use and time of purchase. We met these methods of price segmentation methods in Chapter 3 and Chapters 8–12 provide a systematic analysis of pricing strategies and the various methods of price discrimination.

Notes

1 It is likely that this formula is the reason that economists assume that firms markup marginal, not fixed, costs in surveys of pricing practice.
2 Pigou's "The Economics of Welfare" was first published in 1920. Here, references are to the fourth edition, published in 1932.

References

Cassady R. (1946) Techniques and purposes of price discrimination, *Journal of Marketing*, 11(2), 135–150

Phillips R. L. (2005) *Pricing and Revenue Optimization*, Stanford University Press, Stanford, CA

Phlips L. (1983) *The Economics of Price Discrimination*, Cambridge University Press, Cambridge

Pigou A. C. (1932) *The Economics of Welfare*, 4th edition, Macmillan and Co., London

Schindler R. M. (2012) *Pricing Strategies: A Marketing Approach*, Sage Publications Inc., Thousand Oaks, CA

Simon H. and Fassnacht M. (2019) *Price Management: Strategy, Analysis, Decision, Implementation*, Springer, Cham, Switzerland

Smith T. J. (2011) *Pricing Strategy: Setting Price Levels, Managing Price Discounts, & Establishing Price Structures*, Cengage Learning, Boston, MA

Woodcock R. A. (2017) Big data, price discrimination and antitrust, *Hastings Law Journal*, 68, 1371–1420

7 Behavioural economics

7.1 Introduction

One of the messages of this book is that traditional economic theory offers little practical pricing advice. However, this cannot be said of behavioural economics, a relatively recent development that focuses on theories of actual, observed behaviour. Behavioural economics gained traction in the late twentieth century as Daniel Kahneman, Amos Tversky, Richard Thaler and others showed that human agents are "predictably irrational" (Ariely, 2009).

Kahneman and Thaler received Nobel Prizes in 2002 and 2017 and Tversky would have shared the 2002 Nobel Prize had he not died in 1996. Behavioural economics challenges the key assumptions of traditional theory: that consumers are utility maximisers and firms are profit maximisers with perfect information and the ability to compute optimal courses of action. Behavioural economics has important implications for pricing and this chapter provides an overview of techniques collectively referred to as "the psychology of price" (Caldwell, 2012).

7.2 Origins of behavioural economics

The assumption in traditional economics of utility-maximising, rational agents with prodigious computational skills is unrealistic and Simon (1955) proposed "satisficing" as more realistic and more likely. A solution is accepted, not because it is optimal, but because it is "satisfactory". If initial analysis yields several satisfactory options, then the aspiration level is increased. Conversely, if finding a satisfactory option proves difficult, either the search is expanded, or the aspiration level decreased. Recognising the limitations of human agents Simon coined the phrase "bounded rationality" to describe satisficing behaviour. Satisficing is more realistic than optimising, although exactly how it would work in practice was unclear. Tversky's analysis of "elimination by aspects" is discussed later.

Despite Simon's work and accepting that the assumptions of traditional economics might be unrealistic, economists still assumed that traditional theory was "good enough" to generate valid predictions. The realism of assumptions was not important: the test of a theory was its predictions, and traditional theory had the great advantage that, from a limited number of axioms, a logical body of theory could be deduced.

DOI: 10.4324/9781003272731-7

The next challenge came from the proponents of behavioural economics and Camerer and Loewenstein (2003) identified two landmark papers. First, Tversky and Kahneman (1974) showed that everyday judgements are riddled with biases. People make overconfident predictions based on scant information, assume that familiar (often few) examples are representative of the population and are significantly influenced by their starting point or "anchor" in making estimations. Second, Kahneman and Tversky (1979) demonstrated that losses "hurt" more than equivalent gains and a certain gain is often preferred to an uncertain gain with a higher expected value. The 1974 paper started a stream of research known as "heuristics and biases" while the 1979 paper, labelled "prospect theory,"[1] undermined the utility assumptions of traditional economics.

At about the same time and after working with Kahneman and Tversky, Thaler (1980) described a series of anomalies that illustrate the difference between typical human behaviour (the descriptive orientation of behavioural economics) and normative, utility maximising behaviour (the underlying assumption of traditional economics). He discussed the underweighting of opportunity costs in the endowment effect (reticence in selling or exchanging an item already owned); the overweighting of sunk costs (desire to obtain value from a cost even though it is "sunk"); the importance of a "just noticeable difference" (for example, saving £5 on a £20 purchase but not bothering to save £5 on a £200 purchase); refusing to choose if the consequence might lead to regret; and choosing an "inferior" option because a "superior" option would require will-power to see it through.

The following sections discuss the implications for pricing derived from behavioural economics and the chapter concludes with a discussion of decision-making traditions and their relevance to pricing.

7.3 Satisficing: elimination by aspects

Tversky (1972) considered possible consequences of satisficing in his paper, "Elimination by Aspects" (title). The most important aspect is identified and options not meeting a minimum threshold are eliminated, the procedure is repeated for the next most important aspect and so on. Tversky notes that "elimination by aspects" relies on comparisons and the addition of another choice "hurts" similar options more than dissimilar ones. Sellers can take advantage by providing a product range that makes their preferred option appear to be good value. The author experienced the exploitation of "elimination by aspects" by a bank. A mortgage applicant (the author's daughter) was first asked if she would prefer to pay less mortgage repayments in the early years. To answer "yes" immediately eliminated many less expensive options.

7.4 The endowment effect

Thaler (1980) describes the "endowment" effect: the tendency to put a high value on something that is owned. In one experiment students were given a mug, a bar of chocolate or a choice between the two and then asked if they wished to exchange.

Of those with a choice 55% chose the mug. However, of the group "endowed" with a mug 89% kept it, while of those "endowed" with a bar of chocolate, only 10% exchanged it for a mug (Kahneman et al., 1990). The endowment effect has an immediate commercial implication: a prospective customer may experience the endowment effect if persuaded to "try" a product. I "tried" my current hearing aids before purchasing and, if the seller can persuade the prospective buyer that (to some degree) the product is already "owned," the prospective buyer will feel the pain of "loss" in choosing not to purchase or in opting for a more basic alternative.

7.5 Prospect theory and loss aversion

Kahneman and Tversky (1979) describe experiments that demonstrate that individuals will generally take a certain or probable gain rather than a "gamble" even if the gamble has a greater expected payoff. For example, 80% of participants preferred 3,000[2] with certainty rather than 4,000 with 80% probability. They also preferred 3,000 with 90% probability rather than 6,000 with 45% probability. However, when the choice is about how much the participant is prepared *to lose*, preferences switched. For example, the majority preference was to take a 4,000 loss with 80% probability rather than a certain loss of 3,000: there is risk aversion for gains, but risk seeking for losses.[3]

The findings are neatly summarised in Figure 7.1

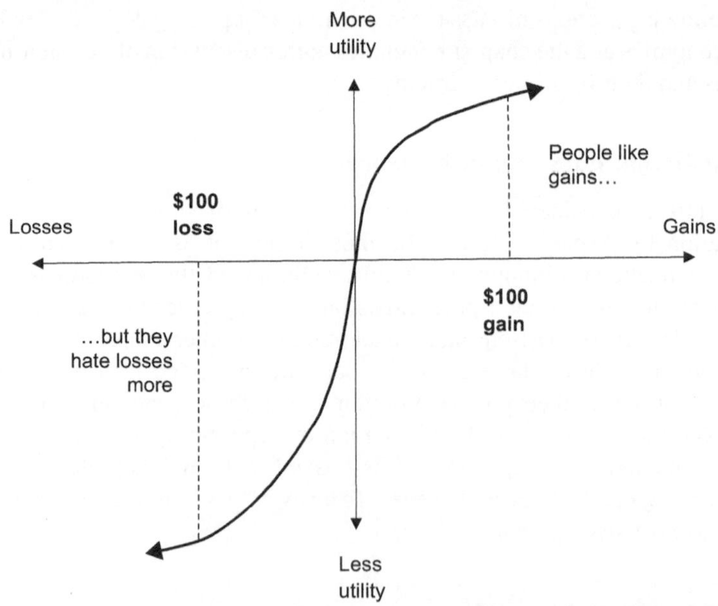

Figure 7.1 The value function

Source: Thaler (2015) *Misbehaving: The Making of Behavioral Economics, p. 31, Exhibit 3*

Reproduced by kind permission of the author

Thaler (2015, p. 31) writes: "There is an enormous amount of human wisdom captured in the S-shaped curve". The graph has three important characteristics. First, the pain of loss is about twice as great as the pleasure from an equivalent gain; second, the sensitivity to gains and losses diminishes as we move away from the status quo; and third, it is the *change* in wealth that matters, not the absolute gain or loss.

The endowment effect stems from loss aversion: once "endowed" with something we do not want to lose it: trying new hearing aids or taking a car for a test drive might lead the prospective customer to become attached to the product. No doubt this also drives many "introductory offers". The "big bundle" of Sky Q, Sky Sports and Sky Cinema currently enjoyed by the author (having been persuaded by the "offer of a lifetime") might be difficult to give up at the end of the contract.

Diminishing sensitivity to gains and losses also has pricing implications, once persuaded to purchase, there may be decreasing sensitivity to increases in price. Many products and services come in a range of options and a car buyer faced with a range of prices from £19,330 to £25,235[4] might be relatively price insensitive once committed to purchase.

Thaler (1985) considers monetary gains and losses in the light of the value function. First, several smaller gains are preferable to a single large gain, but a single large loss is preferable to several smaller losses.[5] Second, if the "gain" (for example a salary) is greater than a "loss" (for example, tax) it is best to combine them so there is a net gain (as in UK PAYE). Third, if the loss far exceeds the gain, there is no point in deducting the gain from the loss (it would not be noticed); it is better to show the gain separately as a "silver lining" or "sweetener". This last point accounts for "cash back" offers on some large purchases.

7.6 Anchoring and transaction utility

Kahneman (2011) discusses how "anchors" influence estimates. Weirdly, experiments show that even irrelevant information, such as the spin of a wheel or the last two digits of a social security number, have an influence. Kahneman explains how anchoring works. First, there is a priming, "suggestion" effect; mere awareness creates a predisposition to estimate high or low. Second, there is an "adjustment effect": adjustments from a reference value are usually insufficient.

Anchoring can be very significant. Asked if the height of the tallest redwood is more or less than 1,200 feet participants then estimated an average height of 844 feet for the tallest redwood. If participants were given a figure of 180 feet (instead of 1,200 feet), the subsequent estimated tallest height was 282 feet. Kahneman goes on to consider the use (or abuse) of anchoring. He describes a 10% off promotion accompanied by a sign, LIMIT OF 12 PER PERSON. The anchor of 12 was sufficient to double the average purchase to 7 cans of soup.

In making a purchase the customer's "anchor" or reference price is very important and Thaler (1983, 1985, 2015) argues that, to understand purchasing behaviour, two kinds of "utility" need to be considered. First, acquisition utility arises if the price paid is less than the "indifference price," the price at which the buyer would be indifferent between the good and the purchase price. (This is the basis of the traditional economic definition of consumer surplus.) Second, *transaction utility* relates to the purchasing experience itself and will be increased if the process is pleasant or if the price paid is less than the price expected.

The "expected price" (or "anchor") depends on circumstances. A relatively high price is expected for a purchase at a luxury resort hotel compared with a convenience store. The expected price in a charity shop is significantly less than a purchase from a high street chain. Transaction utility explains why it is difficult to resist a "bargain" – even though the good is not wanted – and resentment or even anger at a high price considered "unfair".

Transaction utility has several implications for marketing and, in relation to pricing, probably most important is setting the customer's reference or anchor price. Restaurants may offer a very expensive wine, not because they expect to sell it, but to influence the customer's price expectation. The anchor is very important for infrequent purchases where quality is not easy to assess. In such cases, typically consumer durables, Thaler suggests that the recommended retail price (RRP) is likely to be an especially important "anchor". For some products, there are almost perpetual sales designed to persuade buyers that they are getting a bargain. In the UK, SCS, selling furniture and carpets, provides a good example. At the time of writing a "Double Discount Sale" was in progress and, in addition, extra money off vouchers could be downloaded, "worth over £200".[6]

7.7 Fairness

Kahneman et al. (1986) reported experiments to investigate the idea of "fairness" in economic transactions. In the "ultimatum game" participants do not behave as economically rational agents. A is given, say, $10, on condition it is shared with B. If B rejects the offer, neither participant receives anything. Logically, B should accept any amount (something is better than nothing) but, in practice, A tends to be generous, and, typically, B rejects offers judged to be "unfair" (even though B then receives nothing). The "dictator game" goes a step further, B cannot reject the offer. However, even here, A usually makes a "fair" offer. In a subsequent stage of the game other participants show a propensity to "punish" those that made low offers, even at a cost to themselves.

Thaler (2015) describes the results of surveys designed to test the fairness effect. Asked whether it was fair for a hardware store to raise the price of a snow shovel from $15 to $20 after a snowstorm, 82% thought this unfair.[7] Similarly, auctioning the last model of a much sought-after toy (to get the highest price) was considered unacceptable by about 75% of participants. The auction, however, became acceptable if the proceeds were to be donated to charity. Also interesting is a question concerning an automobile in short supply. If the dealer proposes a surcharge on list price of $200, 71% considered this unfair. However, if, instead, the dealer removes a $200 discount, 58% considered this acceptable. Framing a price increase matters!

Thaler provides a real-life example to support the experimental and survey results. First Chicago, the largest bank in Chicago, set out to encourage the use of automatic teller machines by charging $3 if a customer wished to see a human teller to deposit a cheque. There was outrage and the bank became the butt of jokes such as charging for every question – the charge increased if the customer said, "What?!". Further examples are provided by Phillips (2005): Coca Cola ran into a storm of protest when CEO, Douglas Ivester, announced that a new vending machine would increase prices on hot days. And Amazon quickly backtracked when it was discovered that higher prices were charged to loyal customers.

If there is an opportunity to raise prices because of high demand sellers need to be aware of the fairness effect. Setting a high-price risks reputational damage that could affect repeat purchases.[8] Thaler (1985) suggests that the high price might be "disguised". For example, there might be a "package" of products, a three-night instead of one-night hotel stay, or a bundle of hotel, transport and event. The "packaging" of the high-priced product makes assessment of a "fair" price more difficult. For some products, unusual pack sizes can have the same effect, making estimation of a "fair" price difficult. Thaler notes that this behaviour can be observed in the sales of popcorn and candy in cinemas.

If an event is effectively unique, as in a heavyweight boxing championship, then the issue of "repeat sales" does not arise and the seller can charge an exorbitant price with impunity. Thaler (1985) compares the prices at sporting events, finding that, the more important is repeat business, the more reasonable the price. On the other hand, the price for the (one off) Holmes – Cooney fight was, indeed, very high.

7.8 Opportunity costs: surcharges and discounts

Thaler (1980) discusses the propensity of buyers to underestimate opportunity costs. When credit cards were introduced, some stores charged the customer for their use.[9] Customers resented this and, to mitigate the impact of the charge, credit card companies required affiliated stores to grant a "cash discount" rather than a charge for use of a credit card. A surcharge would be seen as an out-of-pocket expense, a "penalty" for credit card users, whereas the cash discount was an opportunity cost associated with credit card use: a saving foregone by using a credit card rather than a direct cash expense. Of course, the "saving" for cash has the same effect, in economic terms, as the surcharge for a credit card, but this was more palatable to the customer. The opportunity cost carries less weight because it is a theoretical saving as opposed to the clear cash outlay of a surcharge.

7.9 Sunk costs

Thaler's (1980) next example concerns "sunk" costs. In economics (and management accounting) these should be ignored as irrelevant. In practice, having purchased a ticket, individuals feel a compulsion to attend even though doing so might be clearly stupid. Thaler mentions a tennis player who carried on playing even though this was making his tennis elbow worse! Sunk costs do not just affect decisions by individuals. One can imagine the difficulty, in the UK, of reversing the decision to proceed with HS2[10] and Thaler (2015) regards continuance of the Vietnam war as related to costs (and deaths) already sustained.

The influence of sunk costs in pricing can be seen in season tickets such as the loyalty card offered by Dobbies Garden centres at £12 per year (£10 if paid by direct debit). This entitles the buyer to two free drinks every month and no doubt increases sales as visitors take the opportunity to make further purchases after consuming the "free" drinks. Two-part pricing might also take advantage of the sunk cost effect. For example, having paid for entry to a theme park the visitor may feel a compulsion to "get their money's worth" by paying for more rides.

7.10 Decoys and extreme aversion

Common-sense suggests that adding another product to a range will take some market share and reduce the market shares of existing products. In addition, the new product will "hurt" similar products the most. This is probably true when a product is inserted into a section of the value-price continuum so that it lies, more-or-less on the value-equivalence line. However, if a new product is completely dominated by an existing product, it becomes a "decoy," instead of "stealing" share it "helps" the similar product to gain share. This is the "attraction effect" or asymmetric dominance.

Huber et al. (1982) used experimental methods to demonstrate the asymmetric dominance effect. Comparison of two products might be difficult because A is better than B on one dimension (for example, quality) but B is better than A on another dimension (for example, price). Introduction of a third, dominated, product increased the market share of the similar product – the attraction effect. Simonson (1989) argued that this might be because the customer could easily justify the choice, the chosen product being clearly better than one of the alternatives. The third, "decoy," product attracts customers to the similar but clearly better alternative.

Ariely (2009 p. 2) describes the annual subscription options for *The Economist:* Online access $59, Print $125, Print plus Online $125. He writes: "I suspect that the clever people at the *Economist's* London offices . . . were actually manipulating me . . . the *Economist's* marketing wizards (and I could just picture them in their school ties and blazers[11]) knew something important about human behavior: humans rarely choose things in absolute terms." The point is that the Print version at $125 is a decoy. No one would choose this option because the Print plus Online option is obviously better and the Print Only option is intended to make it look like a bargain. Ariely found that, in an experiment with MIT MBA students, 84 from 100 chose the Print plus Online option but, when the decoy, Print Only option, was removed, the number choosing Print plus Online fell to only 32 from 100.

Returning to my purchase of hearing aids, I was offered the Level 5 package with an £800 discount at £2,995, the Level 4 package (no discount) at £3,095 and the Level 3 package (£200 discount) at £2,195. I now realise that the Level 4 package was the decoy (and I did purchase the Level 5 package).

Extreme aversion refers to the tendency to prefer the intermediate option rather than one of the extremes. Simonson and Tversky (1992) investigated this in a series of experiments. There was a clear result when a choice of two cameras, Emerson and Sony at $39.99 and $64.99 respectively was supplemented by a top of the range Sony camera at $149.99. Initially, market shares were Emerson 45% and Sony 55%. When the top of the range Sony camera was added the market shares became Emerson 9%, Sony mid-line 48% and Sony top of the range 43%. One might have expected the introduction of the top of the range camera to take market share from the Sony mid-line but, contrary to this "common sense" assumption, it was the low-price, low-quality model that suffered most from the introduction of the high-end camera. The authors report similar results in a series of experiments and concluded that there is, typically, extreme aversion for quality (but not for price).

7.11 Mental accounting

Camerer et al.'s (1997) famous study of New York City cabdrivers showed that they tended to work less on "good" days; after meeting a daily earnings "target," they went home. So, on good days, when demand was high, they stopped early, but, on a "slow day" with few fares, they worked longer. This runs counter to traditional economic theory: plentiful demand should lead to *an increase* in supply. Bracketing a day's earnings in this way is an example of what Shafir and Thaler (2006) call "mental accounting".

Shafir and Thaler consider the purchase of items that will not be consumed immediately. In a survey, more than half the participants would not think of the (economically correct) replacement cost as the "cost" of a bottle of wine when it was consumed or given away. Over half regarded the bottle as "free" (since it was purchased some time ago) or worth its *original* cost (possibly plus interest). Further surveys revealed that most buyers consider the purchase of an item for later consumption *as an investment* or, for a season ticket, possibly as a "saving" compared with the price of buying individual tickets. As Shafir and Thaler (2006) wryly note: [buyers] invest now, drink later, spend never (Title). The "value" attached to an item is more likely to be linked to historical than replacement cost and, in experiments, participants are less likely to sell an item at a "loss" compared to its historical cost and more likely to sell at a "gain" compared to historical cost irrespective of current market value. I guess that any reader who has "invested" in shares understands this last point well.

There are other forms of mental accounting, especially the use of "budgets" for different purposes. These are prevalent in business where "viring" (transfer of money from one budget to another) may not be possible and in everyday life where individuals may even have physical envelopes or jars of money for different purposes (Thaler, 2015).

7.12 The Greek Peak example

Thaler (2015) recounts his experience in helping the ski resort, Greek Peak, to profitability. Prices needed to increase because, although the resort, located in

New York State, offered good "acquisition utility" to a large group of potential customers, prospective skiers might be unhappy if the price was close to that charged by top-of-the-range resorts (negative "transaction utility"). One aim was therefore to deliver more value to customers so that they did not suffer negative transaction value. Free lessons and other amenities helped to do this.

Attracting more local skiers was also important and the existing five-ticket-book for students was the inspiration for a new ten-ticket-book for locals at a discount of 40% to normal price. The discount ensured that there was positive transaction utility, and the up-front payment would be considered an "investment" by purchasers. When the tickets were subsequently used the buyer might regard the experience as "free" or even a "saving" compared to the regular price. The advance sales were a big success, they generated much-needed cash flow before the skiing season started and they provided insurance against a winter with limited snowfall.

7.13 Time

In traditional economic theory it is presumed that future utility is discounted to present utility in the same way as future cash flows are discounted to present value using factors derived from discount rates such as 10% or 20%. The consistency with present value calculations is convenient and, in theory, ensures that individuals make consistent decisions over time. For example, if £120 in one year is preferred to £100 in six months then, six months later, £120 in six months will still be preferred to £100 now.

Unfortunately, behaviour in practice is not like this. Experiments and field studies have repeatedly demonstrated that individuals have a strong preference for instant rewards as opposed to a future, theoretically more attractive, pay-off. At the same time there is relative indifference between future payoffs, £120 in one year might be regarded as little different from £120 in two years. The results imply a steep discount curve that flattens, and hyperbolic (rather than less steep exponential) functions have been found to fit experimental data.

Frederick et al. (2002) reviewed the literature, found a huge range of implied discount rates across studies, and cautioned that the results might be explained by confounding factors in experimental designs. Although Frederick et al. cast doubt on the validity of experimental results, field studies they reviewed also showed high implied discount rates. Given the choice between a lump sum and an annuity with an implied interest rate of 17.5%, ". . . over half of all military officers and over 90 percent of enlisted personnel chose the lump-sum payment" (p. 385). This was despite an interest rate of only 7% at the time. More pertinent, for pricing, were studies of consumer choice where energy efficient equipment would pay back its extra cost in energy savings. The implied discount rates were 17–20% for air conditioners (Hausman, 1979), and 102% for gas water heaters, 138% for freezers and 243% for electric water heaters (Ruderman et al., 1987). Of course, income and cash constraints play a part in the choice of initial purchase, but, clearly, future savings do not weigh heavily in the minds of typical buyers.

7.14 Other behaviours and biases

As behavioural economics became (relatively) mainstream more anomalies and biases were identified and the field has expanded enormously. Bias may be induced by *availability*, news such as mass shootings or child abduction lead us to assume that these happen much more frequently than they do. There is a tendency to overestimate the likelihood of very infrequent events and, conversely, to underestimate the likelihood of common events such as road accidents. Other biases include familiarity and status quo bias (exploited by insurance companies and others that take advantage of customer inertia by increasing prices regularly).

Ariely (2009) discusses the way in which social norms affect decision-making and behaviour. In the latter case he argues that allowing the "social" and "economic" worlds to clash is fraught with danger. Most people help others if asked but will change their behaviour if money enters the equation. In experiments students "worked" hard if they were simply asked to participate. However, a small payment led to *diminution* of effort: a social transaction had been converted into an economic transaction. In social affairs there is an unspoken agreement that good deeds will be "repaid" by good deeds in the future (even if they involve other people).[12] If the market intervenes then the "rules" change. Ariely describes the effect of introducing a fine when parents were late picking up children at a day-care centre. Lateness *increased* as parents now felt that they were paying for a service.

Behavioural economics has found its way into government policy, and, in the UK, the coalition government created the "Nudge Unit" in 2010.[13] One of the most significant interventions concerns pension saving, individuals now "opt-out" rather than "opt-in" to workplace pension schemes and very few choose to opt out. Other countries have adopted an "opt-out" rather than "opt-in" approach to organ donation with similar results. These examples take advantage of inertia and most take the default option.

Behavioural economics is now extensive and influential, and this is only a brief introduction, concentrating on the most obvious pricing implications. In addition to applications in pricing, consumer choice and public policy, behavioural economics has been applied to the behaviour of investors and finance theory. Famously, Alan Greenspan, chair of the Federal Reserve in the US, admitted that his attachment to free markets and deregulation had been (partly) responsible for the 2008 financial credit crunch.

7.15 Integration of behavioural and traditional economics

Kahneman (2003) provided "A Psychological Perspective on Economics" (title). He noted that behavioural economics had shown that people are not selfish utility maximisers, while, in the field of finance, traders are not "economically rational"; they tend to short-termism, "loss aversion" and hasty conclusions. Elements of behavioural economics have been incorporated into traditional economic models. However, "the analytical methodology of economics is stable . . . [and] . . . the number of parameters that can be added is small" (p. 166). This might mean that the findings of behavioural economics are destined to be "noncumulative," adding new insights without radically changing traditional economic theory.

7.16 Traditions in decision making and management accounting

Decision analysis

Fox (2015) provides a history of three strands of decision-making theory. "Decision analysis" is traced to the rise of operational research after WWII. The value of each option is based on "expected utility" (the sum of expected payoffs multiplied by their probabilities) and expected utilities are revised using Bayesian methods (updating probabilities as new information becomes available). Traditional economic theory is based on this model. In B2B transactions negotiation will usually be based on a rational assessment of what is in the (financial) best interest of each party. The seller will aim to demonstrate the value of the product or service to the customer, estimating probabilities of possible outcomes as necessary. This rational analysis, based on traditional economic (and management accounting) theory, requires what Kahneman (2011) calls "system 2" thinking: slow, methodical analysis based on careful, evidence-based assessment of probabilities and outcomes. In B2B transactions the presumption of rational negotiations is not unrealistic and is the recommended approach in the calculation of value to the customer, based on incremental, discounted cash flows.

Value to the customer calculations is based on careful, rational appraisal of the facts and, especially, projected cash flows. The underpinning method is decision analysis and, if several outcomes are possible, then estimations of probabilities are required to calculate expected values. As discussed in Chapter 4, management accountants are well-equipped to support marketing and sales executives in demonstrating value for customers. In doing this management accountants should note the general tendency to underestimate high probabilities but to overestimate very small probabilities. This is important when decision trees, based on customer-estimated probabilities, are constructed.

Behavioural economics

Behavioural economics recognises that the rational model often does not apply in everyday situations. There are a wide range of biases and heuristics (rules of thumb) are used in making a wide range of decisions, either because there is no time for detailed, evidence-based analysis, or because such analysis would be tedious and not worth the effort. Kahneman (2011) refers to this as "system 1" thinking and describes many of its characteristics including jumping to conclusions, loss aversion, the endowment effect, underestimation of large probabilities, overestimation of small probabilities, failure to account for opportunity costs and so on.

One reaction is to see these aspects of human behaviour as warnings of how decision-making can go wrong. Forewarned of typical errors action can be taken to avoid them. A second reaction is to take advantage of the proclivities of human nature. The "nudge unit" in the UK was set up to do just this and, importantly for this book, marketing and sales executives have seized the opportunities thrown up by behavioural insights.

Marketing executives increasingly take advantage of ideas such as anchors, decoys, extreme aversion and transactional utility. As part of the team, management accountants should assess the costs of implementing strategies that require a wider product range and/or the use of discounts and special offers. In consumer goods markets these issues are important and provide the theoretical basis for "*the psychology of price*" (Caldwell, 2012).

Limits of decision analysis and the use of heuristics

There are limits to the use of statistical models in complex situations. For small data samples a complex model can "over-fit" the data. Suppose that the demand for a luxury product is expected to depend on population demographics:

$$\text{Demand} = d_0 + d_1 I + d_2 A + d_3 F + d_4 S$$

where I and A are average income and average age of the population, respectively, F is the average family size and S is the proportion of the population that lives alone. Estimates of the parameters: d_0, d_1, d_2, d_3, d_4, can be derived from a sample of the population. However, if the sample is small, different data samples will yield significantly different parameter values. This model has a high *variance*. It has an appropriate level of complexity, but the small sample size makes it inaccurate.

Now, suppose that, recognising the limitations of a small data sample, a much simpler model is chosen:

$$\text{Demand} = d_1 R$$

Where R is the proportion of "rich" people in the population (earning more than, say, £100,000 per annum). This simple model will have much less variance, repeated trials are likely to generate similar values for the single parameter, d_1. However, it suffers from *bias* because demand depends on much more than one variable. This model is simpler and more stable, but it does not reflect all the relevant aspects of the population.

Artinger et al. (2015) argue that simple models can be preferable even when there is an abundance of data. For example, DeMiguel et al. (2009) compared the performance of a "naïve" investment strategy, splitting funds equally over N portfolios, with 14 "sophisticated" investment models. They concluded that none of the sophisticated models consistently outperformed the simple 1/N model over realistic time scales. From the management literature Artinger et al. (2015) note that classifying a customer as inactive if a purchase has not been made in a fixed length of time is simple and effective and successful entrepreneurs use only simple criteria in determining a new business location. Similarly, Artinger and Gigerenzer (2012) found that car dealers that simply adjusted the price of an unsold car at fixed intervals performed better than more complex approaches.

This research warns of the dangers of complex models in situations of limited data or high uncertainty. Attempts to design complex systems may be doomed to fail and the management accountant should be aware of the limitations of sophisticated models. A good heuristic will be effective in the face of uncertainty and should have the advantage, compared with complex models, of simplicity and understandability. Professionals and managers are likely to be more comfortable with a simple model they understand rather than a clever "black box".

Notes

1 According to Thaler, the term "prospect theory" was chosen because it has no intrinsic meaning.
2 The experiment was undertaken in Israel and the figures relate to Israeli currency.
3 These findings do not hold if the probabilities are very low. Behaviour then changes so that, for example, a 0.1% chance to win 6,000 is preferred to a 0.2% chance to win 3,000.
4 Crossland X Price and Specification Guide 9 October 2020, downloaded from file:///C:/Users/Owner/Downloads/price-guide.pdf 31/05/2021
5 This seems to run counter to the idea of price metrics per day, per month etc. instead of a single annual payment. However small monthly payments may be considered insignificant, and, in addition, they are "bundled" into monthly statements with other payments.
6 www.scs.co.uk/sofa-sale/?gclid downloaded 31/05/2021
7 When the question was posed to MBA students who had studied economics the results were reversed, 76% thought the price increase acceptable.
8 For concerts and sporting events charging a "fair" price leads to "scalping" in the US and ticket touts in the UK. However, the organiser will not be blamed for high prices charged by touts.
9 The practice of charging the customer to use a credit card has been illegal in the EU since 2018.
10 There has, indeed, between an outcry associated with the Government's decision not to proceed as intended with the northern links of HS2.
11 It seems that experts in behavioural economics are not immune to stereotyping.
12 Experiments have demonstrated that most people are "conditional co-operators". They will help so long as their co-operation is reciprocated. If it is not, they will stop co-operating.
13 Now independent of government and known as The Behavioural Insights Team

References

Ariely D. (2009) *Predictably Irrational*, Harper Collins Publishers, London

Artinger F. and Gigerenzer G. (2012) Pricing in an uncertain market, *Working Paper*, Max Planck Institute for Human Development

Artinger F., Petersen M., Gigerenzer G. and Weibler J. (2015) Heuristics as adaptive decision strategies in management, *Journal of Organizational Behavior*, 33, S33–S52

Caldwell L. (2012) *The Psychology of Price*, Crimson Publishing Limited, Richmond

Camerer C. E., Babcock L., Loewenstein G. and Thaler R. H. (1997) Labor supply of New York City cabdrivers: one day at a time, *The Quarterly Journal of Economics*, May, 407–441

Camerer C. E. and Loewenstein G. (2003) Behavioral economics: past, present and future, in: Camerer C. E., Loewenstein G. and Rabin M. (eds) *Advances in Behavioral Economics*, pp. 3–52, Princeton University Press, Princeton, NJ

DeMiguel V., Garlappi L. and Uppal R. (2009) Optimal versus naïve diversification: how inefficient is the 1/N portfolio strategy? *The Review of Financial Studies*, 22(5), 1915–1953

Fox J. (2015) From "economic man" to behavioural economics, *Harvard Business Review*, May, 79–85

Frederick S., Loewenstein G. and O'Donoghue T. (2002) Time discounting and time preference: a critical review, *Journal of Economic Literature*, 40(2), 351–401

Hausman J. (1979) Individual discount rates and the purchase and utilization of energy-using durables, *Bell Journal of Economics*, 10(1), 33–54

Huber J., Payne J. W. and Puto C. (1982) Adding asymmetrically dominated alternatives: violations of regularity and the similarity hypothesis, *Journal of Consumer Research*, 9(1), 90–98

Kahneman D. (2003) A psychological perspective on economics, *The American Economic Review*, 93(2), 162–168

Kahneman D. (2011) *Thinking, Fast and Slow*, Penguin Books, London

Kahneman D., Knetsch J. L. and Thaler R. H. (1986) Fairness and the assumptions of economics, *Journal of Business*, 59(4), Part 2, S285–S300

Kahneman D., Knetsch J. L. and Thaler R. H. (1990) Experimental tests of the endowment effect and the Coase theorem, *Journal of Political Economy*, 98(6), 1325–1348

Kahneman D. and Tversky A. (1979) Prospect theory: an analysis of decision under risk, *Econometrica*, 47(2), 263–292

Phillips R. L. (2005) *Pricing and Revenue Optimization*, Stanford University Press, Stanford, CA

Ruderman H., Levine M. D. and Mcmahon J. E. (1987) The behavior of the market for energy efficiency in residential appliances including heating and cooling equipment, *Energy Journal*, 8(1), 101–124

Shafir E. and Thaler R. H. (2006) Invest now, drink later, spend never: on the mental accounting of delayed consumption, *Journal of Economic Psychology*, 27, 694–712

Simon H. A. (1955) A behavioral model of rational choice, *The Quarterly Journal of Economics*, 69(1), 99–118

Simonson I. (1989) Choice based on reasons: the case of attraction and compromise effects, *Journal of Consumer Research*, 16(2), 158–174

Simonson I. and Tversky A. (1992) Choice in context: tradeoff contrast and extremeness aversion, *Journal of Marketing Research*, 29(3), 281–295

Thaler R. H. (1980) Towards a positive theory of consumer choice, *Journal of Economic Behavior & Organization*, 1(1), 39–60

Thaler R. H. (1983) Transaction utility theory, in: Bagozzi R. P. and Tybout A. M. (eds) *NA – Advances in Consumer Research*, vol 10, pp. 229–232, Association for Consumer Research, Ann Arbor, MI

Thaler R. H. (1985) Mental accounting and consumer choice, *Marketing Science*, 4(3), 199–214

Thaler R. H. (2015) *Misbehaving: The Making of Behavioral Economics*, W.W. Norton & Company, Inc., New York

Tversky A. (1972) Elimination by aspects: a theory of choice, *Psychological Review*, 79(4), 281–299

Tversky A. and Kahneman D. (1974) Judgement under uncertainty: heuristics and biases, *Science*, 185(4157), 1124–1131

8 Pricing strategies

8.1 Introduction

Surveys have consistently indicated the importance of cost, competition and the market in pricing practice and this provides a framework for this chapter. Section 8.2 reviews cost-based pricing showing how activity-based costing can provide new insights in cost-plus pricing. Section 8.3 focuses on the competition-based strategies of price leadership, price followership and the low-price strategy. Section 8.4 focuses on the value-related strategies of market segmentation and product differentiation. The final sections review the use of these strategies in industrial and consumer markets and introduce the Tellis taxonomy of price strategies.

8.2 Cost-based pricing

This is a topic that receives a thorough treatment in management accounting texts and, since the late twentieth century, activity-based costing has added to the management accounting armoury.
A typical example:

Company X operates an activity-based costing system, forecast information for next year:

Cost pool	*Cost*	*Cost driver*	*Number of drivers*
Production batches	£1,750,000	Batches	1,000
Product testing	£900,000	Inspections	5,000
Purchase orders and delivery	£375,000	Component orders	1,000
Customer orders	£1,250,000	Customer orders	25,000

Facility-related overhead, light, heat, insurance etc., is expected to be £3,000,000 in the coming year and these overheads are absorbed on a direct labour hour basis. Total direct labour hours for next year are expected to be 300,000 hours.

240 orders for product X are expected, average 40 units per order. Production will be in batches of 600 units with, on average, 5 inspections for each production

DOI: 10.4324/9781003272731-8

run. Two orders for components are placed before each production run. Additional information for product X:

Component cost £3.00 and £2.50 (two components per unit)
Direct labour 10 minutes per unit at £15.80 per hour
Profit mark up 40% of total manufacturing cost

Solution

Direct costs are readily attributable to product: £5.50 for materials and 10 minutes at £15.80 per hour for labour, total, £8.13 per unit.

This is normally the absolute minimum price. At a price below £8.13 the more units sold the more money lost. Only if the company is desperate, unable to sell inventory, would it sell below this price. We shall see, in Chapter 14, in the Sloan Styles case, that this can happen.

A simple traditional costing system would take total production overhead (in £000), 1,750 + 900 + 1,250 + 375 + 3,000 = £7,275 and calculate an overhead absorption rate based on direct labour hours: £7,275,000/300,000 hours = £24.25 per hour. The production cost per unit would then be £8.13 + (10 minutes at £24.25 per hour) = £12.17 per unit: a traditional production absorption cost suitable for valuing inventory.

An activity-based cost is based on the "drivers" of overhead costs, in this example:

Cost driver	*Cost (£000)*	*Number of drivers*	*Cost per driver*
Batches	£1,750	1,000	£1,750
Inspections	£900	5,000	£180
Purchase orders	£375	1,000	£375
Customer orders	£1,250	25,000	£50
Facility-level overheads	£1,250	300,000	£4.16

Activity-based cost:	
16 production batches at £1,750 per batch	£28,000
80 inspections at £180 per inspection	14,400
32 purchase orders at £375 per order	12,000
240 customer orders at £50 per order	12,000
General overhead 1600 hours at £4.16 per hour	6,656
Total	73,056
Overhead cost per unit 73,056/9,600	7.61
Add: direct cost per unit	8.13
Activity-based cost per unit	15.74

Unit price would be £22.04 (40% markup on activity-based cost) or £17.04 (40% markup on traditional full manufacturing cost): the cost-plus price is obviously dependent on the method used to attribute overhead costs. This is probably the reason that economists assume cost-plus prices will be based on the (economically more meaningful) marginal or variable cost. However, if variable cost is used, the markup needs to not only generate 40% margin but also recover production overhead.

In this example the "traditional" production cost and the activity-based cost are similar. However, this need not be so. The classic case of Schrader Bellows was used by Cooper and Kaplan (1988) to demonstrate the insights that might be generated by activity-based analysis. An activity-based costing exercise led to the product cost examples set out in Table 8.1 and there could be few more graphic illustrations of activity-based costing. A high-volume product such as product 1 has a lower overhead cost compared with the old system but a low volume product such as product 3, with a high volume of activities in relation to its volume, has a very high overhead cost compared to the old system.

Action is needed in relation to the three products that have negative activity-based gross margins. First, their *prices might be increased*, but the very significant increases required might be resisted. Second, there might be ways to *reduce the costs* of the products; ABC analysis identifies which overhead costs are associated with problem products and guides cost reduction efforts. The customer might help by, for example, placing larger, less frequent orders. Third, *unprofitable products might be dropped*, but care must be taken, the "unprofitable" products might be important to complete a product range.

Table 8.1 How activity-based costing changes product profitability

Valve number	*Annual volume (units)*	*Manufacturing overhead per unit*			*Gross margin*	
		Old system	*New system*	*Percent difference*	*Old system*	*New system*
1	43,562	$5.44	$4.76	−12.5%	41%	46%
2	500	6.15	12.86	+109.0	30	(24)
3	53	7.30	77.64	+964.0	47	(258)
4	2,079	8.88	19.76	+123.0	26	(32)
5	5,670	7.58	15.17	+100.0	39	2
6	11,196	5.34	5.26	−1.5	41	41
7	423	5.92	4.39	−26.0	31	43

[Cooper and Kaplan write]: "We are not confident that the table's figures are exactly correct. For example, students of this case have estimated the appropriate overhead charge on valve 3 [listed at $77.64 per unit] to be as low as $64 and as high as $84. Whatever the exact figure the difference between this activity-based cost and the original estimate [$7.30 per unit] suggests that the current labor-based system is seriously flawed."

Surveys suggest that cost-based pricing is prevalent, especially in B2B markets, and management accountants have a key role in providing appropriate costs. Activity-based costing can be important because of (1) more accurate attribution of overhead costs to products; (2) inclusion of distribution and customer-related costs where appropriate; and (3) prices that are defensible in customer negotiations. This last point can be very important if the customer is a government.

8.3 Competition-based pricing

Pricing may be greatly influenced by competitors and, the more competitive the market, the greater the influence. At the extreme, if a commodity is supplied by many firms serving many perfectly informed buyers, "perfect competition" will be the result. Only the most efficient firms will survive, each just making "normal" profit. Every firm will have to accept the market price and all firms will be "price takers".

In practice this is very unusual. First, most goods are not commodities, firms strive to differentiate their products and avoid their commoditisation. Second, the number of firms in markets and, especially, in market segments, is likely to be limited. Third, even in the impossible case of perfect information, buyers still make irrational choices: for example, petrol stations no more than half a mile apart can sell petrol at markedly different prices.

It is tempting to see several firms setting the same or similar prices as operating in very competitive, if not "perfect," markets. However, this conclusion is incorrect. Farm (2020) notes that it is much more likely to be evidence of price leadership and followership: ". . . firms set the same price as another firm and are consequently price takers, but because not all firms can be a price taker, the existence of price takers is an indirect proof of the existence of a price leader" (p. 75).

The key assumption is that "not all firms can be a price taker". A price change must be triggered by one of the firms and, if observed prices are similar across the competing firms, as Farm says, this is not evidence of a very competitive market but of a "managed" market where firms avoid price wars by carefully monitoring competitor actions.

Price leadership and followership are two important strategies and, in their survey, Noble and Gruca (1999) added a third: a low-price strategy, for example, Green Flag in roadside assistance, Aldi and Lidl in supermarkets, EasyJet and Ryanair in airlines. A low-price strategy is consistent with cost leadership, one of the three generic competitive strategies set out by Porter (1980).

Competitive pricing by supermarkets

Supermarkets provide a convenient and familiar example of competitive pricing. Ellicksen and Misra (2008) analysed the pricing strategies adopted by supermarkets in the US. They identified three strategies from the literature: "everyday low price" (EDLP) that corresponds to a low-price or cost leadership strategy; "promotion" where supermarkets offer frequent deep discounts on certain products; and "hybrid" where supermarkets adopt a combination of EDLP and promotion strategies.

They observed that some supermarket chains concentrate on a single strategy. For example, Wal-Mart, Food Lion and H.E. Butt employed a predominantly low-price strategy. However, most chains employed a combination of all three strategies, and, to the surprise of the authors, often strategy was not driven by an overall firm-specific decision but by sensitivity to local competitive actions. There is "strong evidence that firms cluster by strategy by choosing actions that agree with those of its rivals" (Abstract). This supports Farm's analysis that similar prices do not indicate "perfect" or even competitive markets but rather price leadership and followership.

Tesco's advertising (2022) identifies prices that match Aldi's, and this seems to be an example of price followership. When Aldi increased the price of cream from 75p to 79p for a 300 ml carton Tesco *matched the increase* and attached the label "Aldi Price Match".

8.4 Market-based pricing

Consultants have increasingly advocated market-based pricing, identifying the value of the product from the customer's point of view. Examples of market segmentation in consumer markets were introduced in Chapter 3 and typical segmentation variables include *demography* where young, old and certain occupations are expected to be price sensitive and identity can be readily verified; *geography* as lower prices are available in low-income countries and, for example, in out-of-town stores; *random discounts and money-off coupons* where it is assumed the customers prepared to search for offers are more price sensitive; *time of day, week or year* where those taking advantage of off-peak rates are assumed price sensitive; *time of purchase* as early purchasers of, for example, technology or fashion products, are assumed price insensitive; *advance purchases* as early bookers, with time to plan, are offered lower prices; and *quantity discounts* where purchases of large quantities are usually cheaper per unit both because of likely cost savings and because purchasers of large quantities are likely to be price sensitive.

Reflection on these techniques indicates that market segmentation often depends on reasons for purchase, whether commuting at peak times, meeting business commitments by late booking, advance purchase of holidays or "must have" purchasing of the latest technology or fashion. This was the theme for Yankelovich (1964), who emphasised *reasons for purchase* as the best basis for market segmentation and illustrated his point with several examples. For example, watches might be purchased for their function; their quality, durability and style; or for emotional reasons such as a gift; perfumes may be purchased for their scent or to "cancel out" body odours.

Years later Yankelovich and Meer (2006) were disappointed, referring to segmentation theory's emphasis on psychographic variables as a "drift into nebulousness". They blamed the influence of the VALS, "Values and Lifestyle" program, and the identification of the "Nine American Lifestyles" (Mitchell, 1983). Yankelovich and Meer recommended that the way back was to concentrate on "the

Table 8.2 Methods of product differentiation

Strategy	*Examples*	*Targeting price sensitive and price insensitive customers*
Good-better-best pricing	Tesco's value, standard and finest brands; BA's economy, business and first class	Price sensitive customers tend to opt for the value or economy product
Versioning	Zoom's basic, pro and business versions	As good-better-best pricing but usually for information products
Complementary products	Sometimes referred to as "razor and blade" pricing, HP's inkjet printer automatically orders replenishment ink supply	An attractively priced base product attracts customers who then purchase higher margin complements
Price bundling	Providers of broadband, telephone, television services	Price sensitive customers may take more product, a form of quantity discounting
Branding	Branded and generic drugs, "fighting" brands to meet low-price competition	Price sensitive customers will tend to take the low-priced option, others may prefer a "trusted" brand

benefits and features that matter to your customers" (p. 126). The recent value-based revolution may go some way to meeting the criticisms of Yankelovich and Meer by putting customer tastes, behaviours and preferences centre stage.

In addition to the segmentation methods listed earlier there are also a range of product differentiation strategies that serve to segment the market. Advocated by pricing consultants and underpinned by the findings of behavioural economics, product-related strategies, summarised in Table 8.2, have become increasingly important.

8.5 New product pricing strategies

Launching a new product calls for special considerations and we have seen that care should be taken to position a new product carefully in relation to competitors. Moving away from the VEL (value-equivalence line) can be dangerous even if the product is "value-advantaged". If a product is truly innovative then the key decision is whether to swiftly recoup research and development costs or to quickly build market share. Dean's (1950) seminal work identified the two extreme strategies: "(1) a policy of high initial prices that skim the cream of demand and (2) a policy of low prices from the outset serving as an active agent for penetration" (p. 49). A skimming strategy takes advantage of the likely inelastic demand at launch and breaks the market into segments with different demand elasticities as successive price reductions tap more elastic market segments. The alternative, penetration strategy, reaches a wide market quickly, may save production costs due to economies of scale and pre-empts competition.

8.6 Pricing strategies in industrial goods markets

Noble and Gruca (1999) employed a sophisticated survey instrument to investigate industrial goods price setting. Respondents were asked whether they employed any of ten strategies relevant to industrial goods, within the broad categories of cost-plus pricing, competitive pricing, product line pricing and new product pricing.[1] See Table 8.3.

Respondents were asked to identify the strategies adopted in their most recent pricing decision for a single industrial capital good. Reflecting the complexity of pricing decisions up to three strategies could be selected and 270 usable responses were received.

Table 8.3 "Pricing strategy definitions" Noble and Gruca (1999) adapted from Table 1, p. 438, Industrial Pricing: Theory and Managerial Practice, *Marketing Science Vol 18 (3)* reprinted by kind permission of The Institute for Operations Research and the Management Sciences (INFORMS)

Strategy	*Description*	*Related strategies*
New product		
Price skimming	High initial price systematically reduced. Customers expect a falling price	Premium pricing, value-in-use pricing
Penetration pricing	Low initial price to accelerate adoption	
Experience curve pricing	Low price to build volume and accumulate experience	Learning curve pricing
Competitive		
Leader pricing	Initiate price change and expect others to follow	Cooperative pricing, signalling
Parity pricing	Match the price set by the market or price leader	Neutral pricing, follower pricing
Low-price supplier	Strive to have the low price in the market	Parallel, adaptive, opportunistic pricing
Product-line		
Complementary product pricing	Low core product price, higher premiums for accessories, spares, services	Razor-and-blade pricing
Bundle pricing	Bundle usually at an attractive price compared to sum of individual item prices	System pricing
Customer value pricing	A product version offering reduced features, priced very competitively	Economy pricing
Cost-based		
Cost-plus pricing	Priced to give specified percentage profit margin over cost	Contribution, rate of return, target, markup, contingency pricing

The most frequently adopted strategy was cost-based pricing (56%). Competition-based pricing was also frequently adopted (50%) while new product strategies (34%) and product-based strategies (33%) were not so popular. The relative unpopularity of new product pricing is not surprising as it could apply only to new products. However, for those companies that adopted skimming or experience strategies, they were important. Product-based strategies were relatively unpopular *and* relatively unimportant. Difficulty in estimating demand was a reason for the unpopularity of these strategies and the authors noted that this might also account for the popularity of cost-based methods.

8.7 Pricing strategies in consumer goods markets

There is a dearth of survey data concerning pricing strategies in consumer goods markets and reference was therefore made to the household expenditure survey published by the Office for National Statistics[2] in 2019 (the year before the pandemic). The average UK household spent £592 per week and the major categories of spend were:

Expenditure category	*£ per week*
Transport	85.0
Housing, fuel and power	79.4
Recreation and culture	77.2
Food and (non-alcoholic) drink	61.9
Restaurants and hotels	51.4
Household goods and services	41.0
Clothing and footwear	24.5
Communications	21.3
Alcoholic drink	13.0
	454.7

Several examples of segmentation were provided in Chapter 3 and price segmentation is pervasive in most of the categories listed. Food, drink and household goods (£115.9 per week) are typical retail products sold by supermarkets that offer value, regular and premium brands and, if adopting the HiLo strategy, offer frequent promotions. Recreation and culture (£77.2 per week) includes sports, live entertainment, cinemas and package holidays where product ranges and bundles provide options to both price-sensitive and price-insensitive customers. Restaurants and hotels (£51.4 per week) provide separate lunch and dinner menus and may offer set as well as a la carte menus while hotels provide a range of accommodation to suit both price-sensitive and price-insensitive customers. Clothing retailers (£24.5 per week) provide fashion products at full price early in the season and cut prices in end-of-season sales. Suppliers of broadband, television and mobile services (£21.3 per week) have frequent introductory offers and bundle their products. Despite the lack of survey evidence, it is reasonable to conclude that, in consumer markets, segmented pricing strategies are prevalent.

8.8 The Tellis framework

Tellis (1986) created an influential taxonomy of pricing strategies based on two dimensions: the objective of the firm and types of buyers. The firm's objectives were identified as pricing by customer segment, taking advantage of competitive position and exploiting the product line. Buyers were divided into three groups, a price insensitive group with "high search costs," a price-sensitive group with "low reservation prices" and a group that faced "special transaction costs". This group might face purchasing restrictions because of their demographic group, their location or a product that they have already purchased. The two dimensions were used to create a table with nine cells and pricing strategies could then be analysed accordingly, see table 8.4.

Tellis describes and analyses all the strategies, often using simple numerical examples to demonstrate his key point: that the strategies deliver "shared economies". For example, random discounting generates revenue from regular buyers at full-price and from price sensitive buyers when discounts are offered; periodic discounting generates revenue from early purchasers paying full price and from those buying in end-of-season sales; geographic pricing generates revenue in the home market and in other markets with prices dependent on conditions in different areas.

Tellis employs a series of numerical examples to demonstrate shared economies assuming that "full economic costs" for units of product are known. In economic theory economic costs include *all* the costs of producing and delivering the product including "normal profit" as well as direct and overhead costs. In Tellis's examples this means that break-even ensures that the firm is making normal profit. The following examples illustrate typical calculations for geographic pricing and for premium products.

The key point is that penetration of different market segments can create economies of scale. Before leaving Tellis's analysis "price signalling" and "image pricing" should be explained. In Tellis's analysis price signalling takes price to

Table 8.4 Taxonomy of Pricing Strategies, Tellis (1986) "Beyond the Many faces of Price" *Journal of Marketing, (5),* p. 148, Table 1 reprinted by kind permission of The American Marketing Association

Types of buyers	*Objective of firm*		
	Vary prices among consumer segments	*Exploit competitive position*	*Balance pricing over product line*
Some have high search costs	Random discounting	Price signalling	Image pricing
Some have low reservation price	Periodic discounting	Penetration pricing Experience curve pricing	Price bundling Premium pricing
All have special transaction costs	Second market discounting	Geographic pricing	Complementary pricing

Geographic segmentation: shared economies

A firm can sell 40,000 units in the home market at a price of £10 per unit and full economic cost of £12 per unit, making a loss. However, 40,000 units can be sold overseas at a price of £9 per unit and, because of economies of scale, full economic cost falls to £8. Transport and other costs for overseas sales are £2 per unit. Selling in two markets:

> Home market: 40,000 units × (£10 – £8) = £80,000
> Overseas market: 40,000 units × (£9 – £10) = £(40,000)
> And now there is "abnormal" profit of £40,000 despite a loss in the overseas market.

Premium product: shared economies

A firm can sell 40,000 units of a "basic" product at a price of £10 per unit and full economic cost of £12 per unit, making a loss. However, market research identifies a market for a premium product selling 20,000 units at a price of £15. Economies of scale would reduce full economic cost to £10.50 but the premium product would incur incremental costs of £3. Selling both basic and premium products:

> Basic product: 40,000 units × (£10 – £10.50) = £(20,000)
> Premium product: 20,000 units × (£15 – £13.50) = £30,000
> The basic product is still loss making but, overall, abnormal profits of £10.000 are made.

signal product quality and may, indeed, signal high or low quality. However, the seller may also supply low quality at a high price, the price signal will persuade some customers to purchase. Image pricing is similar but high and low-priced versions are differentiated only by branding. We have seen that some customers are prepared to pay more for a brand that they trust (and different packaging means the product is no longer the "same" to the customer).

8.9 Conclusions

This chapter summarises the major pricing strategies and shows how they can be analysed, first, according to their type: cost, competition or market-based; second, according to their application: industrial or consumer markets; and third, following the Tellis framework based on market characteristics and the competitive advantages of the company.

The analysis reveals that value-based methods are extensively employed in consumer goods markets but not in industrial markets where cost-based and competitive strategies seem more important. This finding supports Hinterhuber's

(2008) analysis of the obstacles that face implementation of value-based approaches in B2B transactions.

There are implications for management accounting in Tellis's key point, that pricing strategies are often designed to generate *shared economies*. Increasingly important research and development, infrastructure and fixed costs place a premium on the generation of revenue and market segmentation and pricing strategies may be the key to generating profitable revenue. The following chapters deal with strategies based on market segmentation and price discrimination before we turn to issues associated with competitors and customers.

Notes

1 Segmentation strategies involving discounting and buyer identification were not considered relevant to industrial goods pricing.

2 www.ons.gov.uk/peoplepopulationandcommunity/personalandhouseholdfinances downloaded 14/07/2021

References

Cooper R. and Kaplan R. S. (1988) Measure costs right: make the right decisions, *Harvard Business Review*, Sep–Oct, 96–103

Dean J. (1950) Pricing policies for new products, *Harvard Business Review*, 28, 45–53

Ellicksen P. B. and Misra S. (2008) Supermarket pricing strategies, *Marketing Science*, 27(5), 811–828

Farm A. (2020) Pricing in practice in consumer markets, *Journal of Post-Keynesian Economics*, 43(1), 61–75

Hinterhuber A. (2008) Customer value-based pricing strategies: why companies resist, *Journal of Business Strategy*, 29(4), 41–50

Mitchell A. (1983) *The Nine American Lifestyles*, Warner Books, New York

Noble P. M. and Gruca T. S. (1999) Industrial pricing: theory and managerial practice, *Marketing Science*, 18(3), 435–454

Porter M. E. (1980) *Competitive Strategy*, Free Press, New York

Tellis G. J. (1986) Beyond the many faces of price: an integration of pricing strategies, *Journal of Marketing*, 5, 146–159

Yankelovich D. (1964) New criteria for market segmentation, *Harvard Business Review*, 42(2), 82–90

Yankelovich D. and Meer D. (2006) Rediscovering market segmentation, *Harvard Business Review*, 84(2), 122–131

9 Demographic and geographic pricing

9.1 Introduction

This and the following chapters consider market segmentation and price fences, emphasising the potential management accounting contribution. This chapter concentrates on two *direct* methods of market segmentation: buyer identity and geographic location. These are direct methods because *the seller* sets the prices charged in each market segment.

Demographic and geographic pricing are examples of third-degree price discrimination (setting different prices for different customer groups) and this has received extensive attention from economists, especially its welfare implications. In economics "welfare" is the sum of consumer and producer surpluses and reflects the surplus to both consumer and producer over their costs. Governments and regulators usually aim to increase welfare, so the theory of price discrimination has policy implications. These issues are considered in Chapter 16.

9.2 Demographic segmentation

This is probably the clearest form of price discrimination with discounts for "special" groups such as students and seniors. Arbitrage can be prevented by asking for proof of identity, age, occupation etc. Examples include the Defence Privilege Card for members of the armed services and veterans, "healthservicediscounts" for members of the NHS, "Unidays" for students and railcards for seniors and other age groups.

It is natural to assume that demographic discounts are offered to lower income groups although this is not necessarily true. For example, older people may have more disposable income than younger adults with family and other commitments. However, older adults may be more price sensitive, so a lower price is needed to tempt them to purchase. In addition, it might be necessary to offer discounts to some groups to meet competition and, once offered, discounts may be difficult to remove.

Discounts are usually available for children, especially for travel and holidays. This might be seen as demographic price discrimination, but, often, the discount is not offered because children are a price sensitive group, but because *families* are likely to be price sensitive. The discount might then be better classified as relating

DOI: 10.4324/9781003272731-9

to volume (especially if there is a requirement that children be accompanied by an adult).

9.3 Implications for management accountants

The main implication for management accountants is the importance of increased volume if a new market segment can be opened. As Tellis (1986) points out, in this case, any price that generates additional contribution can be considered – the standard management accounting recommendation when considering truly incremental business that would have no impact on existing sales.

In practice a completely incremental market based on demographic criteria is unlikely and the management accountant should provide advice to management considering a possible demographic discount. For example, suppose that management is considering a 33% discount for older adults travelling at off-peak times. In some industries marginal costs are minimal. For example, if a train will be under-utilised, any extra revenue is additional contribution. The key question is whether increased take-up will outweigh the loss of revenue from full fare paying passengers. If variable cost is negligible then:

$$\begin{aligned}\text{\% increase for break-even} &= (-\Delta P \times 100)/(CM + \Delta P)\\ &(33.3 \times 100)/(100\text{–}33.3) = 50\%\end{aligned}$$

To justify a 33% discount, volume needs to be increased by 50%. Market research is needed to assess whether such an increase is likely.

If marginal cost is not negligible then it must be considered in assessing a proposed discount. For example, suppose that the marginal cost of a cup of coffee is 20p and a regular coffee sells at £2.00. A student discount of 20% is under consideration. For students the price per cup will be £1.60 and contribution will be £1.40 instead of £1.80.

$$\begin{aligned}\text{\% increase for break-even} &= (-\Delta CM \times 100)/(CM + \Delta CM)\\ &40p \times 100/\ (180p - 40p)\\ &28.57\%\end{aligned}$$

An increase of more than 28% is needed to achieve break-even contribution. If 20 students presently visit the coffee shop per day will a price reduction to £1.60 lead to at least 26 students visiting the shop? (This ignores other "complementary" products that they may purchase).

9.4 Geographic segmentation in the home market

Like demographic discrimination, geographic price discrimination is a direct method of discrimination and, if a new market can be opened, any incremental contribution is, in principle, worth having. This means that manufacturing firms find it profitable to expand outside their "home" territories, offering competitive prices in more distant locations. To do this, firms may bear some of the freight costs to more distant locations, a practice known as *freight absorption.* In economic terms this is price discrimination because there are price differences not fully explained by cost differences (the cost to more distant locations suggests that prices should be higher).

Greenhut (1981) found that geographic pricing by industrial firms was prevalent in the US, West Germany and Japan. In the US 67% did not add full freight costs and the corresponding figures of 79% and 82% for West German and Japanese firms were even higher. If freight costs are not borne by the seller, then the product (typically steel, cement, bricks etc.) is sold "free-on-board" (fob) at the factory and freight costs are the responsibility of the buyer. In practice it is more usual for industrial firms to bear freight costs thus gaining control of the "delivered price".

Phlips (1983) sets out the logic of freight absorption by considering a single firm supplying a local market and two more distant markets. The demand is the same in all three markets but, if the product is supplied fob, then the most distant market would not be supplied at all – freight costs, borne by the customer, would be prohibitive. By absorbing part of the freight costs sales are made in all three territories and more profit is made. Having shown that multiple prices based on freight absorption are more profitable than fob prices, Phlips goes on to show that the fob price is, in turn, more profitable than setting a single price (a uniform delivered price) for all three markets.

In practice a single delivered price or *uniform pricing* is common. It can be seen as a special case of freight absorption; the seller absorbs all the "excess" freight charges no matter how distant the buyer. It might arise because of legal obligation as in postal services or because the seller chooses a uniform price. Lederer (2011) reports the practice to be widespread in the US, citing mail order outlets such as L.L. Bean and Lands End as well as in wholesaling where supermarket buyers confirmed that: "Procter and Gamble, Colgate, Palmolive, Clorox and Lever Brothers use uniform pricing almost exclusively" (p. 315). No doubt a uniform price is simpler and, of course, does not prevent volume discounting and negotiations with individual customers.

In consumer markets differential pricing is more closely related to the customer's willingness to pay and this can vary significantly depending on location. For example, Schindler (2012) suggests that sandwiches might be priced differently in local stores, shopping malls and sports stadia. Supermarkets in the UK largely adopt national pricing strategies. However, a survey by Which[1] showed that Sainsbury's Local and Tesco Express charged almost 10% more than their superstores. Customers expect to pay more for snacks and drinks at theatres, cinemas and at sporting events (a pint of beer at an international cricket match is expensive) but sellers do need to consider their reputation if there is a danger that customers consider prices to be unfair.

9.5 Implications for management accountants

As so often, it is not individual margins so much as the profitability of product ranges and business units that matters. For industrial products with significant freight charges the contribution margins should be calculated before and after freight costs for individual customers. Freight costs might seem relatively high for more distant customers, but this can be justified if part of a carefully considered pricing plan that involves freight absorption. Analysis of customer gross margins is a key topic for management accountants, to be considered in detail in Chapter 13. In consumer goods markets margins need to be analysed by retail outlet. Product contribution may be higher in convenience stores, but local rents/leases and business rates need to be deducted in calculating profitability by store.

9.6 Geographic discrimination: international markets

Simon and Fassnacht (2019) draw attention to the significant price differences that can exist between countries, for example, Apple iPhones priced 10% above the average value in Germany and France but more than 10% below the average in the US and Japan; women's leather shoes priced as much as 30% below average in Spain but almost 40% above average in Japan. However, prices that differ significantly across countries provide opportunities for arbitrage: buying by a third party in a cheaper territory to resell in a higher priced area. This practice gives rise to "parallel imports" or "grey markets".

The problem may be exacerbated by movements in exchange rates. In the face of the $ weakening, an exporting firm might increase its $ price to maintain the cash received in its home currency. However, there is no justification for this in the local market, an increased price may lead to a significant fall in volume and much lower profits. The lesson is that prices need to be based on local conditions. Unfortunately, this can lead to significant price differentials between countries and parallel imports may be encouraged.

Parallel imports arise when price differences are sufficient to make it worthwhile for third parties to purchase at the lower price and resell at the higher price. To combat parallel imports or so-called "grey markets" sellers might eliminate price differences across territories by harmonising international prices. However, this would take no account of local conditions and, as noted earlier, would lead to a loss of potential profits. Simon and Fassnacht (2019) recommend, instead, that sellers employ an international "price corridor," reducing price differences between countries so that arbitrage is less attractive. Their example is a pharmaceutical company that estimated optimal prices in the UK, France, Italy, USA and Germany. Increases in the lowest prices and decreases in the highest prices were recommended so that all prices fell within an (arbitrarily defined) corridor. "Compared to the isolated optimal prices, which could not be implemented in practice, the profit sacrifice was acceptable. The price corridor also largely avoided frictions caused by parallel imports" (p. 321).

If international prices diverge so much that this approach is not possible then a different solution is needed. If the low-price markets are important, it may be worth differentiating the product for different markets. A brand with specific markings might be designed to make it difficult to resell in a market for which it is not intended. In this case the cost of branding, packaging and marketing must be carefully considered against the revenue stream generated market by market. In high-priced markets product sold through official channels might be differentiated by a warranty and after-sales support that would not be available for product purchased through the grey market.

9.7 Implications for management accountants

Management accountants are well placed to draw together information relating to prices, volumes and costs across countries and to identify whether parallel imports are taking place. The ease with which the internet makes it possible to purchase in one country and sell in another also makes it possible for the management accountant to access internet prices to assess whether such arbitrage activity is taking place. The fluctuating nature of exchange rates means that a dynamic analysis is needed: an "acceptable" international price corridor might become unacceptable due to changes in exchange rates.

If an exchange rate moves favourably, for example strengthening in an overseas territory, the management accountant needs to consider whether it is desirable to hold the local price constant or reduce it to gain more volume. As well as considering projected cash flows attention needs to be given to possible arbitrage and, if prices are reduced, the consequences of moving to a "value-advantaged" position and likely competitor reaction.

If arbitrage is an issue the management accountant should be involved in considering whether an "international price corridor" should be devised. Consider a product that sells at €1 in the Eurozone, £1.20 in the UK and at $1.50 in the US. At exchange rates of €1 = £0.85 and €1 = $1.20 there would be a clear incentive to purchase in the Eurozone and resell in the UK (UK price in euros 1.20/0.85 = €1.41) and, to a lesser extent, in the United States. A grey market could be expected to emerge. An "international price corridor" would bring prices more into line. The simplest approach would be to increase the euro price to, say, €1.20.

The break-even formula can be used to estimate the impact of volume change. At a variable cost of €0.60:

$$
\begin{aligned}
\text{\% increase for break-even} &= (-\Delta CM \times 100)/(CM + \Delta CM) \\
&- €0.20 \times 100/\ (€1.20 - €0.60) \\
&- 33.4\%
\end{aligned}
$$

A reduction in sales of 33.3% could be sustained without reducing profit in euros. However, as Schindler (2012) points out, this simple calculation is inaccurate. The price increase will make grey market sales less attractive, and we have not taken account of the extra "official" sales that would therefore be made in the UK and US. If, for every unit "lost" in the Eurozone, 0.1 more units would be sold in the UK/US and the contribution from these units is, say €0.6 then the contribution required to break-even would be reduced by €0.06 and the percentage reduction in volume for break-even would be –20/0.54 = –37%. A significant reduction in volume could be sustained without affecting profit in the Eurozone.

If the differences between international prices cannot be bridged by a price corridor, then the management accountant's role is different. If it is worth supplying a low-price territory, then the product probably should be differentiated so that it is not easily resold. The management accountant needs to assess the investment and ongoing costs associated with such a strategy.

Note

1 Information at www.inyourarea.co.uk/news/supermarket-convenience-store-shoppers-spending-320-more-a-year-on-groceries downloaded 6/8/2021

References

Greenhut M. L. (1981) Spatial pricing in the United States, West Germany and Japan, *Economica*, 48(189), 79–86

Lederer P. J. (2011) Uniform spatial pricing, *Journal of Regional Science*, 11(2), 315–342

Phlips L. (1983) *The Economics of Price Discrimination*, Cambridge University Press, Cambridge

Schindler R. M. (2012) *Pricing Strategies: A Marketing Approach*, Sage Publications Inc., Thousand Oaks, CA

Simon H. and Fassnacht M. (2019) *Price Management: Strategy, Analysis, Decision, Implementation*, Springer, Cham, Switzerland

Tellis G. J. (1986) Beyond the many faces of price: an integration of pricing strategies, *Journal of Marketing*, 5, 146–159

10 Quantity-based pricing

10.1 Introduction

In this and the following chapters we consider indirect price discrimination where the seller offers a range of alternatives, and the buyer effectively chooses their market segment by their choice of product or service. This chapter deals with quantity-based discrimination and, in the following chapters, product and time-based discrimination are considered.

Usually, the price per unit falls as more is purchased. This is not surprising; order and batch costs are spread over a larger number of units and the seller, naturally, wishes to encourage the buyer to take a larger quantity.

10.2 Volume-related pricing

Fabiani et al. (2005) found that 42% of European companies employ quantity-based pricing and discounts for volume purchases. They are commonplace in both industrial and consumer markets (where larger package sizes usually mean a lower price per unit). Quantity-related discounts are a form of price discrimination because different customers pay different prices for the same product. The discrimination is indirect because customers select the quantity and therefore assign themselves to a particular "segment".

For a single customer, assuming a linear demand curve, a monopolist setting a single price would maximise profit where the marginal revenue curve meets the marginal cost curve. The standard economic treatment results in optimal price P and output Q as shown in Figure 10.1. For convenience, marginal cost is set to zero.

The monopolist restricts output and raises price above marginal cost thus making contribution PQ. However, if the buyer were offered a series of discounts: 1 unit at £10, 2 units for £19, 3 units for £27, etc. then the buyer would see that each unit was cheaper than the one before, paying £10, £9, £8, etc. for each successive unit and would keep buying right down to marginal cost (the supplier would not, of course offer a price below marginal cost). The monopolist would then make contribution equal to the triangle bounded by P_1, Q_1 and the origin – twice as much as the rectangle PQ. This example demonstrates the advantage of incremental, step-based discounting where each unit is another "step," the price decreasing unit by unit. Note

DOI: 10.4324/9781003272731-10

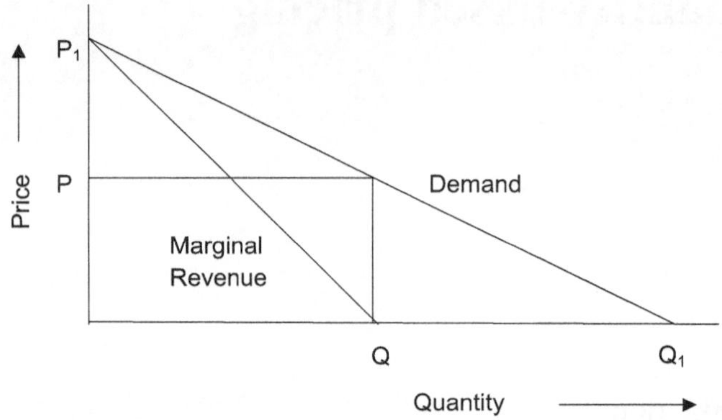

Figure 10.1 Profit maximising price and quantity for a monopolist, marginal cost set to zero

that, to take advantage of lower prices, the buyer must first purchase the preceding units at higher prices. This example presumes either a single customer or a group of identical customers and, in addition, that the demand function is known. It does, though, clearly demonstrate the potential advantage of offering discounts.

Wilson (1993) noted that non-linear pricing can segment the market because low users tend to be price insensitive, willing to pay higher prices per unit, while high volume users are likely to be more price sensitive. Non-linear pricing generates additional revenue, and this may be especially important if a company has high infrastructure costs. It may also be important to encourage larger orders if significant costs are involved in fulfilling an order.

There are several possible discounting arrangements and Nagle and Müller (2018) identify four: first, volume discounts dependent on the total volume taken in a given period, typically a month or year; second, step discounting where the discount applies only to incremental volume; third, two-part pricing where the customer pays a fixed fee and an additional price per unit; and fourth, order discounts that relate to the volume placed in a single order.

10.3 Total quantity versus single-step discount schemes

A multi-step discount scheme, as described earlier, is theoretically ideal. However, a scheme with many steps is difficult to administer and the fewer the number of "steps" the easier the scheme is to both negotiate and communicate. The simplest scheme has only a single step where the seller sets a price per unit for the first tranche of units and then sets a lower price for each subsequent unit. This can be contrasted with a "total quantity" scheme where, again, there is a "threshold" volume above which a lower price is charged but, in this case, the lower price applies not just to the incremental volume but to the whole volume purchased.

The total quantity scheme can be dangerous, offering a discount on the entire volume purchased when the threshold volume is reached. However, the buyer has a clear and strong incentive to purchase at least the threshold quantity so qualifying for the discount. In the UK, supermarket customers are likely to be familiar with vouchers that offer, for example, £9 off if £60 is spent in a single shop, equating to a discount of 15% if spend is precisely £60. This scheme is designed to encourage the customer to purchase significantly more than usual, but this must be weighed against reduced margin. By contrast the step (or incremental) discount scheme offers a discount on only items purchased *above the threshold* and does not impact gross margin and contribution per unit on sales below the threshold. However, the incentive to purchase at least the threshold volume is not so strong. The two schemes have different characteristics, and it is not clear which one might maximise the seller's contribution and profit.

Amornpetchkul (2017) compares a "full unit" discount with an incremental scheme in retail environments assuming a mix of customers with different linear demand functions. She demonstrates that, if the discount percentage is imposed (for example by competition), then either scheme might maximise profit. However, if the seller can set optimal values for the threshold quantity and the discount percentage, then the single step incremental scheme is always more profitable than the total quantity scheme. One might expect incremental schemes to be preferred but the advantage of the all-unit scheme is its simplicity, and, in retail, sellers can set the threshold based on knowledge of each buyer's shopping habits. The seller can ensure that, to receive the discount, the customer must purchase significantly more than a normal shop.

10.4 Two-part tariff schemes

A two-part tariff requires the buyer to pay a lump sum "entry fee" and then a charge per unit. A two-part tariff is a special case of the step discount scheme where the "step" is the initial entry fee and then "subsequent" units are purchased at a price per unit. In the ideal case where the demand schedule of a single buyer is known, the initial lump sum payment can be set equal to the whole consumer surplus (the triangle bounded by P_1, Q_1 and the origin in Figure 10.1) with incremental units supplied at marginal cost.

There are obvious examples such as the standing charge for gas and electricity and then a charge per unit consumed. For example, EON's standard electricity contract for the Eastern region (April 2021) had a fixed tariff of 28.882p per day and a unit rate of 18.096p per kWh. The "price metric" of price per day (rather than, say, £26.35 per quarter) is perhaps intended to make the charge seem less expensive. The utility companies argue that the standing charge is needed to cover the cost of maintaining supplies while the price per unit covers variable costs. In addition, a two-part tariff is also a simple discounting scheme that encourages customers to buy more because the price per unit decreases as quantity purchased increases and the fixed charge is spread over more units.

A two-part tariff may allow a monopolist (or supplier with monopoly power) to make more profit and theme parks provide a perfect example: but which is better, a high entrance fee with low cost per ride, or a low entrance fee with high cost per ride? Oi (1971) addresses this question in: "A Disneyland Dilemma: Two Part Tariffs for a Mickey Mouse Monopoly". He considers the typical case where there are many different customers and, to analyse this case, he first considers a very low entrance fee so that all potential customers enter the theme park. Profits will then be generated mainly by selling rides. If the entrance fee is increased, some customers will drop out of the market and, given "plausible assumptions," Oi shows that optimal profit is achieved by raising the entrance fee to exclude some customers and reducing the price per ride to capture more of the consumer surplus of the remaining customers. He suggests that trial and error might involve raising the lump sum "tax" to see if it drives out some customers and then reducing prices to see if profit is increased or decreased.

It is interesting to trace the pricing policy of Disneyland over the years. In 1955 when Disneyland at Anaheim, California, opened there was a relatively low entrance fee of $1 for an adult and 50 cents for a child. Then there were fees ranging from 25 to 35 cents for an adult and 10 to 25 cents for a child for each attraction.[1] Soon after opening ticket books were introduced with coupons that were exchanged for rides. Initially there were A, B and C class rides but D and E class rides were introduced in 1956 and 1959, respectively. The highest level, E class, ride was priced at 50 cents per ride. In 1982 Disney eliminated pricing per ride and moved to an entrance fee and no charge per ride. The entrance fee rose quickly from $12 in 1982 to $25.50 in December 1989 for an adult one-day pass.[2] Disneyland continues to charge a single-entry fee but now prices depend on the season, varying from $104 (tier 1) to $154 (tier 5) for a single park adult pass.[3]

Oi's seminal work related to the use of two-part pricing by a monopolist and Harrison and Kline (2001) investigated two-part pricing in oligopolies citing health clubs, telephone services, credit cards and public utilities as examples. They assumed a homogenous product and homogenous customers and concluded that, unlike the monopoly case analysed by Oi, firms would set prices equal to marginal cost. Profits would be generated by the fixed "entry" fees set by the competing firms. As the number of firms increased these fixed fees would fall and eventually approach zero. Not surprisingly homogenous products and customers together with many competing firms leads to perfect competition.

In practice customers are likely to have varied preferences and price sensitivities. This case was investigated by Jensen and Sorgard (2005) and they found that, assuming just two types of customers with high and low demand, price per unit could be *below marginal cost* and the fixed fee could be positive no matter how many firms competed. Firms that charge an entry fee and then do not charge per unit as in the Disney example or "all-you-can-eat" restaurants follow this policy. (A zero price per unit must be below marginal cost.)

10.5 Total quantity schemes: implications for management accountants

Perhaps the simplest scheme is to offer a percentage reduction on all units if some threshold volume (or value) is purchased. We have seen that such discounts are offered by retailers where sellers have customer-by-customer data based on loyalty cards and simple communication of the scheme is important. However, such schemes are also not uncommon in B2B markets. Firms with heavy infrastructure costs may depend on significant volume to cover these costs and, for example, Nagle and Müller (2018) refer to steel manufacturers that offer auto companies significant discounts for their high-volume business. Discounts may be applied to specific products, or they may be linked to the total sales purchased.

Management accountants should be sceptical of total volume discounts *because the discount applies to the entire volume sold*, or, in the case of some retail schemes, on all sales up to the threshold. If sales at "normal" prices generate 40% contribution, then a volume discount of 10% requires a 33% sales increase to compensate for the discount and a 20% discount would require a 100% sales increase. The dangers are highlighted by Nagle and Müller who point out that a canny buyer might offer to take, say, 10% more volume for a discount of "only" 2%, nothing wrong with that if the discount relates only to the incremental volume. However, if the seller applies the discount to the total volume, incautiously giving the buyer a total quantity discount, then the buyer receives a 22% discount on the incremental volume.

If an all-unit scheme must be employed it can be improved by tying discounts to the percentage increase from the buyer's order quantity *before discount* (Wang and Wu, 2000). Undoubtedly supermarkets adopt this approach based on their knowledge of their customers shopping habits. Nevertheless, it is not clear why supermarkets offer all-unit discounts. Retailers in general generate gross margins of 25–30% and, at these levels, volume increases of more than 50% are needed to compensate for a 10% all-unit discount.

10.6 Step discounts: implications for management accountants

Armornpetchkul's analysis demonstrates that optimal step schemes are better than optimal total quantity schemes and her review of prior literature reinforces the key point that step schemes are more effective than total volume discounts. They increase order quantities and seller's profit (Lal and Staelin, 1984; Kim and Hwang, 1988) while Chen and Robinson (2012) showed that, if there are heterogeneous buyers, most savings can be captured by a limited number of step breakpoints. Management accountants are advised to recommend incremental, step, schemes rather than "all unit" discount schemes.

10.7 Two-part pricing: implications for management accountants

It was noted that a two-part tariff is a special case of the simplest step scheme with an initial fee and then an incremental price per unit. Coffee shop pricing provides an unusual example on this theme. In 2019 Costa charged £2.15 for a small latte (12 fl oz), £2.45 for its medium cup (16 fl oz) and £2.75 for its large cup (20 fl oz). One could see this as a £1.85 "entry fee" for 8 fl. ozs. and then a variable price of 30p for 4 fl oz. of coffee. The customer is tempted to purchase a larger size by the relatively low incremental price. In this case the management accountant needs to check the incremental costs associated with the larger sizes, but these are surely small, minimal extra preparation time, possibly an extra shot of coffee and some milk. Costa received adverse publicity in 2019 when it trialled revised prices based on a smaller "small" latte at £2.25, a smaller medium (the old small) at £2.55, a new large (the old medium) at £2.85 and an extra-large (the old large) at £3.05.[4] Apparently, Costa was considering a new "entry fee" of £1.95 together with a greater range of prices for incremental cup sizes (but maintaining the additional price for 4 fl. ozs. at 30p for the new medium and large cups).

The aim is to maximise incremental contribution and the management accountant should identify the contribution generated by the "entry fees" or fixed charges and by units sold, whether units of electricity, rides in a theme park or fl.ozs. of coffee. In general, the aim is to increase the "entrance fee" and, usually, to reduce the price per unit. One can see this in the Disney policy which now has a high entrance fee and free rides.[5] It seems that Costa has flirted with increasing its "entrance fee" (the price of its small cup) and extending its volume range. In this case the company must consider whether a higher "entrance fee" might deter customers (especially in view of adverse publicity). Energy companies might wish to increase the daily "standing" charge while setting relatively low prices per unit. However, in this case, other factors come into play, especially government pressure to discourage excessive energy use.

Management accountants need a good understanding of the issues involved in these schemes, in particular the inter-relationship between "entrance fee" or standing charge, price per unit and variable cost per unit. There are standard treatments of the theory of two-part pricing such as Wilson (1993, pp. 136–141). However, the analysis presumes detailed knowledge of potential customers and their demand functions. In practice, it is likely that Oi's advice to proceed by trial and error, testing combinations of standing charges or entrance fees and unit prices is most practical. Understanding the issues is, of course, important if the management accountant is to contribute to policy setting.

10.8 Transfer pricing: implications for management accountants

The analysis of discount schemes has a possible implication in transfer pricing where one division buys from another division in the same company. Theory shows that, to maximise total profit, the buying division should purchase at the supplying division's marginal cost, plus opportunity cost per unit. However, if the selling division has spare capacity there is no opportunity cost and sales between divisions "should" be made at marginal cost. A marginal cost price means the supplying division makes losses equal to its fixed costs and all the contribution from sales is captured by the buying division. To overcome this problem, the two divisions might negotiate a lump sum payment by the buying division to the selling division. This is a two-part tariff, the lump sum being the equivalent of an "entry fee" that permits the buying division access to product at marginal cost.

The transfer pricing problem is unusual in that, in its simplest form, it is close to an "ideal case" in that there are only two parties, the buying and selling divisions, and the demand function and the cost structures of both divisions can be estimated.

The analysis of discounting schemes suggests an alternative to the lump sum payment: the selling division could offer a step discounting scheme designed to persuade the buying division to purchase down to marginal cost. Consider a simple example. Division A with fixed costs of £10,000 per week supplies Division B with product, marginal cost £5 per unit. Division A is required to supply 800 units per week at £5 per unit and Division A makes a loss equal to its fixed cost of £10,000. Now suppose that A can set its own price schedule, say:

Units	*Price per unit (£)*	*Revenue (£)*	*Variable cost (£)*	*Contribution (£)*
400	£23.75	9,500	2,000	7,500
600	£20.625	12,375	3,000	9,375
700	£19.06	13,342	3,500	9,844
800	£17.5	14,000	4,000	10,000

Division B will realise that the last 100 units costs only £658, £6.58 per unit, and will be encouraged to purchase its (presumed optimal) quantity of 800 units. Division A will generate £10,000 of contribution and cover its fixed cost. A discount schedule is an alternative to a lump sum payment of £10,000 by Division B in return for purchases at marginal cost. If Division B refuses to purchase 800 units in the step scheme or to pay £10,000 lump sum in the two-part tariff scheme the product is not viable because Division A is unable to cover fixed costs.

There is likely to be negotiation as the selling division tries to gain more contribution and the buying division tries to concede less. However, this approach would maintain divisional autonomy without necessarily deviating unduly from the overall optimal quantity transferred. Tomkins (1990) suggested a scheme along these lines based on an initial price that allowed the selling division a "fair" contribution to fixed cost and profit and then a further negotiation at lower prices so that the total transfer of product approached the optimum level (800 units in the above example).

10.9 Price schedule taking account of batch/order-related costs: implications for management accountants

In the previous sections a simple split between fixed and variable cost has been assumed but, in practice, the relationship between cost and volume could be complex. The management accountant has long had a role in analysing the relationship between cost and volume and this is obviously critical in analysing the profitability of discounting schemes. Activity-based costing might identify unit, batch, product, customer and facility-related costs and then cost per unit at different levels of volume can be derived. For example:

Quantity (units)	100	1000	5000	10000	20000
Unit-related costs at £2 per unit (£)	200	2000	10000	20000	40000
Order related costs at £50 per 100 units (£)	50	500	2500	5000	10000
Batch related costs at £3000 per 600 units	3000	6000	27000	51000	102000
Attributable product costs £5000	5000	5000	5000	5000	5000
Total costs (£)	8250	13500	44500	81000	157000
Cost per unit (£)	82.5	13.5	8.9	8.1	7.85

These unit costs provide an indication of the lowest prices that might be charged at different levels of volume: a vital input to the pricing decision and an issue we meet again in the Sloan Styles case; see Chapter 14.

Notes

1 Source: www.cnbc.com/2015/07/17/this-is-how-much-disneyland-cost-when-it-opened.html downloaded 12/03/2022
2 Source: www.latimes.com/archives/la-xpm-1989-12-13-fi-382-story.html downloaded 12/03/2022
3 Source: www.wdwinfo.com/disneyland/tickets.htm downloaded 12/03/2022
4 www.thesun.co.uk/money/9684681/costa-shrinks-cup-sizes-at-the-same-time-as-putting-up-its-prices/
5 Disney has refined its policies in recent years so that the entrance fee varies with season and day of the week, effectively rationing demand in line with capacity of the theme park.

References

Amornpetchkul T. (2017) Threshold discounts comparison: all-unit or incremental? *Journal of Revenue and Pricing Management*, 16, 265–294

Chen R. C. and Robinson L. W. (2012) Optimal multiple-breakpoint quantity discount schedules for customers with heterogenous demands: all-unit or incremental? *IIE Transactions*, 44(3), 199–214

Fabiani S., Druant M., Hernando I., Kwapil C., Landau B., Loupias C., Martins F., Mathä T. Y., Sabbatini R., Stahl H. and Stokman C. J. (2005) The pricing behaviour of firms in the Euro area: new survey evidence, *Working Paper Number 535*, European Central Bank, downloaded from: www.ecb.int or http://ssrn.com/abstract_id=825628

Harrison M. and Kline J. J. (2001) Quantity competition with access fees, *International Journal of Industrial Organization*, 19, 345–373

Jensen S. and Sorgard L. (2005) Two-part pricing, consumer heterogeneity and Cournot competition, *SSRN Electronic Journal*, http//doi.org/10.2139/ssrn.900306

Kim K. H. and Hwang H. (1988) An incremental discount pricing schedule with multiple customers and single price break, *European Journal of Operational Research*, 35(1), 71–79

Lal R. and Staelin R. (1984) An approach for developing an optimal discount pricing policy, *Management Science*, 30(12), 1524–1539

Nagle T. T. and Müller G. (2018) *The Strategy and Tactics of Pricing*, 6th edition, Routledge, New York and Abingdon, Oxon

Oi W. Y. (1971) A Disneyland dilemma: two-part tariffs for a Mickey Mouse monopoly, *The Quarterly Journal of Economics*, 85(1), 77–96

Tomkins C. (1990) Making sense of cost-plus transfer prices where there are imperfect intermediate good markets by a 'pragmatic-analytic' perspective, *Management Accounting Research*, 1(3), 199–216

Wang Q. and Wu Z. (2000) Improving a supplier's quantity discount gain from many different buyers, *IIE Transactions*, 32, 1071–1079

Wilson R. B. (1993) *Nonlinear Pricing*, Oxford University Press, Oxford

11 Product differentiation and pricing

11.1 Introduction

Product variants provide a very important method of separating customers that have different requirements. Some customers require a high specification product while others need only a "value" version. Some customers are interested in add-ons and accessories while others prefer just the basic product. Customers may differ in their product preferences: some opt for a high-performance car while others put the priority on space and safety; some like to watch sport on television while others have no interest in sport but like to watch films. There is an endless variety in customer needs, desires and preferences and understanding the various customer segments is key to product design, marketing and pricing.

11.2 Complements, substitutes and bundles

Complementary products may be necessary to the function of the base product as in the well-worn example of razors and razor blades or they may be optional extras as products to "enhance" a new car such as treatments to protect fabric, car wash/wax materials and top-up insurance arrangements. Complementary products can also be linked by convenience as in supermarkets that offer low-priced staples such as bread and milk but then tempt customers with an enticing range of products, or by association as in the snacks offered by cinemas. The nature of complements means that the seller may find that it pays to offer a "base" product at a very competitive price if the customer is then likely to purchase complements that generate high margins and contribution. The growth of the luxury cruise industry (pre-COVID-19) provides an illustration as customers, attracted by low cabin ("stateroom") prices, then spend on excursions, drinks, beauty treatments and so on.

Substitute products are different. Instead of giving the customer the opportunity to purchase additional products, the customer is invited to choose from a range of products. Products may be vertically differentiated as in the example of roadside assistance where some versions are better than others; or they may be horizontally differentiated as in iphones, cars and clothes offered in a range of colours. Branding can also differentiate the product as in the example of branded versus generic drugs or the sale of chemicals for use in the agricultural, medicinal or cosmetic industries.

DOI: 10.4324/9781003272731-11

Many products are clearly either substitutes or complements but, if product add-ons are bundled with the base product, then the various product bundles (made up of complementary products) can become substitutes for each other. Product bundling has become both ubiquitous and important with, for example, product bundles offered by Sky and Virgin in broadband provision, telephone service and television entertainment. "Pure" bundling arises when only the bundle is offered and, in this case, groupings of complementary products become substitutes. "Mixed" bundling occurs when products can be purchased separately or as part of a bundle, usually at a discount to the sum of the individual prices.

11.3 Substitute products

The theory of vertical product differentiation is based on differentiation by "quality". There are several versions, and the buyer self-selects their market segment by their choice of product. Price sensitive buyers will tend to purchase value or basic products while price insensitive buyers tend to purchase premium or luxury versions.

The theory can be understood using the same diagram as for quantity discrimination, see Figure 11.1. Here, the quantity increases as the price falls not because individuals purchase more, but because more price sensitive customers are tempted to purchase. Taking marginal cost as zero for convenience, a monopolist will maximise profits by setting price at $P_1/2$, and quantity at $Q_1/2$ units. Revenue will be $P_1/2$ x $Q_1/2 = P_1Q_1/4$ and, if marginal cost is zero, this will also be the contribution generated.

Now, if a second, "value" product is introduced with less functionality than the standard product, at a price of, say, $P_1/4$, this product will generate more sales as customers not prepared to pay $P_1/2$ decide to purchase; see Figure 11.2. In

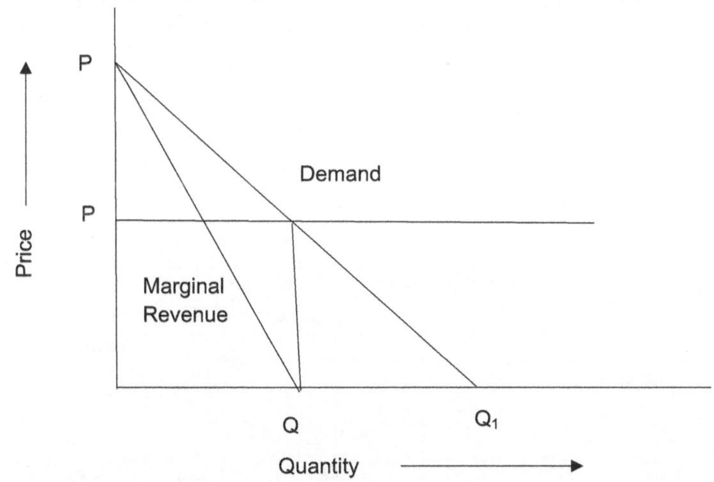

Figure 11.1 Profit maximising price and quantity for a monopolist, marginal cost set to zero for simplicity

economic terms the "deadweight loss" (neither producer nor consumer surplus) is reduced to just the triangle with base Q_1–$3Q_1/4$. Smith (2011) analyses the case for two products and shows that the introduction of a value product increases profits by serving a wider market but also reduces profits by "cannibalising" sales of the regular product: some customers trade down to the value product. To ensure that contribution is increased a good product fence is needed so that regular customers are not tempted to trade down.

If a "value" version can be introduced, then why not consider a new premium product as well? Such a product would be better than the first product, attracting price insensitive customers willing to pay more for extra product features. A new premium product at a price of, say, $3P_1/4$ might be introduced, and "high value" customers would purchase this version. This would transfer some of the consumer surplus from buyers that previously purchased the "standard" product to the producer.

The next question is, of course, if two products are better than one, and three better than two, why not add more products at either the top or bottom of the range? This could generate yet more contribution. In principle, any number of product variants could be introduced to target all the different types of customers (just as, in theory, there could be many "steps" in a quantity discounting scheme). However, if too many variants are introduced, there is more cannibalisation, costs are likely to increase significantly, and customers become confused.

For physical products, product costs increase as new features and functions are added and, perversely, sometimes, instead of designing a value product, it makes sense to remove functions from the regular product: it may cost more to produce a product that has *less* functionality! It is not just production costs that increase. Even if, as in the case of information products, production cost is unaffected, a more complex product range means increased costs of marketing and communication. In addition, aside from possible confusion and cost, an increased product range means (even) more attention must be given to the price fences that differentiate

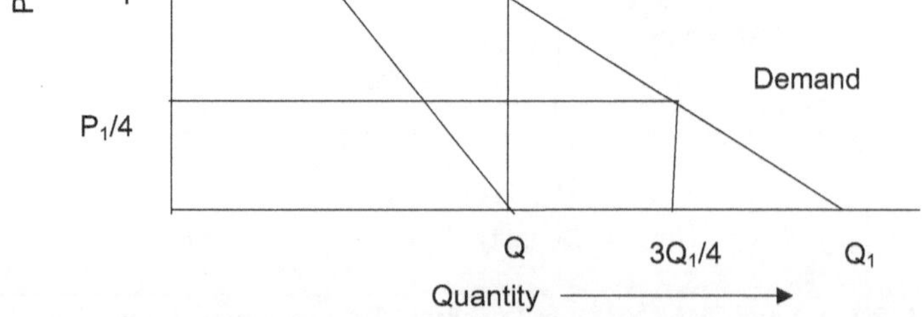

Figure 11.2 Vertical product differentiation with two products, prices P and $P_1/4$

products. The issue can hardly be better described than in the oft-quoted passage by Depuit, published in 1849:

> "It is not because of the few thousand francs which would have to be spent to put a roof over the third-class carriages. . . . What the company is trying to do is to prevent the passengers who can pay the second-class fare from traveling third class; . . . And it is again for the same reason that the companies, having proved almost cruel to third-class passengers and mean to second-class ones, become lavish in dealing with first-class passengers. Having refused the poor what is necessary, they give the rich what is superfluous."
>
> (quoted by Ekelund, 1970, p. 275)

Clear fences are obviously very important and the more product variants the more attention is needed to ensure that the variants are clearly separated. Mohammed (2018, p. 110) notes that: "I often suggest other pricing strategies but wind up implementing G-B-B [good-better-best] because it's the option managers find the easiest to understand, explain, and get behind." However, this is not to say that "good-better-best" is always adopted. Several airlines have introduced a "premium economy" class which provides increased legroom and other benefits. No doubt the logic is that passengers that would have booked economy can be tempted to pay more for premium economy while, at the same time, business and first-class passengers are unlikely to trade down.

Our discussion has concentrated on the purely economic reasons for introducing a range of product variants of clearly increasing quality. In addition, there are important behavioural and psychological reasons for expanding the product range. First, there is "anchoring," the existence of a relatively highly priced variant can help to anchor expectations – so the other variants appear to offer good value. Second, there is uncertainty reduction or "extreme aversion" which leads customers to choose the middle option, it seems "safer" than the more extreme variants. Third, a product may be a decoy, not intended to be sold but to direct customers to one of the other products in the range.

Once alerted to the existence of product ranges they can be seen everywhere: RAC's standard, advanced and ultimate roadside assistance; economy, business and first-class air travel; supermarket value, standard and premium ranges and so on. Expanding the product range can increase market share by introducing a new high-end product or tapping a new market with a new low-end product. Mohammed (2018) refers to these as "offensive" reasons for adopting a good-better-best approach. He also refers to a "defensive" motivation, defending against competitors entering the market with cheaper products by introducing a "good" version of the product that appeals to price sensitive customers. We saw that this could be important in the DEC minicomputers case. Mohammed differentiates this from the development of a "fighting brand". A fighting brand such as the launch of Go by British Airways requires considerable marketing and promotion expense and Mohammed suggests that an additional, value-oriented product at the bottom of the range might be a better option.

11.4 Versioning of information products

Product differentiation is pervasive in many industries but is especially important for firms providing digital services. Shapiro and Varian (1998) point out the "dangerous economics" of information-based firms. Software can be extremely expensive to produce but, once written and tested, copies are extremely cheap to replicate. In the twenty-first century there may be no physical product at all as users simply download applications. Fixed costs are often "sunk" in the development of the product and variable costs might be unaffected by scale, there is no need to expand facilities, build new factories or invest in extended distribution chains. Thousands, millions or hundreds of millions of units can be distributed at the same variable cost per unit.

Cost-plus approaches are obviously irrelevant, and pricing *must* be based on value as perceived by the customer. In the software, communications and entertainment streaming industries companies seek to avoid commoditisation because, with variable costs close to zero, competition would then drive prices toward zero. This is perhaps most obvious in competition between companies offering television streaming services. Netflix developed a huge number of subscribers by online streaming of films. However, following the entry of Amazon (Amazon Prime) and Disney (Disney+) the major players now invest huge sums in developing original content and securing rights to live sport aiming to differentiate their product offerings.

Shapiro and Varian provide several examples of differentiated products, PAWWS Financial Network offered real-time and delayed stock quotes; The New York Times and Business Week made fresh content free but sold access to their valuable archives; Adobe provided Photoshop software at a premium to professional designers but also as a value version for everyday users. Perhaps one of the best current (2021) examples is Zoom with basic, pro and business versions at different price points: the basic version is free but limited to 40 minutes for more than two participants, the pro version is priced at £11.99 per month with meeting durations up to 24 hours and the business version allows up to 10 hosts and provides services such as meeting transcription.

11.5 Implications for management accountants

The most important implication for management accountants is the importance of analysing the whole range of substitute products. Analysis should identify contribution by individual product variant, then costs attributable to the whole range should be deducted to establish range profitability. Investment decisions should be based on volume, revenue and cost projections for the whole range.

Changes in the profitability of individual products and the range over time should be tracked carefully. Changes in price differentials can have serious consequences. Smith (2011) argues that discounts are likely to be most effective for the low-end product because this targets price-sensitive customers who are likely to be influenced by a lower price. In contrast, discounting the best product might be ineffective because the discounted top-of-the range variant will generate less contribution per unit and, in addition, might steal sales from lower priced versions.

This might be seen as a typical product mix problem with price, volume and mix variances versus budget. However, the author is uncomfortable with budget variances because they might reveal not variances that should be addressed, but problems with the budget which might be optimistic or have become out-of-date. Instead, analysis should be based on prior year versus current year results to reveal the dynamic relationships at work.

For example, assume a service can be provided at different grades at rates of £144, £168 and £204 per year. Over time the total volume of customers served has fallen from 4 million to 3.2 million and the composition of the product mix has changed so that relatively fewer customers opt for the basic service. Contribution from each grade used to be £50, £70 and £100 but inflation in prices and costs has seen these figures change to £55, £77 and £110. A standard analysis, comparing the previous contribution generated to that generated at current volumes might appear as in Table 11.1.

Table 11.1 shows that the reference contribution is £262m and the current contribution is much less at £240.9 million, £21.1 million less than the reference contribution.

Margin variance: £240.9 million – £219 million = £21.9 million (current volume at current margins less current volume at reference margins)

Mix variance: £219 million – £209.6 million = £9.4 million (current volume at reference margins less current total volume in reference mix)

Table 11.1 Price, volume and mix variances: calculations

	Basic service	*Standard service*	*Premium service*	*Total*
Reference volume (millions of customers)	1.2	2.6	0.2	4.0
Reference average contribution per unit (£)	50	70	100	
Total contribution (£ million)	60	182	20	**262**
Current volume (millions of customers)	0.7	2.2	0.3	3.2
Current contribution (£ million)	38.5	169.4	33	**240.9**
Current volumes at reference contribution (£ million)	35	154	30	**219**
Current (total) volume in reference mix (millions of customers)	0.96	2.08	0.16	3.2
Current (total) volume in reference mix and at reference contribution (£ million)	48	145.6	16	**209.6**

Volume variance: £262 million – £209.6 million = £(52.4) million (current total volume in reference mix and at reference margins less previous reference volume in reference mix and at reference margins)

Total variance: £21.9 million + £9.4 million – £52.4 million = £(21.1) million

The total variance of £(21.1) million is comprised of a negative volume variance of £(52.4) offset by positive margin and mix variances of £21.9 million and £9.4 million, respectively.

These calculations should be only a starting point for analysis. It is obvious that loss of volume is a major problem. Although this has been mitigated by a better product mix the loss of 20% of total customers is a matter of great concern. It should be noted that the loss of customers is greatest, as a percentage, for the basic service, down from 1.2 million to 0.7 million customers, a fall of over 40%. Managers might think that loss of customers in the "value" segment is not particularly important, a reduction worth only £12 million in contribution. However, if competitors are taking market share in the most price sensitive section of the market, this could have a knock-on effect to other segments.

The example is loosely based on the experience of AA plc, previously the Automobile Association, which has lost 20% of its personal members over the years. The company seems to be reacting by introducing more premium extras such as "smart breakdown" cover, at an extra £49 per year. At the other end of the market the cheapest AA cover, basic roadside assistance for one person, is advertised at £6 per month, but cheaper if purchased annually at £59 per year. Despite this low-end product the AA is losing share: for comparison Green Flag offer roadside cover for two vehicles for less than £53.

11.6 Complementary products

Smith (2011) notes that the pricing of complementary products is influenced by several effects. First, the signpost effect where products advertised as good value persuade customers that this also applies to other products. Retail stores offer competitive prices on, for example, fruit and vegetables, tempting customers to also purchase higher margin products. Second, customers "locked in" after purchasing the base product also purchase optional extras, sometimes because it is difficult to evaluate their prices. Third, the complementary products themselves can also "lock in" customers. For example, applications based on computer and iphone operating systems can make the customer reticent about changing the operating system when the opportunity arises.

For some products the seller might be able to lock in the buyer to the purchase of related products and services by leasing rather than selling the product. For the purchaser a lease smooths payments and removes uncertainty associated with expensive and complex equipment. In the past, IBM and Rank Xerox in the markets for computers and photocopiers leased, rather than sold, their products. For a new high technology product, buyers might find the decision to purchase difficult and leasing would reduce their risk. In addition, an operating lease would reassure the buyer because the seller would deal with any operating problems.

Theoretically, a lease can reduce transaction costs because, if a new, unknown, product is sold, the contract of sale might become complex as efforts are made by the buyer to ensure that possible future problems are anticipated in the contract. An advantage of leasing, for the seller, is facilitation of contact with the customer and ability to monitor usage (for example number of copies made). If the seller can sell the service (computer time used or copies taken) then it also becomes possible to price discriminate based on quantity. Levy (1988) traced the use of leasing by IBM and noted that, as competitors entered the computer market in the 1980s, IBM's policy switched from leasing to outright sale.

There are more recent examples in the market for jet engines, complex, high value products that require constant monitoring, frequent maintenance and overhauls. In the 1990s Rolls Royce developed the TotalCare® package and it has since been very successful. In 2016 Rolls Royce Director of Services, Tom Palmer, commented: "A total of 90% of our Trent engine fleet is under TotalCare". Prior to the introduction of TotalCare the interests of supplier and customer conflicted. The customer wanted airtime while the supplier only profited from the lucrative aftermarket when the engine broke down. With TotalCare the customer has the option of a charge by engine-flying-hour, a metric that reflects the customer priority. Interests of supplier and customer are aligned: both want to keep the engine flying.[1] From the supplier's point of view TotalCare has the advantage of tying the customer and fending off third party providers.

The economic analysis presented by Smith (2011) is based on two complementary products with linear demand curves. He shows that the optimal, profit maximising, prices are given by the usual formula for independent products, $p = (s - v)/2$. In this formula, p is the optimal price, s is the maximum that any consumer is willing to pay, and v is the variable cost per unit. However, crucially, the demand curve for a complementary product *is linked to the demand for its complement*. If the price of the base product falls, more will be purchased and demand for complementary products will increase.

11.7 Implications for management accountants

The main implication for management accountants is the importance of not looking at products in isolation. If there are complementary products it becomes important to assess the profitability of the complements as a group not as individual products. Marginal costs are still important, not least in the calculation of contribution margin for individual products and for groups of products, and activity-based costing still permits assessment of profitability and may point to potential operational savings and improvements. However, failure to make contribution or even sustain losses on the base product(s) might be justified by sales of higher margin complements.

In some cases, assessing whether a base product and its complements are profitable might be straightforward. For example, gross margin and net margin for individual retail stores, cruise ships, bank branches etc. can be established. Analysis by customer might also be possible, store loyalty cards provide retail data, purchases on cruise ships require the use of a charge card issued on boarding and banks have records of customer transactions. Analysis would allow contribution by customer to be calculated, identifying which customers are clearly profitable and which are not. If a large group of customers makes little contribution, then pricing policy needs to be reviewed.

In other cases, the calculations might not be so easy. A particular problem arises when the base product is sold at a low margin in the expectation that this will lead to after-sales that are highly profitable. In the automobile industry cars/trucks may be produced in original equipment divisions while separate divisions serve the after-market. The latter tend to be highly profitable while the original equipment divisions are not.

A different problem arises if production divisions sell to separate sales divisions. Dugdale and Lyne (2010) reported the case of Finrock, a company engaged in production and sale of heavy earth moving equipment. Product divisions sold to country-based sales companies and the profitability of both product and sales divisions was heavily influenced by negotiated transfer prices. This problem was resolved by booking all sales to product divisions and charging them an allocation of sales costs. (Transfer prices still existed because sales companies were legal entities, but the parent company concentrated on the profitability of its production divisions in strategic decision-making.) In this case the complementarity was between production and sales and the artificial barrier of transfer prices could be avoided, not all such problems can be solved so easily.

11.8 Substitutes and complements: the Niehans formula

Smith (2011) develops formulas for the cases of two products whether substitutes or complements and, implicitly, the analysis takes account of cross price elasticities between products. Simon and Fassnacht (2019, p. 241) present the general Niehans formula for the optimum price of product j in a range of n products and this formula relates to both substitutes and complements:

$$P_j^* = \frac{\varepsilon_j}{(1+\varepsilon_j)} C_j' - \sum_{\substack{i=1 \\ i \neq j}}^{n} (p_i - C_i') \frac{\varepsilon_{ij}}{(1+\varepsilon_j)} \frac{q_i}{q_j}$$

This formula looks complicated, but it is very informative. If all the variables on the right-hand side of the equation are known, then it gives the optimum price of the jth product in a range of n products.

The first term is just the optimum price for product j in the absence of other interacting products. If the elasticity of the jth product, ε_j, is very large, that is, the product is very elastic, then the first term is close to C'_j, the marginal cost. On the other hand, if demand is relatively inelastic, say, $\varepsilon_j = -1.5$, then the optimal price is significantly greater than marginal cost. As one would expect the more monopoly power the supplier has, the higher the price that can be charged.

The second term adjusts the optimum price by taking account of the other $n - 1$ interacting products. The absolute value of this term is larger: (1) the more products (q_i) there are, (2) the larger the contribution margins, ($p_i - C'_i$), of the other i products, (3) the larger the cross-price elasticities (ε_{ij}) and (4) the greater the ratio of the sales volumes q_i/q_j.

The cross-price elasticity is the percentage change in the quantity of product j when the price of product i changes by 1% and it may be either positive or negative. If products are substitutes then the cross-price elasticity is positive, an increase in the price of one will cause demand for the other to increase because it will represent better value than before. On the other hand, if products are complements then an increase in the price of one will cause demand for the other to fall because sales of the second product are linked to the volume of sales of the first product.

The Niehans formula is easily understood in the case of complements where the cross-price elasticities are negative. The second term is then subtracted from the first and reduces the single-product monopoly price. If the products are substitutes, on the other hand, then the second term will be negative and therefore, when subtracted from the first term the price will be higher than the single-product monopoly price.

11.9 Implications for management accountants

The complicated looking Niehans formula makes it clear that the optimal prices for all the products in a range depend on each other and, in principle, it is only possible to calculate optimal prices for all the products at once. In practice this is unlikely both because existing prices will be a major constraint and because estimating some of the parameters in the Niehans equation, especially the cross-price elasticities, is difficult.

Realistically the management accountant is unlikely to be involved in attempting to set "optimal" prices. However, understanding the implications of the Niehans formula is important. Since the development of activity-based costing, management accountants have been conscious of the costs of complexity and a wide product range. The Niehans formula on the other hand points to the advantage of a range of substitute products and we have seen examples of good-better-best pricing and the use of enlarged product ranges. In determining the extent of the product range, the management accountant has a key role in establishing the trade-off between extra contribution from incremental sizes/models and the incremental costs of extending the product range.

In relation to complementary products the formula makes it clear that the price of the base product will be lower the more linked complements there are and the greater the profitability of the complementary products, exactly as one would expect. The management accountant, at the very least, can furnish key information, the contribution margins of the various products and relative volumes.

Schindler (2012) shows how the break-even formula discussed in Section 4.8 can be adjusted to take account of substitutes and complements. The key point is that, if the price of a product is increased or decreased, its volume will be affected *but so will the volumes of any substitute or complementary products*. The new contribution margin of the "target" product should be adjusted to include the impact on associated products. If a change of one unit in the target causes 0.2 units of an associated product to be gained or lost, then the new contribution margin needs to be adjusted by 0.2 × C, where C is the contribution of the associated product. The adjustment will be positive for a substitute, negative for a complement.

For example, if a price decrease of £5 is considered for a product with contribution margin £30 currently selling 1,000 units per month, a simple calculation suggests that an increase of 200 units will be needed to break-even. However, if sales of an associated product are affected, say by 0.2 units for each unit of the target product, and the associated product generates £20 of contribution then the contribution of the target product should be adjusted by 0.2 × £20 = £4. The adjusted contributions are £21 and £29 for substitutes and complements respectively. For substitutes the break-even volume becomes 238 units but for complements it falls to 172 units:

$$BE = \frac{\Delta FC - (\Delta CM \times \text{Base sales})}{CM}$$

BE (substitutes) = – £5,000/21 = 238 units; BE (complements) = £5,000/29 = 172 units.

The figures highlight, once again, the importance of careful attention to price differentials for substitutes and the potential advantage of low prices for some complementary products.

11.10 Product bundling

Finally, in this chapter, we consider product bundling: offering a group of products at a discounted price. The bundle may be based on complementary goods but, equally, a bundle may comprise unrelated products: a kind of quantity discount, based not on quantity of the *same* product but a grouping of *different* items.

In Figure 11.3 the demand curves for products A and B are shown together with optimal prices, P_A and P_B.

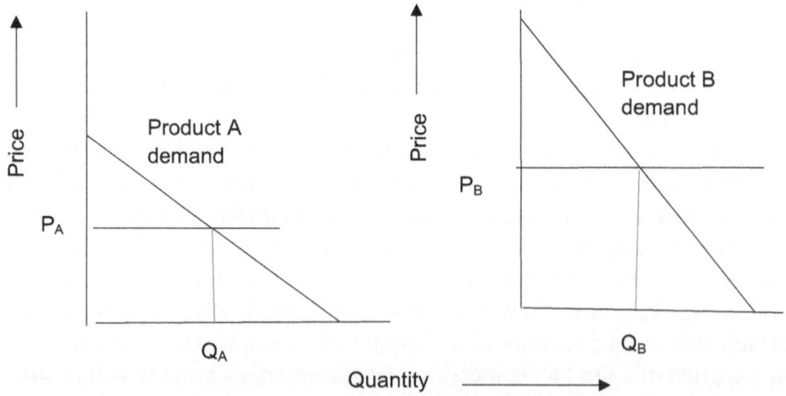

Figure 11.3 Demand for products A and B, marginal costs set to zero for convenience

The optimal monopoly prices are P_A and P_B generating quantities Q_A and Q_B. Some customers, not prepared to pay the monopoly price, will not purchase one of the products. However, if the products are offered together at price P_{Bundle} customers purchasing product A at P_A now see the price of product B as $P_{Bundle} - P_A$ and may purchase. By persuading "one-product" customers to buy the bundle the seller increases sales and (if the bundle price is set correctly) contribution.

Pure bundling

Pure bundling means offering products only as a bundle, individual items are not offered separately. Nagle and Müller (2018) note that a pure bundle reduces costs compared with offering several variants and, in addition, "research shows convincingly that people are less sensitive to the cost of value-added features and services when bundled as a single expenditure" (p. 81). The reason could be loss aversion with a single larger payment (loss) being preferable to several smaller payments. Similarly, Eppen et al. (1991) note that pure bundling can be effective for items that have high setup costs: the aim is to reduce variety in the product range by offering a pure bundle instead of multiple options. They describe the actions taken by Chrysler in the 1980s to reduce millions of possible combinations of options on two of their models to just 42. This permitted streamlined production, reduced costs and more competitive prices.

A pure bundle also provides a means of segregating price sensitive and insensitive customers. If the sensitive group will pay £100 but the less sensitive group will pay £120, the (pure) bundling of an accessory might permit prices of £100 (base product) and £140 (base plus accessory). The price sensitive group will still take the original product at £100 but the price insensitive group might be attracted to the superior product at £140 (if this group values the accessory at £20).

Mixed bundling

There are cost and psychological reasons for pure bundling, but mixed bundling also makes sense. Additional contribution is generated from customers prepared to buy one product but placing little value on the other. Smith (2011) mentions MacDonalds Value Meal (burger, fries and a drink) while Nagle and Müller (2018) refer to Cable TV operators offering bundles focused on families, sports fans and film enthusiasts. In the latter example sports fans might pay £15 per month for sports but only £5 per month for cinema while the reverse might be true for a cinema fan. A bundle of sports and cinema could be offered at £20, and both would purchase compared with only £15 per customer if sports and cinema are not offered as a bundle.

A pure bundle would lose some potential subscribers because a sports fan valuing cinema at less than £5 per month would not be prepared to pay £20 for the bundle. In general, economic theory leads to the conclusion that mixed bundling is more profitable than pure bundling. Hitt and Chen (2005) refer to Schmalensee (1984) and Salinger (1995) in noting that mixed bundling aids price discrimination while also "capturing residual demand through unit sale" (p. 1483).

To illustrate the issues that arise we can extend the sports and cinema example. The valuations of different sports by sports fans set out in Table 11.2 show that different fans place a range of values on different sports.

Table 11.2 shows that individual pricing to maximise revenue would generate £58 but, would a bundle price be better? To include all customers the bundle price would be set at £14; all six customers would purchase the bundle and, indeed, this would yield more revenue: £84. However, Table 11.3 shows how a mixed bundling strategy can increase total revenue.

If the bundle price is £15, customer E, valuing the bundle at £14 will not purchase, instead just purchasing Motor Racing at £10. Total revenue will increase to 5 × £15 = £75 for bundle sales plus £10 from customer E, £85 in total. Increasing the bundle price step by step shows that the revenue-maximising price for a bundle is £18. Customers A, B and F purchase the bundle while customers C, D and E purchase individual items, and total revenue is £92. This example shows that revenue is increased but setting the bundle price is not straightforward, even in this simple example where all customer valuations are known.

Table 11.2 Willingness to pay for different sports by six sports fans, A to F

Sports fans	*Football (£)*	*Cricket (£)*	*Athletics (£)*	*Motor racing (£)*	*Total value (£)*
A	12	3	2	2	19
B	6	5	2	6	19
C	8	8	0	0	16
D	3	0	12	0	15
E	2	0	2	10	14
F	3	15	0	0	18
Revenue maximising price for each sport separately	6	8	12	6	
Number of customers	3	2	1	2	
Revenue	18	16	12	12	58

Table 11.3 Possible bundle prices and consequences for revenue

	Bundle price (£)			
	£14	*£15*	*£16*	*£18*
Bundle purchases (£)	84	75	64	54
C single product purchases (£)				16
D single product purchases (£)			12	12
E single product purchases (£)		10	10	10
Total revenue (£)	84	85	86	92

The complexities of bundle pricing lead some authors to set out general "rules". On one thing they are agreed, bundling works best when products have low marginal costs and/or good contribution margins. Indeed, Bakos and Brynjolfsson (1999) demonstrate that, if individual items are costless (specifically, information goods delivered over the internet), bundling large numbers of items (such as many television channels) is "surprisingly profitable".

Smith (2011) notes that, ideally, each bundled product will have an independent market, but the markets overlap in the sense that groups of customers are interested in several products. At the same time the distribution of reservation prices between customers is broad and contrasting with respect to their desire for different products. Finally, the consumption of one product does not subtract from the value in consuming the other product(s).

Some of these conditions are captured in Eppen et al.'s (1991) recommendation that the bundle be targeted at an aggregate market with higher priced individual items offered to unusual customer segments. Ideally the aggregate market will target a group of customers with overlapping tastes and wide disparity in valuations while separate products cater for niche tastes. The aim is to expand the market by, for example, offering a bundle that targets sports fans in general, but high prices are charged in "unusual" segments such as fans of skiing.

Customised bundling

Hitt and Chen (2005) study the use of customised bundling where the customer selects options from a menu to construct a "personal" bundle. They conclude that customised bundling often outperforms pure bundling and includes individual sales as a special case. Interestingly, the AA (AA plc.) now allows customers to build their personal bundle of services from a range of options: an example of customised bundling.

A customised bundle can include a variety of services, raising customer switching costs and helping to build customer loyalty. The author purchased Sky's "big bundle" (26/11/2020) with the following structure:

There seems little doubt that this offer is partly intended to maintain customer loyalty, the added features might be difficult to give up.

	Individual price (£ per month)	*Bundle price (£ per month)*
Sky signature (basic package)	30	21
High definition	6	–
Sky sports	30	15
Sky cinema	15	9.50
Sky Q recording box	16	7
Total	97	52.5

11.11 Implications for management accountants

The first implication for management accountants is that developing and selling product bundles can be both sensible and profitable. Ensuring that the bundle generates a good contribution margin is very important and companies in the cosmetics industry provide nice examples. For example, the Advanced Génefique Serum by Lancôme carries a price tag of £60 for 30 ml.[2] However, the serum is also part of a set that includes eyelash and face creams for £60 or even less.[3] The set of three items appears to offer good value but no doubt the aim is to sell more of the serum. (In this example the single unit price of £60 is a decoy, encouraging the buyer to see the set as good value.)

A second implication is the importance of understanding the company's product range and strategy. If, as in many information goods industries, marginal costs are close to zero then bundling becomes an attractive marketing strategy. In these circumstances the aim is to maximise revenue and theory suggests that it is highly desirable to (1) bundle products to increase sales and (2) develop small bundles to target specific market segments if there is diversity in the market. The management accountant might undertake activity-based costing analysis to understand the nature of infrastructure and fixed costs. Short-run marginal costs might be close to zero, but this must not be an excuse for the escalation of medium term "fixed" costs.

A third implication concerns understanding the role of marginal costs if these *are not* close to zero. The important metric is contribution margin: a high contribution margin suggests that bundling might be advantageous. While the bundle price will be at a discount to the sum of item prices, for high contribution products the incremental volume needed to justify the bundle is small. The reverse is true for low margin products. To take an example, two products, A and B, with prices £20 and £30, respectively, and corresponding marginal costs of £5 and £10 might be bundled at a price of £40. At present 100 units per month of each product are sold generating contribution of £3,500. The bundle volume required for break-even is £3,500/£25 = 140 units, an increase of 40%.

11.12 Unbundling

Lest the reader think that companies always create bundles of products it is also possible to unbundle products. Perhaps the most notorious example is Ryanair's unbundling of services that were previously part of the fare. There was even a suggestion that Ryanair might charge for a visit to the toilet! Other airlines followed Ryanair by charging for checked baggage and, for example, EasyJet charge £9.49 – £42.49 (depending on the route) for a bag weighing 15–23 kg if paid when booking online. The price is £48 if paid at check-in.[4]

These examples are driven by the airline's desire to increase revenue and, for many travellers, hold baggage will be necessary and their demand will be inelastic, so a relatively high price can be charged. In addition, the unbundling of services such as checked baggage and in-flight meals means that the basic flight price is cheaper and more competitive. As Nagle and Müller point out, this is a key point because airlines that continue to provide checked baggage and other services as part of their offer risk attracting high cost-to-serve passengers while losing passengers that do not value these services highly. Nagle and Müller also note that customers tend not to value services that appear to be "free," it can be desirable to place a price on services even if they are elements in a bundle. (An example of this can be seen above in the author's purchase of Sky's "big bundle".)

Simon and Fassnacht (2019) provide further interesting examples of unbundling. They refer to publishers offering individual chapters of textbooks, a practice made possible by the ease with which information goods can be sold and downloaded, iTunes offering individual tracks without the need to purchase the whole album and the practice at some service stations of charging for use of the bathroom unless the customer buys other goods and services.

It is also important to identify all the elements of a product bundle when negotiating in B2B environments. Understanding the price/cost relationships of all the elements of a product or service is vital to a successful negotiation, a topic we consider in Chapter 15 dealing with different types of customer and negotiation strategies.

11.13 Implications for management accountants

The key implication is the importance of a good understanding of the costs of services provided and, hence, the price that should be charged or imputed in calculating the price of the bundled product. The airline example is instructive because there are costs associated with checked baggage, in-flight meals and the use of agents (rather than online booking). The management accountant can employ activity-based techniques to estimate these costs thus providing key information both in setting the price of the service (if a pure bundle is employed) and in setting the price of individual services if they are unbundled.

While cost information indicates a pricing floor it does not, of course, indicate the price to be charged. In the airline industry competition is likely to have a determining effect on pricing strategy. While the pricing of baggage checks and in-flight meals is probably inelastic once the decision is taken to fly with a particular airline, the pricing of the flight itself will be heavily dependent on competition.

Notes

1 Report by Bill Read FRAeS (2016) for the Royal Aeronautical Society entitled *Aftermarket Revolution,* downloaded November 2021 at www.aerosociety.com/news/aftermarket-revolution/

2 www.lancome.co.uk/skincare/by-range/genifique/advanced-genifique-serum (6/10/2021)

3 www.fragrancedirect.co.uk/lancome-advanced-genefique-serum-skincare-routine-set-30ml (6/10/21)

4 www.easyjet.com/en/terms-and-conditions/fees, 6/10/2021

References

Bakos Y. and Brynjolfsson E. (1999) Bundling information goods: pricing, profits, and efficiency, *Management Science*, 45(12), 1613–1630

Dugdale D. and Lyne S. R. (2010) *Budgeting Practice and Organisational Structure*, Elsevier/CIMA Publishing, Oxford

Ekelund R. B. (1970) Price discrimination and product differentiation in economic theory: an early analysis, *The Quarterly Journal of Economics*, 84(2), May, 268–278

Eppen G. D., Hanson W. A. and Martin R. K. (1991) Bundling – new products, new markets, low risk, *Sloan Management Review*, 32(4), Summer, 6–14

Hitt L. M. and Chen P. (2005) Bundling with customer self-selection: a simple approach to bundling low-marginal-cost goods. *Management Science*, 51(10), 1481–1493

Levy D. T. (1988) Short-term leasing and monopoly power: the case of IBM, *Journal of Institutional and Theoretical Economics*, 144(4), 611–634

Mohammed R. (2018) The good-better-best approach to pricing, *Harvard Business Review*, Sep–Oct, 106–115

Nagle T. T. and Müller G. (2018) *The Strategy and Tactics of Pricing*, 6th edition, Routledge, New York and Abingdon, Oxon

Salinger M. A. (1995) A graphical analysis of bundling, *Journal of Business*, 68(1), 85–98

Schindler R. M. (2012) *Pricing Strategies: A Marketing Approach*, Sage Publications Inc., Thousand Oaks, CA

Schmalensee R. L. (1984) Gaussian demand and commodity bundling, *Journal of Business*, 57, S211–S230

Shapiro C. and Varian H. R. (1998) Versioning: the smart way to sell information, *Harvard Business Review*, Nov–Dec, 106–114

Simon H. and Fassnacht M. (2019) *Price Management: Strategy, Analysis, Decision, Implementation*, Springer Nature, Cham, Switzerland

Smith T. J. (2011) *Pricing Strategy: Setting Price Levels, Managing Price Discounts, & Establishing Price Structures*, Cengage Learning, Boston, MA

12 Time-based pricing

12.1 Introduction

We have considered indirect segmentation strategies based on volume and product and, in this chapter, the focus is on time-based methods, sometimes referred to as periodic pricing. It is important to distinguish between differences based on the time of *use* and differences based on time of *purchase*. We will consider these in turn.

12.2 Time-based pricing: time of use and peak-load pricing

Time-based pricing is commonplace when there is a peak-period. It makes sense to manage demand at the peak-time by increasing prices and then to utilise off-peak capacity by reducing prices. The most obvious examples are in the transport industry where infrastructure needs to be sufficient to cope with peak demand but then there is excess capacity at off-peak times. Electricity generation provides another example, peak demand must be met but then more electricity than is needed is generated at off-peak times.

Figure 12.1 shows the marginal revenue curves (based on the respective demand curves) for peak and off-peak customers. A simplified marginal cost curve shows a discontinuity when capacity is reached, at this level of volume no more can be produced and marginal cost rises steeply, vertically in the diagram. The consequence is that the price at the peak time should be set sufficiently high to ensure that demand does not exceed capacity. In the diagram this is where peak marginal revenue crosses the (vertical) marginal cost curve. At off-peak times, by contrast, the price should be set to marginal cost to encourage more customers.

There are many examples of companies that adopt peak and off-peak pricing. Rail companies offer much lower fares during the day compared with the prices charged during the morning and evening rush hours, electricity companies offer cheaper rates on the "Economy 7" tariff (during the seven off-peak hours at night), matinee performances in the afternoons are cheaper than evening performances at theatres, Disneyland passes are cheaper during weekdays than at weekends or during holiday periods and so on.

The reduction in price at off-peak times can lead to "peak-reversal" where the volume of "off-peak" sales creates a new peak. As Simon and Fassnacht (2019)

DOI: 10.4324/9781003272731-12

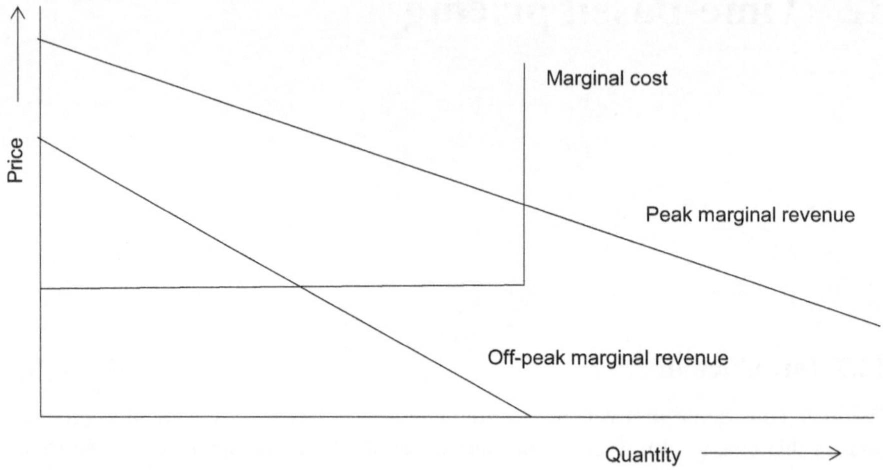

Figure 12.1 Peak and off-peak pricing

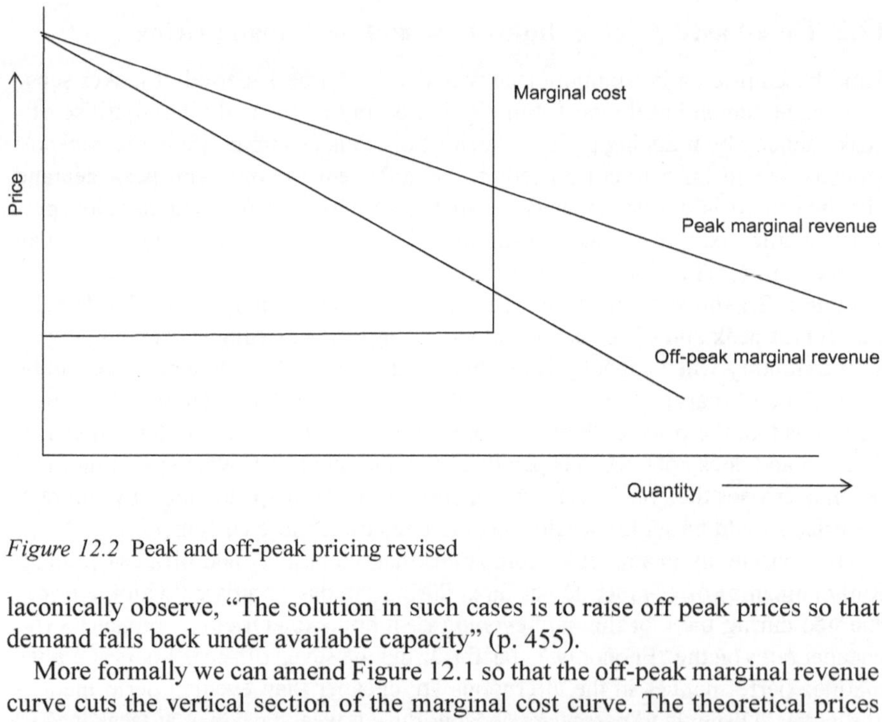

Figure 12.2 Peak and off-peak pricing revised

laconically observe, "The solution in such cases is to raise off peak prices so that demand falls back under available capacity" (p. 455).

More formally we can amend Figure 12.1 so that the off-peak marginal revenue curve cuts the vertical section of the marginal cost curve. The theoretical prices for both peak and off-peak periods are now determined by the points where the marginal revenue curves meet the vertical marginal cost curve.

There is debate in the economic literature as to whether peak and off-peak prices reflect price discrimination. At face value different prices are charged for essentially similar services so there is price discrimination. However, if price discrimination is defined as price differences that are not justified by cost, then Figures 12.1 and 12.2 make it clear that the different prices do, indeed, reflect differences in marginal cost so, strictly speaking, this is not price discrimination. As usual, the niceties of economic debate need not concern us, the key point is that different prices are needed to deal with peak and off-peak demand.

12.3 Implications for management accountants

There are two key implications for management accountants. The first concerns the estimation of marginal costs in price setting. If there is significant spare capacity then marginal costs may be negligible. The cost of another passenger is likely to be close to zero for a scheduled train or flight that has empty seats. In other circumstances this is not so, a unit of electricity cannot be produced without expenditure on fuel and conversion to electricity. Management accountants obviously have a role in determining the marginal costs that should be considered. Such calculations may not be simple, an electricity distributor might rely on coal, gas, nuclear and renewable resources and, perhaps, an average marginal cost should be calculated. However, if the base load is supplied by nuclear power, then, off-peak, the appropriate marginal cost would be the cost of nuclear generated electricity.

The situation is different if peak-load pricing is under consideration. Now the marginal cost should include any material and directly attributable labour and other expenses, and, in addition, any opportunity cost associated with an extra unit or customer. Hirshleifer (1958) notes that, if there is a "hard" limit on capacity as in Figures 12.1 and 12.2, then taking the final customer means no more customers can be taken and the opportunity cost is therefore simply the contribution generated at the price where marginal revenue meets the vertical marginal cost curve. The issue, therefore, is estimation of the price that should be charged to exactly use all the capacity available.

A second implication for management accountants concerns investment decisions. Typically, transport, utilities, entertainment and communications industries have low marginal costs but high fixed and infrastructure costs. Deciding to invest in increased capacity is a major decision and involves both assessment of the costs involved and estimation of the incremental revenue that will be generated. New investment should be justified by the incremental revenue that will be generated from peak-load customers and should include off-peak revenue only if prices above marginal cost can be charged (as in Figure 12.2, but not Figure 12.1).

12.4 Time-based pricing: time of use and price discrimination

There are two major marketing strategies that are linked to pricing over time: the skimming strategy and the penetration strategy. Skimming refers to charging a high price for a new product and then reducing the price over time; penetration refers to charging a low price for a new product, building familiarity with the product and market share. Although the strategies are very different, both may aim to maximise contribution and profit. In the first case, early customers are prepared to pay a high price, while others are prepared to wait, satisfied with an older product but at a reduced price. In the second case the aim is to build share, possibly at the expense of profitability, in the expectation that economies of scale and learning effects will, in due course, generate contribution and profits.

Skimming

The skimming strategy is prevalent in the fashion and technology industries. Lazear (1986) analysed mark-down policies in the retail fashion industry concluding that more rapid mark-downs are associated with a high initial price and uncertainty about the value of the good. In a simple example he showed that, if mark-downs are planned, the initial price will be higher than a single planned price and, for a uniform distribution of customer valuations, the optimal mark-down price is half the initial price. Pashigian (1988) extended Lazear's work by deriving optimal values for both uniform and triangular distributions. If the range in customer values is small, then initial markup on cost is relatively small and mark-down is small. If the range in customer values is large (maximum customer value three or four times the minimum customer value) then the optimal markup on cost rises significantly and the optimal mark-down is about 40% for a triangular distribution and (consistent with Lazear) 50% for a uniform distribution.

Pashigian also analysed US fashion data over several decades. His graphical analysis showed that markdown sales had increased from about 7% of total revenue in 1925 to about 16% of total revenue in 1985. At the same time the markup percentage in the original prices had increased from about 38% to about 50%. He argued that an increasingly variable product mix was linked to these changes in pricing and markdown policies. As the variety of fashion goods increases so does uncertainty associated with the range of customer valuations. This suggests higher initial prices but with more readiness to mark-down if sales are less than expected.

There has been an explosion of theory in relation to fashion pricing and the competitive landscape has changed dramatically. One of the most innovative fashion retailers is Zara, part of the Inditex group. Caro and Gallien (2012) describe Zara's "fast fashion" business with short life-cycle products rarely discounted during the selling season. This leads to significant stock in the two-month "sale period" at the end of the summer and winter seasons.[1] The authors developed an automated discounting system that tended to mark-down expensive items more quickly but, conversely, did not mark-down cheaper items as much as the existing manual approach. Overall, revenue and profit improved, and Zara adopted the automated approach after careful comparison with the existing method.

As regards a skimming strategy for technology products an obvious example is provided by Apple. The iPhone XR was released in 2018 at $749 for the basic model. With the launch of the iPhone 11 in 2019 at $699[2] the price of the iPhone XR fell to $599 and when the iPhone 12 was released in 2020 the price of the iPhone XR fell again, to $499. The iPhone XR therefore fell in price from $749 at launch to $499, a fall of 33% over two years from October 2018 to September 2020.[3]

Penetration

Penetration pricing can be important to establish a new product. Simon and Fassnacht (2019) cite several examples. Toyota's Lexus, aimed at the premium car market, was launched in the US at a price of $35,000. After good reviews sales of the car increased and so did prices, by "a total of 48% over the next 6 years" (p. 275). Intel sold its x86 chip at $429 in 2007, subsequently raising the price in several steps to $629 in 2014. Amazon hardly reported a profit from its foundation in 1994 but "in late 2017 . . . enjoyed a market capitalization of $571 billion" (p. 277).

These examples serve to illustrate two of the main reasons for pursuing a penetration strategy. First, as in the cases of the Toyota Lexus and Amazon, to build market share. In Amazon's case this has translated into considerable monopoly power and a powerful brand. Second, as in the case of the Intel chip, to generate volume and so gain the advantage of learning effects. There are several arguments to support penetration pricing and Simon and Fassnacht list, among others, establishing a long-term market position, generating economies of scale, benefiting from the learning or experience curve and warding off potential competitors. Nagle and Müller, meanwhile, identify circumstances that might favour penetration pricing: a cost or benefit advantage that would dissuade competitors from entering the market, use of the penetration price as a "loss leader" in a range of complementary products and, finally, when a firm is small relative to competitors so that a penetration policy will not disturb the market.

Despite the reasons that support penetration pricing, pricing texts are suspicious of a penetration strategy. Marn et al. (2004) consistently advocate increasing industry prices so, naturally, see penetration pricing as sensible only on "rare occasions". Their main concern is that a low-priced new product may fail to generate profit and never build anticipated market share as competitors enter the market with a "newer, slightly better product". (p. 107). Smith (2011) also sees penetration pricing as potentially dangerous as it might: "not only fail to capture potential contribution margins but also . . . strongly . . . [encourage] . . . a competitive response" (p. 71). As we saw, the position of a new product on the price-value map should be carefully considered in the light of possible competitive reaction. Simon and Fassnacht (2019) also offer a word of warning. While recognising the impact of learning effects in the electronics industry and citing the rapid fall in costs of sequencing the human genome, they also note that firms have run into difficulties because "It appears that experience spreads to competitors faster than formerly believed" (p. 269).

12.5 Implications for management accountants

Price skimming

Price skimming runs the risk that buyers wait for the price to fall before purchasing. For consumer goods the usual solution is to limit the life of the product. Some products have a limited life because they are only "fashionable" during the summer or winter seasons. Apple launches new products every year thus rendering older products "obsolete" to some extent. These examples emphasise the importance of company strategy with Zara's innovative "fast fashion" approach to production and Apple's constant innovation, the former leads to the need for a unique approach to managing mark-downs, the latter permits Apple to charge premium prices for the latest iPhone versions before later reducing prices when new models are launched.

If a company relies on markdowns during periodic sales management accountants should collect and analyse data for products and product groups. Tracking the relationship between price, sales volume, contribution per unit and total contribution through normal and mark-down sales to final liquidation should reveal vital intelligence to guide future pricing policy. Smith and Achabal (1998) describe an algorithm to guide price markdowns based on the inventory available, time to the end of the season and sales rate per week. They implemented the system in three retailers with good results in two of them. A particular feature of the model was taking account of the fact that, as inventory declined, sales rates also declined because the "assortment" of products became less complete, and a much-reduced range could not be as attractively presented. The authors note that the model indicated initial mark-downs greater than was usual and preparedness to have some stock unsold at the end of the season. Management accountants working in "mark-down" environments need familiarity with the methods adopted by store managers and the potential for automated systems.

For industrial goods sellers may face a problem in selling highly innovative or very complex products. In the first case buyers may be suspicious of a new technology and, in the second case, the high ongoing repair and maintenance costs may be a deterrent to purchase. Leasing may be an effective alternative to selling, reducing the risk associated with a new product and/or eliminating hefty and unpredictable repair costs, replacing them with an ongoing, defined payment per month.

Penetration

Management accountants are likely to be more in favour of a skimming strategy with higher prices and early recovery of sunk infrastructure and development costs. However, we have seen examples of the penetration strategy, and, for some products, it is appropriate. A key issue is marginal costs, and, for penetration pricing, marginal costs will, ideally be low. The penetration strategy itself may be important in reducing marginal costs if a learning effect takes place.

The author's experience in a company that manufactured computer peripherals indicates that, for some products, learning is very important and can be predicted by an appropriate learning curve. The usual approach is to model the learning curve by an equation of the form $y = ax^b$ where y is the cumulative time taken per unit to produce x units; a is the time taken to produce the first unit and b depends on the rate of learning. For a 90% learning rate b would be set equal to $\log 0.9/\log 2 = -0.152$. b is always negative so ensuring that the cumulative time per unit falls as x increases. The rate of learning is faster for an 80% rate than for a 90% rate because the rate indicates how the cumulative time per unit falls every time output doubles. With 80% learning, if the cumulative average time is 1 hour, the cumulative average will fall to 0.8 hours if output doubles and to 0.64 hours if output doubles again.

Penetration pricing is also important if market share is particularly important and marginal cost is zero or negligible. Internet communication and streaming products fall into this category. Suppliers of broadband, telephone, video conferencing, television and live entertainment face very high development and setup costs but very low marginal costs per customer. For companies that have invested very significantly in development and infrastructure, building market share is crucial and, if marginal cost is close to zero, this can lead to the product even being given away, both to build share and to develop familiarity with a new product. Examples of products that are offered free, at least in basic versions, include Hootsuite,[4] MailChimp and Dropbox. The aim is to have customers develop familiarity with the product and then add paid for services. For example, Dropbox offers free but limited cloud storage, and this can easily encourage users to pay for significantly more storage. Zoom offers video conferencing for two users free and 40 minutes free but this can persuade organisations to expand their usage, subscribing to paid-for plans.

In relation to communication products "network effects" can be important. Network effects come into play if a product becomes more attractive as more users join the network. Facebook, Twitter, Snapchat, LinkedIn and other social media sites dominate partly because, once a critical market share is established, more and more users see the benefit of joining. For such companies the penetration strategy is almost mandatory.

12.6 Time-based methods: time of purchase and yield management

An important class of companies deliver a perishable service, typically purchased in advance and subject to capacity constraints. These companies can take advantage of price variation during the period before the service "expires," aiming to maximise utilisation. The most obvious examples are in the travel, hospitality and entertainment industries as airlines, rail companies, hotel chains and cruise lines aim for maximum utilisation. These companies face high investment costs together with heavy infrastructure and fixed costs but low variable costs per customer so long as capacity is not breached. For these companies it is important to manage demand by varying prices during the period before the service "expires": before the flight or train leaves.

The emphasis on yield management was first seen in the airline industry. Phillips (2005, p. 6) writes:

> In 1984, American Airlines was threatened on its core routes by the low-fare carrier People Express. In response American developed a revenue management system based on differentiating prices between leisure and business travellers. A key element of this program was a 'yield management' system that used optimization algorithms to determine the right number of seats

to protect for later-booking, full-fare passengers on each flight while still accepting early-booking low-fare passengers.

Airlines have long differentiated two segments in the market: leisure and business travellers. Leisure travellers tend to be price sensitive and have the flexibility to book early. On the other hand, business travellers tend to be price insensitive and may have to arrange flights at short notice. It is therefore important to make sure that, in the few days before a flight leaves, seats are available for passengers who simply *must* book a flight. Whilst there is a tendency to see these as "business travellers" in practice, of course, there are other reasons for late booking such as attending a funeral.

Airlines face competing pressures, making sure "full fare" seats are available while also aiming to sell all seats. Historically, the problem was solved by making empty seats available to passengers who arrived at the airport without a ticket, prepared to wait for spare seats. Such passengers were on "standby". However, increased security means that passengers must now purchase a ticket in advance. Some airlines have therefore resorted to over-selling the number of seats available. The consequence is that, sometimes flights are overbooked and not all passengers can fly as intended. Passengers are therefore given incentives to forego their intended flight and go to "standby" for an alternative flight.[5]

It is obvious that a profit maximisation algorithm could be very complex as price over time is recalculated to take account of price sensitive and price insensitive customers, cancellations, no-shows and possible overbooking. Airlines have different policies, but low-cost airlines are not immune to the use of overbooking. Following a rather harrowing story reported in the Guardian (12 Aug, 2017, downloaded 5/2/21) EasyJet stated: "We sometimes sell more seats on a flight . . . We will always ask for volunteers to give up their seats in the first instance . . . On average . . . we will only overbook by one or two per flight".

In principle the theory of yield management is easy to understand, the distribution of customer arrivals is known from previous data and an algorithm can be devised to determine how the price should change over time to maximise revenue from available capacity. The calculation is complicated by the need to hold back some seats for last-minute bookers and by policies such as overbooking, and a further complication arises if there are "network effects": some customers may wish to book flights that have several legs or to book a hotel room for several nights. Phillips (2005) analyses the problem of reserving capacity for high-paying customers when this might result in turning away customers that wish to book several linked flights or several nights in a hotel.

Much of the theory of yield management was developed for the airline industry but yield management is also applied in other industries where customers book in advance such as hotels, car rental, cruise lines, theatres, theme parks and so on. There are industry specific issues so, while overbooking is possible in the airline industry, it would not be employed by, for example, cruise lines: the cost of informing a customer that their cabin was not available would be prohibitively high. Some hotel chains, such as Travelodge, charge different rates for a non-refundable room and one which can be cancelled without charge. On 5/2/2021 a one-night stay at Travelodge, Knutsford on 13/2/2021 would cost £30.99 non-refundable but £33.99 for the flexible option – cancellation or amendment without charge until noon on the day of arrival.

12.7 Implications for management accountants

In industries that have a perishable, fixed capacity product or service management accountants need to understand the imperatives of pricing. In these industries, sometimes maximising revenue will also lead to the maximisation of contribution because marginal costs are low. Increasingly, yield management is finding application in a range of industries for the techniques apply in industries such as retail where a given stock of perishable goods must be sold by the "sell-by" date.

Management accountants are well-placed to gather key information such as revenue, utilisation and contribution generated for each flight or hotel. A comparison with competitor revenues and utilisation statistics would be particularly revealing and an exercise could be undertaken to track competitor prices over time to estimate performance.

Notes

1 After the clearance period any remaining stock is "liquidated" by selling to wholesalers that sell through low-priced channels, typically, in developing countries.
2 https://9to5mac.com/guides/iphone-11/
3 www.techradar.com/uk/reviews/iphone-xr-review
4 Hootsuite's free version changed on April 5, 2021, from managing up to 3 social accounts and 30 posts to 2 social accounts and 5 posts; accessed at: https://help.hootsuite.com/hc/en-us/articles/1260804307389-Changes-to-the-Hootsuite-Free-plan-April-5-2021 downloaded November 6, 2021.
5 The author joined a flight that was ready to take off when the steward asked for a volunteer to leave the plane. No one moved. The compensation offered was increased until, with hotel accommodation, a free flight and cash compensation on offer, there was a cry of "I'm here, I'm here." A seat was freed for (presumably) an important passenger and the flight could depart.

References

Caro F. and Gallien J. (2012) Clearance pricing optimization for a fast-fashion retailer, *Operations Research*, 60(6), 1404–1422

Hirshleifer J. (1958) Peak loads and efficient pricing: comment, *The Quarterly Journal of Economics*, 72(3), 451–462

Lazear E. P. (1986) Retail pricing and clearance sales, *The American Economic Review*, 76(1), 14–32

Marn M. V., Roegner E. V. and Zawada C. C. (2004) *The Price Advantage*, Wiley & Sons, Hoboken, NJ

Pashigian B. P. (1988) Demand uncertainty and sales: a study of fashion and markdown pricing, *American Economic Review*, LXXVIII, 936–953

Phillips R. L. (2005) *Pricing and Revenue Optimization*, Stanford University Press, Stanford, CA

Simon H. and Fassnacht M. (2019) *Price Management: Strategy, Analysis, Decision, Implementation*, Springer Nature, Cham, Switzerland

Smith S. and Achabal D. (1998) Clearance pricing and inventory policies for retail chains. *Management Science*, 44(3), 285–300

Smith T. J. (2011) *Pricing Strategy: Setting Price Levels, Managing Price Discounts, & Establishing Price Structures*, Cengage Learning, Boston, MA

13 Competition

13.1 Introduction

The second chapter reviewed pricing practice and identified three main factors in pricing decisions: cost, markets and competition. In previous chapters we have considered how cost-based methods can be used and how markets might be analysed using value-maps, market segmentation and value analysis. In this section we consider the role of competition and recommendations for anticipating and responding to competitor actions.

All authors[1] agree that price wars are to be avoided if possible. The logic is easy to understand, the company cutting prices may gain market share and a short-term advantage; however, competitors are likely to respond with price cuts and a price war may ensue. This would be disastrous because, if prices settle at a new, lower, level, all firms are worse off than before.

This argument accounts for the "kinked demand curve" in economics textbooks. The kink reflects current prices. There is reticence about raising prices because competitors may fail to follow and the price-raising company risks losing market share: prices are relatively elastic above the kink. On the other hand, if prices are reduced, others are likely to follow with price cuts. If all companies reduce their prices, then each company's market share may be only marginally increased and so, despite reducing prices, the price cutter finds that market share has hardly changed: prices are relatively inelastic below the kink.

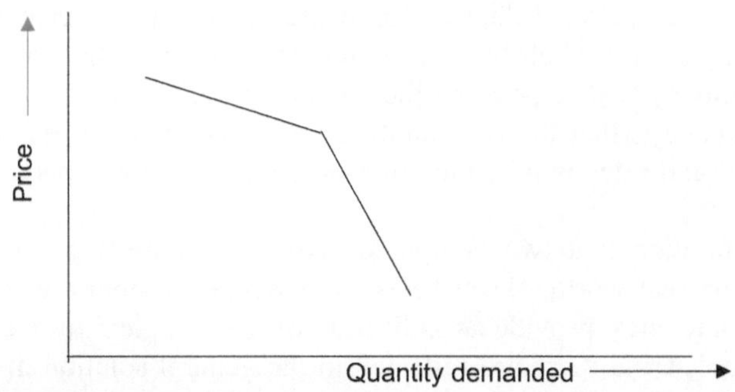

Figure 13.1 The kinked demand curve

DOI: 10.4324/9781003272731-13

The kinked demand curve is illustrated in Figure 13.1. Given the likely behaviour of demand if prices are raised (significant fall in demand for company raising price) or lowered (little impact on demand for company lowering price) oligopolists tend to refrain from price competition. Instead, they try to differentiate their products by adding distinguishing features or compete through advertising, special offers and promotions. Economic theory has considered the consequences if companies do compete, and this is covered in the next section. We then turn to competition in practice and the avoidance of price wars, a particular theme for Marn et al. (2004). They place considerable emphasis on the use of value maps, an idea we introduced in Chapter 5.

13.2 Economic theory

There are two simple theories that deal with duopoly competition – where just two companies compete for the same market. The first theory is the Cournot model where each firm *assumes that the other will not vary the quantity it produces*. The firms then see themselves as monopolists but based on a reduced market and each then sets its price to maximise profit. A monopolist would restrict output to $Q_C/2$ where Q_C is the quantity produced in a competitive market. However, a duopolist, following the Cournot model, would set its quantity, Q_A, at $(Q_C - Q_B)/2$, where Q_B is the quantity produced by the other duopolist. However, if we assume that the two firms are identical, then they will produce identical quantities, so $Q_A = Q_B$ and we can write: $Q_A = (Q_C - Q_A)/2$ and therefore $Q_A = Q_C/3$.

This model indicates that, while a monopolist would produce half the quantity supplied in a perfectly competitive market, identical duopolists would supply two-thirds of the market. The same logic suggests that an oligopoly with three firms will produce, in total, 3/4 of the competitive output (each firm produces one quarter of the competitive output). Obviously, a competitive oligopoly with several firms will produce most of the output generated in a perfectly competitive market. This explains why regulators take pains to try to ensure that there is no collusion and markets are as competitive as possible.

The consequences of competition become even more evident in the second basic economic theory: the Bertrand model. Here it is assumed that the two companies compete on price. If the two companies have equal market shares, if one company reduces price slightly it will immediately take all the market. However, the other company will respond by reducing its price and so take all the market. The consequence is that the two companies will compete all the way down to marginal cost and price will be the same as would be set in a perfectly competitive market.

The presumption that two companies produce identical products is highly unlikely in the real world. Nevertheless, the simple economic theories, leading to different outcomes, provide an indication of the complexities that face a real-world oligopolist and these are reflected in the general solution of the oligopolist's pricing problem. The following comment is based on Simon and Fassnacht (2019), page 193. Optimal price is given by:

$$p^* = \frac{\varepsilon + \sigma\varepsilon_k \; C'}{1 + \varepsilon + \sigma\varepsilon_k}$$

In this equation ε is the direct price elasticity for the product, (% change in quantity/% change in price), ε_k is the cross-price elasticity between the product and the competitor's price (% change in quantity/% change in *competitor's* price); σ is the reaction elasticity (% change in competitor's price when the product price changes by 1%). Simon and Fassnacht (2019, p. 193) note that "the markup to marginal costs is determined not only by the direct price elasticity, but rather by an "adjusted" elasticity which incorporates competitive reaction".

13.3 Product differentiation

Not surprisingly practical advice for oligopolists and companies competing in monopolistic markets is not based on the Cournot or Bertrand models and the complexity of the optimal price formula makes its use unlikely. Instead, writers have concentrated on the importance of differentiating the product and managing industry prices. Shapiro and Varian (1998) describe methods of versioning information goods and Mohammed (2018) describes the advantages of "good-better-best" pricing. They list several ways in which products might be differentiated. Higher prices might be charged for:

(1) Convenience: for example, availability 24/7 and/or unrestricted access.
(2) Features: for example, multiple users; next-day appointments; same-day delivery.
(3) After-sales service: for example, dedicated technical helplines; extended warranties.
(4) Fixed-price contracts: price certainty for utilities such as gas and electricity.
(5) The brand: a premium brand and a value version under different labels.
(6) Removal of annoying features such as advertisements.

Lower priced versions might face a variety of restrictions, perhaps available only during off-peak period periods or with limits on downloads or storage or, in the case of hotel and car rental bookings, not being refundable. There are many ways in which products and services can be differentiated so that relatively price-insensitive customers can be offered a better product at a higher price while price-sensitive customers can opt for a more limited or inflexible product but at a lower price. These possibilities may make it possible to reach segments of the market that might not be served by a single "standard" product or service and may avoid direct price competition.

13.4 Managing industry prices

The key point here is the difference between *industry* price elasticity and *brand* price elasticity. Table 13.1 reports estimates of industry elasticities for broad food

Table 13.1 Own price elasticities, extracted from Table 7, p. 24 Tiffin et al. (2011) Estimating Food and Drink Elasticities[2]

	2002	*2006*	*2009*
Dairy and Eggs	−0.430	−0.391	−0.505
Fats and Starches	−0.830	−0.867	−0.847
Fruit and Nuts	−0.806	−0.756	−0.698
Meat	−0.860	−0.824	−0.804
Fish	−0.351	−0.360	−0.441

categories. They are stable over several years, between zero and -1: industry price demand for these food products is inelastic.

On the other hand, Smith (2011) reports estimates of *brand* elasticities that are significantly greater than 1 (in absolute terms) and a study by Krishnamurthi and Raj (1991) reported brand elasticities ranging from -2.0 to -8.2. As might be expected, brand elasticity is relatively elastic, an increase in the price may cause some customers to switch to other brands. This is, of course the underlying reason for the oligopolists' kinked demand curve and their general aversion to price competition.

We saw, in Chapter 5, Leszinski and Marn (1997) demonstrate the use of value maps in analysing product position and, using the dynamic value map, Baker et al. (2010) used the Gild-tech case to demonstrate the danger of launching a product in a value-advantaged position. It is safer to position a product along the VEL. In this case only competitors close to the new product on the VEL will be threatened and the VEL for the whole industry is likely to be little affected.

Price-based competition can easily be disastrous for the industry and Baker et al. (2010) devote a whole chapter to the topic. They note that any decrease in price "drops straight off the bottom line" (p. 134) and, in a price war, with all competitors reducing prices together, it is unlikely that any volume increases will compensate for price reductions. In addition, a reduction in price distorts customer price expectations and increases their price sensitivity. Finally, Baker et al. note that, even in a price war, it is rare for competitors to be driven out of the market and, even if they are, their assets are likely to be picked up at bargain prices by the remaining competitors.

All this leads Baker et al. to emphasise the importance of discipline in price leadership and price followership. This means avoiding price wars that move the VEL to the right. Instead, they recommend actions that aim to move the VEL to the left, creating more profitability *for the whole industry*.

13.5 Avoiding Price wars

Baker et al. (2010) suggest that, to avoid destructive price wars, strategies should avoid shifting the competitive playing field. Any price cut to meet competition should be delayed until the full facts are known and over-reaction should be avoided. They recommend clear communication of pricing policy and the avoidance of head-to-head competition by identification of market niches: products, segments or even channels.

Similar suggestions are made by Nagle and Müller (2018). They note that price wars are a "negative sum game," the loser might lose everything, but the winner can also be hurt in the process. A common trap is the pursuit of market share even though this can be a "beggar-my-neighbour" policy that leads to price competition. To avoid price competition Nagle and Müller suggest differentiation, concentrating on niches in the market; meeting price competition by other actions such as improving quality, warranties, service etc.; targeting competitors only in the specific markets that they attack; assessing how much damage the competitor might do before responding and so on.

Although Akshay et al. (2000) title their article "How to Fight a Price War" much of their advice concerns *how to avoid* a price war. They first advise *diagnosing* the problem referring to customer, company, competitor and "contributor" issues, the latter are other players in the industry (such as labour unions) affected by a price war. Rather than reduce prices during a recession some companies may be able to persuade governments to help or staff to cut salaries for a time. (In 2020, responding to the COVID-19 pandemic, 5 executive officers at AON agreed temporary pay cuts of 50% and 70% of the company's employees saw 20% reductions in their salaries[3]).

If price action is necessary Akshay et al. recommend *selective* price action. They mention McDonalds introduction of the "value lunch" to avoid direct price competition with Taco Bell; product bundling, quantity discounts and loyalty schemes may also be devices for avoiding direct price competition. In some cases, price competition may be limited to particular products or services, Akshay et al. imply that it was no coincidence that NorthWest Airlines cut prices on services that competed with those offered by discount carrier Sun Country Airlines. Fighting brands may be a means of fighting a low-price entrant to the market without disturbing the main market, 3M launched the "Highland" brand of diskettes so as not to disturb the market for customers loyal to the 3M brand.

Akshay et al. note that selling off excess inventory or using spare capacity to market products through value brands can be attractive. However, they caution that such actions can start a price war. If the value brand is functionally equivalent to the main brand it can destabilise the market (effectively placing a value-advantaged product on the price-value map with consequent risk of shifting the VEL).

13.6 Understanding the competition

Common to advice given by pricing academics and consultants is the importance of understanding competitors' products and their positioning on price-value maps. In addition, competitors' motives for their pricing policy need to be carefully analysed. Obviously, the key to this is an external focus. This was the recommendation by Simmonds (1981, 1982), who showed how management accountants could contribute to pricing and marketing policy by analysing competitor cost structures and their likely responses. Simmonds (1981) demonstrated that an investment that might seem marginal could be easily justified if its impact on market share and the relative positions of the company and its competitor were carefully assessed.

The essence of the analysis was that the investment would ensure continued dominance in the market and a cost advantage through the learning curve.

Simmonds (1982) continued his theme but this time concentrating on the implications of price policy. He first reviewed a much-used case study where contribution could be as high as $236,000 if competitors followed the lead to a higher price but as low as $99,000 if they did not. Simmonds argued that detailed analysis of likely competitor responses was needed and, using another case study, demonstrated the use of decision tree analysis. In this case market share might be as high as 60% (if a lower price was set) but as low as 33% if competitors chose to also set a lower price. The decision would be influenced by company strategy, "Immediate reduction of the price to £0.5 is the recommendation of those who believe in maintaining leadership in the industry. . . . Others, however, conclude that BES should announce its prices at £0.6 and give competitors a chance to increase their price" (p. 214).

13.7 Games and bidding

Simmonds demonstrates the importance of anticipating competitor responses and game theory has become an important part of economic theory. Landsburg (2002) devotes a chapter to the theory of games and shows how, among other things, a Nash equilibrium can arise. A Nash equilibrium is a situation whether the players in a game cannot improve their current outcomes by shifting strategy. The idea is usually demonstrated by the "prisoner's dilemma". In this game two prisoners are separately interrogated and offered a light sentence (say 1 year) if one confesses and the other does not. In this case the prisoner that does not confess receives a heavy sentence (say 10 years). If both confess, they each receive a 5-year jail sentence but, if neither confesses, they each get two years on lesser charges.

The dilemma, for prisoner A, is whether to stay silent (in which case both prisoners go down for two years) or to confess. A reasons that, if B confesses, it will be best to confess as well, reducing the sentence from 10 to 5 years; if B does not confess, it is still in A's interest to confess so as to get the lightest, one year sentence. B reasons in exactly the same way and both prisoners confess. This is an example of a Nash equilibrium. From the equilibrium position of both confessing neither will choose to change and take the heavier sentence. Both prisoners are worse off than if they had remained silent. This explains the "code of silence" enforced by criminal organisations such as the Mafia.

Suffice it to say that game theory can lead to a variety of outcomes, and, in some games, there may be several Nash equilibria or no equilibrium at all. Game theory can be applied to competitive behaviour such as the duopoly already discussed. The Cournot solution where both companies produce one-third of the competitive output is a Nash equilibrium because neither company would wish to deviate. However, as in the prisoner's dilemma, if the companies were to collude to restrict output to the monopoly quantity, agreeing to split the profits, they would both be better off. Samuelson (2016) provides an overview of the development of game theory and its application in economics. He notes that the outcome of some games is very dependent on how the game is framed and this has limited the application of game theory in areas such as bargaining where, amongst other things, each player may or may not have the option to withdraw before or after the other party has bid. However, game theory has found application in other areas of competitive behaviour such as auctions and, for example, governments now routinely auction licences in the fields of telecoms, transport and oil exploration while requiring sealed bids for some government contracts.

13.8 The "winner's curse"

Auctions and sealed bids are competitive situations that can easily lead to what economists call the "winner's curse": whoever wins the auction can easily discover that they have paid too much. The reason is obvious, if several companies compete with apparently sensible bids, the winner makes the highest, most optimistic offer. The winner subsequently discovers that they over-valued the contract.

Economists have studied this problem using experimental methods. Typically, they ask participants to bid for a project knowing that the bidder places more value on the item than the seller. The crucial point in the experiment is that the seller has more knowledge than the buyer and will only accept a bid that is higher than their own valuation. The consequence is that, unless the value to the bidder is much higher than the value to the seller, the odds are against the buyer making the profit they assumed. The problem is intensified when there are many bidders so only a "high" bid is likely to win. Experiments have been designed to encourage participants to learn from experience, but the results are surprisingly robust, participants usually fail to improve despite repeated trials. Attempts to stimulate learning are typified by the comments of Foreman and Murnighan (1996), who concluded: "Although we originally doubted Ball et al. (1991), our results strengthen their conclusions . . . [there was] considerable feedback and many opportunities to learn to be a cautious bidder. Yet this was still not enough" (p. 178).

Thaler (1988) provides an excellent description of the winner's curse together with a review of field studies from the literature. Dessaur (1981) found that most of the books auctioned to publishers did not cover their advances; Cassing and Douglas (1980) concluded that most of the free agents in baseball were overpaid; Capen et al. (1971) found that, typically, the highest bids from companies for oil licences to explore the Gulf of Mexico were 5 to 10 times the lowest bids and the "winners" usually did not make the returns expected; Roll (1986) studied corporate takeovers and, though Roll is cautious, Thaler (p. 199) notes that "it seems clear that bidding firms are making very little money (if any) through take-overs"

Further examples are provided by Ferris and Petitt (2002). Eli Lilly purchased PCS Health Systems for $4.1 billion but, three years later, wrote down the value of PCS by $2.4 billion. Quaker Oats paid $1.7 billion for soft drinks company, Snapple in 1994. Ferris and Pettit comment that the losses made by Quaker were much greater than the direct loss of $1.4 billion when the company was sold for only $300 million. In 1989 Sony Corporation purchased Columbia Picture Entertainments Inc. but wrote off 80% of the investment just three years later.

A high-profile UK example is furnished by the demise of GEC, built into a global conglomerate by Arnold Weinstock who retired in 1996. His successor, Lord Simpson aided by finance director, John Mayo, refocused the company, selling the company's defence businesses, spending the company's cash pile and building debt to purchase US telecom companies, Reltec, Fore and others. Reltec and Fore were purchased at premiums to their market values of 36% and 43%, respectively (Abdel-Kader and Mentzeniot, 2007). The collapse of the dot.com boom in 2001 and downturn in the telecommunications sector saw GEC, renamed Marconi Corporation, making losses, Simpson and Mayo were ousted and the company folded in 2006.

The problem persists. Mcgrath (2009) discusses the Kraft takeover of Cadbury, mentions the AOL-Time-Warner merger and discusses the "recipe" for a winner's curse in a M&A (merger or acquisition): a highly motivated, well-funded acquirer, a reluctant target company prepared to play hard-to-get, and competitive bidding. Emotions might run high, spreadsheets are used to justify rather than inform decisions and the result is predictable.

Of course, one cannot be sure that underpricing is a consequence of the winner's curse but there is ample evidence to suggest its prevalence. Carillion went into administration in 2018 as its debt burden mounted and cost over-runs on three of its biggest contracts were cited as contributing to the company's downfall: the £350 million Midland Metropolitan Hospital in Sandwell, the £335 million Royal Liverpool Hospital and £745 million Aberdeen Bypass.[4]

13.9 Implications for management accountants

The key message of this section is the importance of understanding competitors and how the company's products and strategy interact with those of the competition. Management accountants have the skills to contribute to an understanding of competitors through analysis of their financial statements and by supporting marketers in tracking competitor price and product activity. Simmonds demonstrates how analysis of competitor cost structure and market position can affect investment decisions and management accounting skills linked with insights from this section can lead to more business partnering in several areas:

(1) As we have seen in previous sections management accountants have a key role to play in evaluating product differentiation proposals. Such proposals may be vital in avoiding direct competition, but they need to be costed, including the possible increase in cost of product range complexity. Management accountants should be involved in assessing the impact of new product variants including their likely effect on existing sales of the product. As we have seen before, evaluation of the whole range is vitally important, taking account of shared economies as well as phenomena such as extreme aversion in good-better-best pricing.
(2) Management accountants should be involved in the development of new products and their launch. Price-value maps are an excellent tool for

understanding the competitive landscape and management accountants could have a key role to play in analysing value (to customer) for a new product and assessing its likely location on a dynamic value map.

(3) Faced with aggressive competition the management accountant should provide the voice of moderation in considering response. Pricing consultants are at one in recommending the avoidance of price wars and the management accountant should evaluate the likely consequences of alternative courses of action including the cost of competing in other ways (quality, service etc.), the value of the business at risk and whether retaliation is worthwhile, consideration of selective price cuts only to target the competitor, analysis of the competitor's motives and so on.

(4) The management accountant will be involved in setting bid prices if the company is considering the acquisition of another company or bidding for a contract. In these situations, knowledge of the winner's curse is important, the general rule is to make a bid at less than the value placed on the acquisition or contract and be prepared to lose if necessary. Ferris and Petitt (2002) provide a thorough review of company valuation methods pointing first to the importance of estimating future cash flows and, second, to the careful consideration of an appropriate discount rate. Crucially, the discount rate should not be the acquirer's cost of capital but *a rate that reflects the riskiness of the estimated cash flows* of the company acquired. One would expect a higher return from a risky investment. In Sony's acquisition of Columbia, the appropriate rate needed to reflect the risky nature of the entertainment business, not the relatively low cost of capital available to Sony in Japan at the time of the acquisition.

(5) If the company has the opportunity to sell an asset or a company then the advice is reversed, it would be desirable to sell via an auction, to set a relatively optimistic "fair value" below which no bid will be accepted and to be prepared to be patient or reluctant to sell.

(6) Finally, management accountants know only too well that spreadsheets can easily be manipulated to "justify" specific course of action. The salutary examples mentioned reinforce the importance of making assumptions clear and undertaking some sensitivity analysis on key variables. Assumptions about costs, revenues, time scales and as noted above, discount rates, can make significant differences when evaluating bid targets or possible contracts.

13.10 Regulation

Introduction

We have seen that companies can benefit from monopoly power and from collusion to restrict output and raise prices (as when duopolists agree to restrict output to the monopoly quantity). This is *horizontal* price-fixing where members of an industry collude to "fix" prices. *Vertical* price fixing arises when a supplier influences or controls the prices set by companies that resell its products. *Resale price maintenance* is an example of vertical price fixing. Governments have generally acted to limit monopolies, prevent abuse of monopoly power and make price fixing illegal. The regulations vary between jurisdictions; here we sketch an overview of practice in the US, EU and UK.

The United States passed legislation (the Sherman Act) as long ago as 1890 that made both abuse of monopoly power and collusion to fix prices illegal. Nor must companies collude in related areas such as discounting, finance terms, warranties and so on. EU competition regulation similarly limits monopolies, mergers and restrictive practices and dates from the founding of the European Economic Community in 1957. It is now governed by Articles 101 and 102 of the 2009 Treaty on the Functioning of the European Union (the "Lisbon treaty"). UK regulation dates from the Monopolies and Restrictive Practices Act, 1948, which established the Monopolies Commission, now the Competition and Markets Authority (CMA). The CMA investigates mergers, entire markets, cartels and anti-competitive behaviour, and aims to protect consumers from unfair trading practices.[5]

Merger policies are similar

Practice in relation to mergers that might lead to less competition, higher prices, less choice etc. are similar across the three jurisdictions. In the US the Department of Justice can prevent mergers that would significantly reduce competition and, in the twenty-first century, has prevented mergers/takeovers between AT&T and T-Mobile; Nasdaq and the New York Stock Exchange; US Airlines and United Airways among others.[6] Similarly, both the EU and the UK assess mergers and can block those that are deemed anti-competitive. In 2019 the EU Commission blocked the takeover of Aurubis by Wieland in the market for rolled copper and, on the same day, announced that the proposed takeover of Alstom by Siemens in the rail industry would also be blocked.[7] In 2019 the UK's Competition and Markets Authority (CMA) blocked a proposed merger between Sainsbury's and Asda, supermarket chains that often competed directly with each other while, in 2020, the proposed merger of JD Sports and Footasylum was blocked, the CMA judging that the removal of one of these direct competitors would not be in consumers' interest.

Collusion can lead to harsh penalties

There is also similar practice in relation to collusion leading to "horizontal" price fixing. Price fixing by competitors has been illegal in the US since 1890 and, in the US, if convicted, participants face a fine and/or prison. In 2020 the Department of Justice requested the extradition from Italy of Maria Ullings, a marketing executive, indicted in 2010 on charges of price-fixing associated with surcharges on heavy air freight. Before the twenty-first century, in the EU and UK, price-fixing was a civil offence punishable by fines on the companies involved. However, the UK criminalised cartel activity in 2003 and, in June 2008, three former executives received significant prison sentences for their participation in a global cartel fixing the prices of marine hoses. The EU relies on fining companies for involvement in price-fixing cartels and the Commission reported a series of fines in industries including car part suppliers, ethylene purchasers, Atlantic salmon and canned vegetables among others.[8] The EU does not have the power to fine or imprison individuals but the UK provides an example of national remedies and, increasingly, national governments within the EU have introduced legislation that criminalises individuals for participation in price-fixing cartels.

Vertical price fixing is (usually) illegal

Vertical price-fixing is, broadly speaking, illegal across the US, EU and UK. All such price fixing was illegal in the US under the Sherman Act, 1890. However, if there was **no agreement** resellers could follow the manufacturer's recommended resale price. Further, following the Colgate case (1919), supplies could be with-held from a reseller failing to charge the recommended price. In principle, a further relaxation followed from the case of Leegin, 2007: an agreement could be permitted if it stimulated competition *between* brands by eliminating reseller competition of a particular brand. The ruling is controversial and there are few examples of companies following the Leegin example which depends on the application of the *rule of reason* in judging a case (Nagle and Müller, 2018).

In the UK vertical price fixing or resale price maintenance has been illegal in most areas since the Resale Prices Act in 1964. Exemptions for books and over-the-counter medicines were removed in 1997 and 2001. The CMA enforces the law with, for example, fines for two musical instrument manufacturers, Roland and Korg, totalling £5.5 million in 2020 and a fine for online musical retailer, GAK, for an agreement with supplier Yamaha to fix resale prices. In the UK **both suppliers and retailers** can be in breach of the law if they agree to set retail prices.[9]

EU practice in relation to vertical price fixing is similar to the UK. The intent to prohibit resale price maintenance dates from the founding of the European Common Market and has been clarified and strengthened since. After a long period without much activity, in 2017 the European Commission fined four consumer electronics groups for fixing retail prices. The investigations were initiated by concern about the use of e-commerce software to monitor retail prices.[10] Under Article 101 (1) there are just three exemptions: a new product launch where dealers may be encouraged to provide extra promotion activity; a short-term, low-price campaign; and to address the "free-rider" problem where distributors might offer low prices but limited sales service.

Abuse of monopoly power is illegal and, in the US, price discrimination may be illegal

The US introduced anti-trust legislation in the nineteenth century, long before the UK and the EU. And the Sherman Act was strengthened by the Clayton Act, 1914, which outlawed practices that might lead to monopoly or might result from it: in the twentieth century there were high profile cases involving Standard Oil, AT&T, Kodak and Microsoft concerning alleged abuse of monopoly power. The Robinson-Patman

Act, 1936, went further by outlawing certain forms of price discrimination and the Cellar-Kefauver Act, 1950, legislated against companies merging to form large conglomerates.[11] In the provisions of these later Acts US anti-monopoly and restrictive practices diverge from practice in the UK and the EU.

In the context of pricing policy, the Clayton Act is especially important. It was intended to protect small businesses that might be driven out of the market by larger competitors using discriminatory, or predatory pricing (deliberately low prices to undercut the competition), promotional allowances or advertising:

"A seller charging competing buyers different prices for the same "commodity" or discriminating in the provision of "allowances" – compensation for advertising and other services – may be violating the Robinson-Patman Act. This kind of price discrimination may give favoured customers an edge in the market that has nothing to do with their superior efficiency. Price discriminations are generally lawful, particularly if they reflect the different costs of dealing with different buyers or are the result of a seller's attempts to meet a competitor's offering" (FTC web-site: www.ftc.gov/tips-advice/competition-guidance/guide-antitrust-laws/price-discrimination-robinson-patman, downloaded 28/03/21).

Nagle and Müller set out five conditions that must be present for price discrimination to be proved: different prices for different customers; at about the same time; goods (not services) must predominate; the goods must be essentially the same; there must likely be competitive injury. Even if all conditions are met there are three main defences: cost difference (for example freight); prices set to meet competition; goods are perishable, obsolete or distressed.

In the EU regulations relating to abuse of monopoly power are set out in the TFEU Article 102 Guidance Paper. Since the early twenty-first century the EU has used a dominance test to determine whether there is potential abuse with about 40% of the market for particular goods typically required for "dominance". The Commission is active and has recently accepted commitments by Broadcom to end exclusivity and quasi-exclusivity agreements in systems on a chip for set-top boxes and modems; by Transgaz to make gas capacity in Rumania available to neighbouring states and by Aspen to reduce prices in Europe for six cancer drugs.[12]

The UK transferred the relevant EU regulations into UK law and following Brexit its anti-abuse activities have, to date, continued to closely mirror EU regulations.[13]

Final comments

This is only the briefest overview, intended only to alert managers and management accountants to the legal framework that varies from country to country. The US has had anti-trust and restrictive practices for over a century and has famously draconian penalties for some infringements of its laws. The EU has levied significant fines on companies but not on individuals. However, in relation to price fixing, *national governments* have taken their lead from the US and price-fixing is a criminal offence, punishable by prison, in several jurisdictions.

Finally, in the US, the Robinson-Patman Act banned some forms of price discrimination and companies operating in the US need a thorough understanding of the law to ensure their discounting and promotional activities are legal.

13.11 Implications for management accountants

There are a number of points to remember for management accountants involved in pricing policy.

(1) If the aim is to manage industry prices or avoid a price war it is very important to avoid any hint of collusion with competitors. The US has had draconian penalties for secret collusion and European countries are catching up. It is not EU law but *national law* that needs to be understood to avoid criminal charges. The extradition of Maria Ulling from Italy to the US is a salutary reminder of the risks involved in price-fixing, not only for companies but also for individuals.

(2) Care should be taken with statements such as: "Simply imitating a competitor's pricing behaviour . . . *conscious parallelism* . . . is lawful in the United States and the European Union as long as there has been no agreement among the companies involved" (Marn et al., 2004, p. 185). Note that this is an old reference (2004) and practice in the field of regulation can change rapidly and management accountants and marketing managers need to make sure they are aware of current legislation and practice in those jurisdictions where their companies operate.

(3) It is also important to avoid any hint of collusion with resellers if it is intended to try to maintain downstream prices. Resale price maintenance is illegal in the UK and the EU and regulators in both jurisdictions have been active in fining companies attempting to control prices. Practice in the UK makes it clear that both producers and resellers need to avoid price-fixing.

(4) In the US especially certain forms of price discrimination are illegal and, if operating in the US, understanding the regulations is important. Difference in prices can be justified on cost grounds and Nagle and Müller (2018, p. 304) note that dynamically changing cost structures can make a defence based on cost difficult but: ". . . the sophistication of activity-based costing holds a great deal of potential . . ."

(5) In the US the most likely price discrimination problem relates to volume discounts, and, in this area, management accountants need to be very careful. On the other hand, discrimination in relation to services (such as versioning), dynamic pricing over time, discrimination based on variation in the quality of products (such as good-better-best pricing) are usually legal.

(6) In the EU it would be wise to avoid any suggestion of resale price maintenance, this is especially the case for a "dominant" firm, one that holds more than, say, 30% market share.

(7) Finally, if mergers or acquisitions are considered it would be wise to take legal advice before spending significant sums if there is any likelihood that a regulator might block the transaction.

Notes

1 Strictly, all authors of which the author is aware.
2 Accessed at https://assets.publishing.service.gov.uk/government/uploads/system/uploads/attachment_data/file/137726/defra-stats-foodfarm-food-price-elasticities downloaded 18/07/2021
3 www.insurancejournal.com/news/international/2020/04/27/566445.htm downloaded 21/11/2021
4 Downloaded from www.bbc.co.uk/news/business-42666275, downloaded 20/03/2021.
5 CMA web-site: www.gov.uk/government/organisations/competition-and-markets-authority downloaded 26/03/2021
6 Splinter News: https://splinternews.com/4-corporate-mergers-shot-down-by-the-government downloaded 27/03/2021
7 EU Commission: https://ec.europa.eu/commission/presscorner/detail/en/STATEMENT_19_889 downloaded 27/03/2021
8 EU Commission https://ec.europa.eu/competition/cartels/cases/cases downloaded 27/03/2021
9 Downloaded from www.pinsentmasons.com/out-law/news/resale-price-maintenance-cma-crackdown, Out-law News, 24/03/2021
10 Downloaded from www.whitecase.com/publications/alert/rpm-comes-back-dead-eu-commission-tackles-pricing-e-commerce: RPM comes back from the dead – European Commission tackles pricing in e-commerce, 25/03/2021
11 Encyclopaedia Britannica www.britannica.com/event/Clayton-Antitrust-Act, downloaded, 27/03/2021
12 https://thelawreviews.co.uk/title/the-dominance-and-monopolies-review/european-union downloaded 21/11/2021
13 https://thelawreviews.co.uk/title/the-dominance-and-monopolies-review/european-union downloaded 21/11/2021

References

Abdel-Kader M. and Mentzeniot V. (2007) The effect of corporate restructuring on the stakeholder's value: the case of GEC/Marconi, *World Journal of Business Management*, 1(1), 28–46

Akshay R. R., Bergen M. E. and Davis S. (2000) How to fight a price war, *Harvard Business Review*, Mar–Apr, 107–116

Baker W. L., Marn M. V. and Zawada C. C. (2010) *The Price Advantage*, 2nd edition, Wiley & Sons, Hoboken, NJ

Ball S. B., Bazerman M. H. and Carroll J. S. (1991) An evaluation of learning in the bilateral winner's curse, *Organizational Behavior and Human Decision Processes*, 48, 1–22

Capen E. C., Clapp R. V. and Campbell W. M. (1971) Competitive bidding in high-risk situations, *Journal of Petroleum Technology*, 23, 641–653

Cassing J. and Douglas R. W. (1980) Implications of the auction mechanism in Baseball's free agent draft, *Southern Economic Journal*, 47, 110–121

Dessaur J. P. (1981) *Book Publishing*, Bowker, New York

Ferris K. R. and Petitt B. S. P. (2002) *Valuation: Avoiding the Winner's Curse*, Prentice Hall, Upper Saddle River, NJ

Foreman P. and Murnighan J. K. (1996) Learning to avoid the winner's curse, *Organization Behavior and Human Decision Processes*, 67(2), 170–180

Krishnamurthi L. and Raj S. P. (1991) An empirical analysis of the relationship between brand loyalty and consumer price elasticity, *Management Science*, 10(2), 172–183

Landsburg S. E. (2002) *Price Theory & Applications*, 5th edition, South-Western, A Division of Thomson Learning, Cincinnati, OH

Leszinski R. and Marn M. V. (1997) Setting value, not price, *McKinsey Quarterly*, Feb, 1–27 downloaded 15/04/2021

Marn M. V., Roegner E. V. and Zawada C. C. (2004) *The Price Advantage*, Wiley & Sons, Hoboken, NJ

McGrath R. G. (2009) Kraft, Cadbury and Hershey: a not so sweet deal? *Harvard Business Review Press*, November, downloaded 20/3/2021 from: https://hbr.org/2009/11/watch-out-kraft-a-war-of-attrition

Mohammed R. (2018) The good-better-best approach to pricing, *Harvard Business Review*, Sep–Oct, 106–115

Nagle T. T. and Müller G. (2018) *The Strategy and Tactics of Pricing*, 6th edition, Routledge, New York and Abingdon, Oxon

Roll R. (1986) The Hubris Hypothesis of corporate take-overs, *Journal of Business*, 59, 197–216

Samuelson L. (2016) Game theory in economics and beyond, *Journal of Economic Perspectives*, 30(4), 107–130

Shapiro C. and Varian H. R. (1998) Versioning: the smart way to sell information, *Harvard Business Review*, Nov–Dec, 106–114

Simmonds K. (1981) Strategic management accounting, *Management Accounting (UK)*, 59(4), 26–29

Simmonds K. (1982) Strategic management accounting for pricing: a case example, *Accounting and Business Research*, 12(47), 206–214

Simon H. and Fassnacht M. (2019) *Price Management: Strategy, Analysis, Decision, Implementation*, Springer Nature, Cham, Switzerland

Smith T. J. (2011) *Pricing Strategy: Setting Price Levels, Managing Price Discounts, & Establishing Price Structures*, Cengage Learning, Boston, MA

Thaler R. H. (1988) Anomalies: the winner's curse, *Journal of Economic Perspectives*, 2(1), 191–202

Tiffin et al. (2011) downloaded 18/07/2021 from: https://assets.publishing.service.gov.uk/government/uploads/system/uploads/attachment_data/file/137726/defra-stats-foodfarm-food-price-elasticities-120208.pdf

14 Customer profitability

14.1 Introduction

We have considered the important factors in setting prices: costs, market demand and the impact of competition. The focus has been on estimating the value of products and services from the customers' point of view, how the company might position its products in relation to its market segments and how these segments might be exploited by the methods of price discrimination. The impact of competition was considered in the last chapter. In this chapter we analyse the profitability of customers and transactions. In the next chapter we discuss negotiating strategies for different types of customers.

This chapter deals with subjects close to the heart of management accountants: customer profitability and the price that customers pay compared to list or invoice price. Detailed analysis is likely to reveal that some customers are not profitable, that some sales practices lead to massive erosion of margin and company systems might encourage volume and market share rather than profit. This chapter is important not only because it may reveal significant profit opportunity but also because all the careful "strategic" thinking about product positioning and market segmentation can be undone by unfortunate policies and misguided incentives at the detailed sales and transaction level.

14.2 Customer profitability

The emergence of activity-based costing in the 1980s was based on practice in manufacturing companies. However, the potential of the new technique across a range of industries and applications was quickly explored with ABC finding an important application in customer analysis. The Kanthal case, first published in 1989, demonstrated the power of activity-based analysis and was used by Kaplan and Cooper (1998) to show how the profitability of customers could vary dramatically. Kanthal had some very profitable customers, many customers that were near break-even and a few very unprofitable customers. Only large customers could create large losses, so these customers were both unprofitable and large and, because of their size and perceived importance, the company did not want to lose them. The problem was that these companies were placing large volumes of expensive-to-process

DOI: 10.4324/9781003272731-14

small orders. However, once the problem was understood, the solution was found: an automated system so the customer could place orders directly.

A second example concerned warehousing costs where activity-based analysis revealed that two methods, "full pallet" and "layer and case," had very different cost driver rates of $0.015 and $0.08, respectively. The price, however, was based on an average cost of $0.04 for all customers. The "layer and case" customers were unprofitable. As in the Kanthal case, a solution was found, one company even discovered that switching to the full pallet option would be cheaper: a win-win situation.

Kaplan and Cooper (1998) devote a chapter to the use of activity-based management in customer profitability analysis. They note that traditionally, sales, marketing, distribution and administration costs have been treated as "fixed". However, as a percentage of sales, they may not be just variable, they may be "super-variable": *increasing* as a percentage of sales over time. One reason can be the pursuit of market share leading to an increase in smaller customers with relatively high costs to serve. Kaplan and Cooper (1998) set out some of the key differences between high and low cost-to-serve customers. The high-cost-to serve customers are more likely to customise products, take small and unpredictable orders, customise and change delivery schedules, require manual processes, call on pre- and post-sales support, expect inventory to be on-hand and may delay payments. The low-cost-to-serve customers tend to take standard products on predictable delivery schedules, use information technology and so on.

The issue of customer profitability has been understood for decades. Cokins (2015) quotes an article from the 1922 National Association of Cost Accountants yearbook in which Castenholtz notes that the cost of production might be accurately ascertained but losses still incurred if there is poor control of selling and administrative expenses. The difference, now, is that with the development of new techniques and the emergence of sophisticated information technology, it is possible to analyse expenses and trace them to customers.

14.3 The Sloan Styles case

The issues surrounding customer profitability are well illustrated by the case of Sloan Styles (Shank, 2006). Sloan Styles supplied women's fashion wear to department stores, speciality retailers and catalogue-based sellers. The company worked with customers to design their private label styles and then organised production through a network of contract factories. The loss of a major customer had seen Sloan take on more small accounts to make up the lost volume and, in addition, in 1997, Sloan launched its own branded apparel. The results in 1998 were disappointing, income before tax slipped from its 1993 high of $2.6 million to near break-even at $104,000. Much of the own brand inventory had to be sold through discount outlets and overall contribution margin of 28% was below the target of 30%. The detail is set out in Table 14.1.

The concern, in Finance, was that contribution margin had slipped below the 30% target. However, perusal of Table 14.1 reveals that this was because a significant volume of inventory had to be off-loaded through discounters at low prices.

Table 14.1 Sloan Styles 1998 sales and contribution data by customer adapted from Shank (2006) Exhibit 2, p. 232 *in Cases in Cost management: a Strategic Emphasis 3rd Ed.* Cengage Learning Inc. Reproduced by permission. www.cengage.com/permissions

	Talbots	*Nordstrom*	*Dillards*	*J Jill*	*Lands end*	*Stein Mart*	*Orvis*	*Discount outlets (3)*	*Others (175)*	*Total*
Avge price ($)	45.1	38.6	41.9	32.9	46.8	42.5	41.3	14.4	39.6	39.4
Sales (units 000)	536	158	75	62	56	56	22	135	122	1,221
Cont'n margin ($000)	7,468	1,953	946	673	749	703	295	(862)	1,628	13,553
%CM	31%	32%	30%	33%	28%	29%	32%	(44)%	34%	28%
Styles (number)	229	240	43	64	46	60	49	486	65	1,282
Shipments (number)	3,799	9,544	1,067	200	357	1,786	140	59	20,769	37,721

Contribution margins for other customers were consistent and, indeed, excluding the discounters, the average contribution margin was 31%. The company seemed to be operating a consistent pricing policy that followed the founder's "rule" based on estimating the wholesale price at 50% of the expected retail price. In previous years the 30% contribution margin thus generated had been sufficient to ensure good profitability.

Gary Sloan, the founder's son, was concerned that an increasing number of styles was weighing heavily on the company. Each style could be expensive to design, sample and deliver. Gary instigated an ABC analysis and the cost drivers of $4,002 per style[1] and $23.2 per shipment were derived. There was also a cost driver per equivalent yard of cloth, administration costs were allocated at 6.8% of sales and customer service costs were directly attributed to customers. ABC-derived customer profitability is presented in Table 14.2.

Table 14.2 lays bare some of the problems facing the company. First, there is overwhelming dependence on one company, Talbots, for profitable sales. Second, the "own brand" experiment has proved extremely costly, revenue has not even covered direct costs and, in addition, the activity-related costs, including designing and delivering 486 styles, cost more than $2 million. Third, the sales to "other" (small) outlets have been unprofitable with heavy customer service and shipment costs. Fourth, the second biggest customer, Nordstrom, is unprofitable.

The company obviously needed to attend to both strategy and pricing policy. In 1998 66% of the 1,262 styles designed and delivered sold fewer than 500 units each and, when one considers that sales of over 300 units are needed just to recoup the $4,002 style-related costs, action was needed to cut the number of styles and/or increase the prices for these low-volume orders.

Customer profitability analysis can lead to surprising results. One might expect that the customers receiving the better prices would be larger, more important or both, but Kaplan and Cooper demonstrate that this might not be so, and the Sloan Styles case is a perfect example: larger companies are treated in the same way as smaller ones. Holden and Burton (2008) suggest that a plot of customer requirement versus price can yield surprising results: some small companies receive low prices and larger companies often do not receive especially low prices, see Figure 14.1.

Figure 14.1 shows the price versus total requirement plot for a commodity product. Prices paid per lb tend to fall as total requirements increase, but there is an enormous scatter around the price-requirements trend line; some relatively small customers are paying less than the price paid by much larger customers. The Sloan Styles case is exceptional in that both large and small customers receive much the same prices. The analysis almost screams the importance of Talbots, but this company receives the same pricing treatment as all the others.

14.4 The pocket-price waterfall

In the Sloan Styles case there was an implicit policy that all customers be treated equally, large and small customers received similar prices and customer service. This was probably the consequence of a rigid pricing policy that took no account

Table 14.2 Sloan Styles 1998 Customer profitability analysis

$000	*Talbots*	*Nordstrom*	*Dillards*	*J Jill*	*Lands end*	*Stein Mart*	*Orvis*	*Discount outlets (3)*	*Others (175)*	*Total*
Cont'n margin	7,468	1,953	946	673	749	703	295	(862)	1,628	13,553
Activity-related costs	3,519	2,115	617	642	561	551	334	2,214	1,799	12,352
Customer "profit"	3,949	(162)	329	31	188	152	(39)	(3076)	(171)	1201
Profit (% revenue)	16.3%	(2.7)%	10.5%	1.5%	7.1%	6.3%	(4.2)%	(159)%	(3.6)%	2.5%

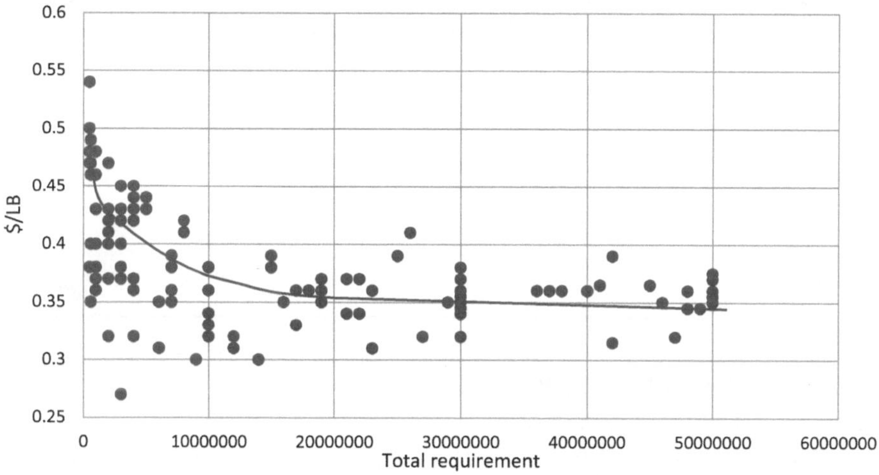

Figure 14.1 Prices paid by total requirements

Source: Copyright (2008) Wiley. Used with permission from (Holden and Burton, Figure 1.1, p. 7, Prices by Total Requirements, Pricing with Confidence, Wiley)

of the importance of the customer, the service delivered or the size of the order. It is obvious that the policy, though successful in the past, needed to change. At Sloan Styles, there was little evidence of discounting from "target" price – except for the swingeing reductions needed to sell unsold inventory through discount chains.

It is much more common to see a range of discounts, especially in B2B transactions where list prices may be just the starting point for negotiations. Marn and Rosiello (1992) demonstrated just how much the price actually paid, the "pocket price," can differ from the invoice price. In their example of the "pocket-price waterfall" they first noted that invoice price differed from list price because of order size and competitive discounts. Then further concessions reduced the invoice price to pocket price: payment terms discount, annual volume bonus, off-invoice promotions, co-operative advertising (funds to support local advertising) and freight costs. Marn et al. (2004) mention further customer-related costs: extended credit terms that mean increased cost to fund receivables; holding consignment inventory for specific customers and price reductions for ordering online. These "revenue leakages" are especially dangerous if sales and margin reports are based on the invoice price, with obvious potential for misleading managers and executives.

The presentation of the various discounts as a "waterfall" increases the impact of the presentation and Table 12.3 shows how effective this can be. A reduction on list price of 20% as shown in Table 12.3 is significant given that any price reduction "falls straight to the bottom line". Marn and Rosiello report invoice to pocket-price gaps of this magnitude in several industries.

Table 14.3 Example of a pocket-price waterfall

List price	*Competitive discount*	*Invoice price*	*Quick payment discount*	*Volume discount*	*Off-invoice promotions*	*Consignment costs*	*Pocket price*
100							
	(5)	**95**					
			(2)				
				(5)			
					(6)		
						(2)	
							80

14.5 The pocket-price band

Just as revealing as the pocket-price waterfall is the "pocket-price band". Baker et al. (2010) note that, at any time, there are likely to be many different effective prices charged to different customers for the same product and they illustrate a pocket-price band analysis in the Monnarch battery case (see Figure 14.2).

The analysis shows a histogram of pocket prices in $ per battery for different customers. The range of pocket prices varies from less than $30 to more than $63 per battery with most customers receiving a price between $42 and $54 per battery. A further analysis of pocket price versus account volume revealed no correlation between prices paid and size of customer: smaller companies were just as likely to receive a good price as larger ones. In the Sloan Styles case the important point was that such a pocket-price band did *not* exist. The surprising point was that all customers were treated similarly. One would expect large and important customers to receive discounts and/or excellent service and it should be surprising when this is not the case.

The profit opportunities are obvious if the pocket-price band *can be managed.* In fact, Marn and Rosiello (1992) note that managers are often surprised both by the range of the band and by the identities of the customers at each end of the range. These ideas are further explored by Marn et al. (2003, 2004) who note that securing a 1% increase in price might be achieved, not by an across-the-board price increase, but by incremental management of the pocket-price waterfall.

Armed with analysis of the price waterfall and the pocket-price band Baker et al. (2010) describe more cases. At the Castle Battery Company better management of prices at the detailed transaction level allowed the company to significantly improve profit on products that managers had assumed were becoming increasingly commoditised. At Tech-Craft the price waterfall was "engineered" to good effect and a quarterly report summarised the price waterfall for major product lines. The various revenue leakages are interesting (percentages are approximate): standard distributor-dealer discount (15%), order size discount (2.5%), exception discount (8%), cash discount (1%), receivables carrying cost (1%), cooperative advertising (3%), merchandising allowance (2%), annual volume rebate (2.5%) and freight (1%).

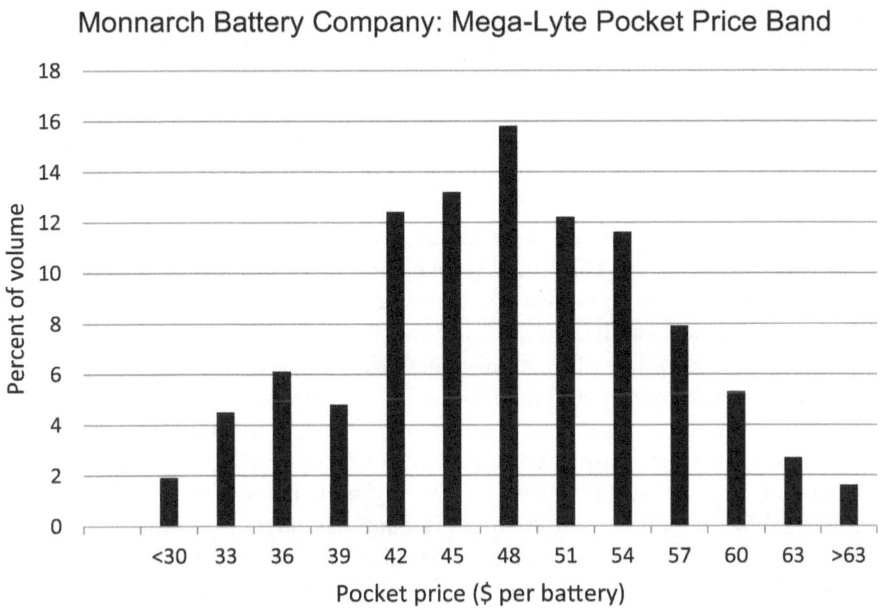

Figure 14.2 The pocket-price band

Source: Copyright (2010) Wiley. Used with permission from (Baker, Marn and Zawada, Exhibit 16–4, Monnarch Battery Company: Mega-Lyte pocket-price band, *The Price Advantage*, John Wiley & Sons, Inc.)

In both editions of their book, Marn et al. (2004) and Baker et al. (2010), include a chapter and an Appendix setting out examples across industries ranging from breakfast cereals to vinyl flooring. There are several examples of price waterfalls and of "pocket margin" waterfalls. In the latter cases the waterfall is expressed not as a percentage of price but as a percentage margin (price less cost of goods sold). If the impact of leakages on price can be surprising, the impact on margins can be dramatic. For example, if the expected margin is 40% but leakages mean that, on average, 25% of revenue is lost, then margin shrinks, on average from 40% to 15%. The pocket margin band could easily show that some customers are unprofitable.

14.6 Implications for management accountants

The implications for management accountants are among the most important in this book. Management accountants have access to raw data, and they have the analytical tools, such as activity-based costing that are needed for customer profitability, pocket-price waterfall and pocket-price band analyses. Items such as promotion, advertising and freight may need to be apportioned and the cost of items such as consignment and seasonal inventories and receivables require an appropriate cost of capital. Importantly, management accountants can take the initiative by presenting the results to marketing managers, pricing professionals and senior executives and, since the results can be both easily understood and may have significant implications, there is considerable scope for business partnering between management accountants and sales and marketing executives.

It is obvious that there is a close link between customer profitability analysis and pocket-price waterfall analysis and care must be taken to include all the relevant items but without double counting. One "solution" in the Sloan Styles case would have been to make sure that important customers received preferential treatment and small customers were dissuaded from placing unprofitable orders in uneconomic volumes. This could be achieved by raising list prices but offering significant volume and order size discounts. The existing price structure for Talbots and a typical small customer is shown in table 14.4.

If prices were raised by 20% but discounts were offered for large volumes and order sizes, then Talbots would qualify for significant discounts while small customers would not. A revised price structure might appear as shown in Table 14.5.

A discount structure permits considerable flexibility so that, for example, Nordstrom with high volume but small numbers of units per style and per shipment would qualify for only a total volume discount. The layout of Table 4.5 shows how the analysis can combine activity-based cost analysis and price waterfall profit leakages such as the discounts offered. There is considerable scope for managing the pocket-price waterfall so that, for example, price increases can be imposed on unprofitable customers without damaging profitable customers.

The management accountant can contribute both by making recommendations to deal with immediate issues and by identifying longer-term strategic issues. There may be unintended revenue leakages and some customers might be revealed as unprofitable. Options might include pricing and order size policies as at Sloan Styles, the use of technology to reduce order costs as at Kanthal or changes to customer behaviour as in the pallet loading case. There may also be opportunities for "engineering" the pocket-price waterfall that might lead to increases in pocket-price without an across-the-board change to list prices.

Table 14.4 Existing price structures for Talbots and typical small customer

$	*Price*	*Variable cost*	*Activity-based costs*	*Pocket price*
Talbots	100	69.1	14.6	16.3
Small customer	100	66.3	37.2	(3.5%)

Table 14.5 Suggested price structure for Talbots and typical small customer

$	*List price*	*Volume & Order discounts*	*Invoice price*	*Variable cost of goods*	*Activity-based costs*	*Pocket price*
Talbots	120	20	100	69.1	14.6	16.3
Small customer	120	-	120	66.3	37.2	16.5

The analysis may also have longer-term, strategic implications. For example, consistency is needed between the three levels of price policy: industry, market strategy and transaction-level pricing. A premium product should carry a premium list price, but care must be taken not to undo the product positioning by a lax discounting regime.

Note

1 The cost driver per style was comprised of four elements relating to selling support, purchasing, sample manufacture and product support.

References

Baker W. L., Marn M. V. and Zawada C. C. (2010) *The Price Advantage*, 2nd edition, Wiley & Sons, Hoboken, NJ

Cokins G. (2015) *How to Measure and Manage Customer Value and Customer Profitability*, downloaded 2/4/2021 from: https://www.researchgate.net/publication/289410908_How_to_Measure_and_Manage_Customer_Value_and_Customer_Profitability

Holden R. K. and Burton M. R. (2008) *Pricing With Confidence*, John Wiley and Sons, Hoboken, NJ

Kaplan R. S. and Cooper R. (1998) *Cost & Effect: Using Integrated Cost Systems to Drive Profitability and Performance*, Harvard Business School Press, Brighton, MA

Marn M. V., Roegner E. V. and Zawada C. C. (2003) The power of pricing, *McKinsey Quarterly*, Feb, downloaded 31/03/21 from: www.mckinsey.com/business-functions/marketing-and-sales/our-insights/the-power-of-pricing

Marn M. V., Roegner E. V. and Zawada C. C. (2004) *The Price Advantage*, Wiley & Sons, Hoboken, NJ

Marn M. V. and Rosiello R. L. (1992) Managing price, gaining profit, *Harvard Business Review*, Sep–Oct, 84–94

Shank J. K. (2006) Sloan Styles Inc, in: *Cases in Cost management: A Strategic Emphasis*, 3rd edition, pp. 227–241, Thomson South Western, Cincinnati, OH

15 Segmentation, customers and negotiations

15.1 Introduction

A major focus throughout this book has been on the importance of understanding the customer and designing company systems that exploit this understanding. We have seen how markets can be segmented by buyer identity, geography, quantity and time and how products can be designed and marketed to appeal to different customer groups. In this chapter we first consider segmentation of the market based on what customers value and then why it is important to understand how different customers behave. As usual there is a major difference between consumer markets and B2B markets. In consumer markets the aim is to identify customer groups that are sufficiently large to be targeted. In B2B markets individual customers become the focus and specific approaches are required to identify what they value, whether they should be targeted and how to prepare for negotiations.

15.2 Segmenting by customer needs

The identification of customer "needs" has become central to marketing and: "One of the basic tenets of marketing is that customers don't buy products; rather they buy benefits" (Sheth and Mittal, 2004, p. 177). This means, for example, that customers do not so much buy a car as a means of transport together with other benefits such as comfort or the thrill of acceleration. This widens the definition of "needs" to include more than just functions; while products may provide physical benefits, they can also meet emotional and aspirational needs.

We saw, in Chapter 3, how companies in several consumer industries segmented their markets and, increasingly, companies have moved from a production toward a marketing orientation: "The philosophy that marketing strategies must be based on customer needs and wants has come to be known as the marketing concept" (Michman, 1991, p. 3). This idea is central to the concept of market segmentation as the needs of customer groups are identified and then the company sets out to meet those needs more effectively than competitors. Michman mentions left-handed golf clubs, decaffeinated coffee and diet soft drinks as examples of products catering to the needs of specific customer groups.

DOI: 10.4324/9781003272731-15

The importance of identifying customers' needs was well-exemplified by Ohmae (1988). After diagnosing the problem Japanese industry faced, unable to compete easily with lower-cost producers in countries like South Korea and unwilling to emulate the high quality of German manufacturers, they were "caught in the middle". The answer, argued Ohmae, was to analyse customer needs and then design products to meet those needs. His examples were the digital piano developed by Yamaha; Babu, a new bath additive that wiped out traditional additives in the Japanese market; coffee percolators that improved the taste of coffee; redesigning the lens-shutter camera; and a microwave oven that was part of a regular oven to save space, a precious commodity in Japanese households. In each case the product was developed after analysing customer needs: excellent piano music, the effect of a hot spring, great tasting coffee, excellent photographs and kitchen equipment that economised on space.

15.3 Buyer behaviour

Customers can have the same "needs," but very different approaches to buying, some want the highest quality product, some want a bargain while some want good value, trading off quality and price. Mitchell and Bates (1998) analysed the various shopping styles revealed by five previous research studies. Almost all the studies found that some buyers are "perfectionists," they simply want the best quality; some are brand-loyal; some are confused by the choice of goods on offer; some want good value (price-quality conscious); some are impulsive; and some shop as a recreational activity. Sproles (1985) also identified a group that do not want to shop at all (shopping avoiding).

A later study by Stamer and Diller (2006) revealed broadly similar categories of buyer behaviour. A survey of German households' price behaviour across five fast-moving consumer goods revealed five consumer groups:

(1) Optimisers, concerned with both price *and* quality
(2) price seekers who will search for discounts and deals without being overly concerned with quality
(3) brand conscious with high-quality expectations and tending not to search for low prices
(4) discount buyers, not especially concerned with quality or price and preferring a simplified shopping experience at acceptable prices
(5) high-price shoppers who value their time and tend to use high prices as an indication of quality.

These studies show that there are several types of shoppers, some are likely to be price sensitive (price seekers and price-value conscious shoppers) and some are likely to be price insensitive (high quality, high price, brand conscious, fashion conscious and impulsive shoppers). However, price sensitive and insensitive customers do have something in common: they probably know what they want. By contrast recreational shoppers do not shop for specific products, rather, they enjoy shopping and are probably more likely to indulge in impulse buying.

It should be noted that individual behaviour may switch depending on what is purchased. Someone may want very high-quality fashion garments and footwear but may take a very price sensitive approach when shopping for food. Companies need to understand the behaviour of their target customers and need to tailor their marketing strategies. Oversimplifying, supermarket chains are generally clear about their target customers. Aldi and Lidl with the everyday low-price strategy target discount buyers and price seekers. Tesco, Sainsburys and Morrisons adopt a hi-lo strategy that can attract value buyers that will purchase well-known brands at discount prices as well as those that simply buy their favourite brands. Waitrose aims for high price and brand loyal customers. The major chains, Tesco, Sainsburys, Morrisons and Waitrose adopt a hi-lo strategy and also offer value ranges aimed at low-price shoppers: even Waitrose offers an "Essentials" range. The importance of understanding the customer is exemplified by the demise of Woolworth, a company that found it difficult to keep up with changing shopping habits.

15.4 Types of business customer

B2B pricing is obviously very different from pricing consumer goods, one would not expect to see, for example, impulse or high-price behaviours in business buying. Nevertheless, business buyers have distinct characteristics, and these were analysed by Nagle and Müller (2018) and Holden (2012). Nagle and Müller categorised business buyers into price, value, brand and convenience and, similarly, Holden (2012) categorised business buyers into price, value, relationship and "poker-players". Nagle and Müller also discuss "power buyers" a subcategory of value-driven buyers.

It is perhaps strange to see "brand" buyers in the Nagle and Müller analysis of B2B customers, but the definition of this category is very close to Holden's relationship buyers: a brand or relationship buyer trusts the seller based on experience of products and services previously delivered. Nagle and Müller's convenience buyer is hardly interested in price, the purchase is probably so small in relation to the end-product that it is not worth negotiating. Table 15.1 combines the Nagle and Müller and Holden categories and provides the framework for the following discussion.

15.5 Negotiating with price buyers

Price buyers may qualify several suppliers that can meet their requirements and ask for bids against a carefully determined (minimal) specification. Procurement professionals have control, access to other members of the buying centre is denied, there is no interest in value or developing relationships and a "sealed bid" process may be employed. The advice is to make a bare-bones offer or service, strip away all value-added features and be sure to have a clear "walk-away" deal. If the buyer requires extra services, they can be added but only at a price. The deal must be based on a tight specification and contract "creep" avoided.

Table 15.1 Types of business buyer

Buyer type	*Description*
Price	The price-buyer simply wants the lowest price and is not interested in building a relationship with the supplier. Governments may insist on this and some companies have policies that ensure emphasis on price.
Value	Value buyers carefully weigh the value that the product or service can deliver versus its costs.
Brand/relationship	These buyers depend upon the supplier for expertise and the value they can deliver. They will continue to purchase the "brand" or deal with the same supplier so long as expected standards are maintained.
Power	A special category of value-buyer that have enormous purchasing power and may therefore be able to insist on lower prices because of their size and market share.
Poker-player	These are value-buyers masquerading as price buyers, they want a high value product but at a low price, they are "poker-players" because, in threatening to walk away from their preferred supplier, they are bluffing.

Neither Nagle and Müller nor Holden recommends doing business with price buyers, though both note that price buyers can offer an opportunity if there is excess inventory or spare capacity. Still, Holden cautions that fixed costs should be excluded from the price *only* if there is spare capacity *and* the customer can be "*bumped*" if better business comes along.

15.6 Negotiating with value buyers

Here the key is understanding the customer's requirements and providing different price levels offering different levels of service. Holden (2012) emphasises the need to establish the value offered versus competitors with detailed, customer specific, calculations of value delivered and ROI for the buyer. Similarly, Nagle and Müller emphasise ways that the product can add value. Value-adding services can be unbundled so that trade-offs can be offered and aspects of the product or service that the buyer values identified.

Keiser's (1988) advice is also relevant. He also emphasises excellent understanding of the product or service value together with insight into the customer's requirements. He suggests that value might be provided by, for example, assurance of quality, convenience, priority treatment if there is shortage, sharing new technology, credit terms, timing of delivery, customisation and service. The aim is to focus negotiation on areas of common interest rather than the one issue where seller and customer must be at odds: the price.

15.7 Negotiating with brand/relationship buyers

The approach to relationship customers seems rather similar, be prepared to offer a low-priced option together with a higher priced full-service option. This gives the salesperson the ability to negotiate what the customer needs, but, in this case, the aim is to ensure a reliable service, building trust with the customer over time. High pressure selling is to be avoided; quality and delivery should be as agreed and there should be careful understanding of customer needs by responsive, reliable, expert salespeople. Both Nagle and Müller, and Holden emphasise respect for brand/relationship buyers. If such a buyer expresses disappointment the seller must make every effort to repair relations, offering extra services if necessary.

15.8 Negotiating with power buyers

Power buyers have such a large share of the market that they can exert considerable pressure on the seller. If the decision is taken to deal with powerful customers Nagle and Müller suggest offering exclusivity to force these buyers (such as powerful supermarket chains) so they compete with each other; eliminating unnecessary costs; differentiating the product sold from that sold through other outlets; offering lower prices but only if the buyer takes other products as well and, finally, being prepared for bullying tactics, possibly from a higher manager; and remember: "the power buyers that get mad are those that need something from you" (p. 125).

15.9 Negotiating with "poker-players"

The "poker-players" are most difficult to deal with. These buyers want low prices but also try to obtain good service. They are referred to as poker-players because they do not intend to carry out the threat to "walk away". However, the seller does not know this and, all too often, gives in and agrees a reduced price. Holden and Burton (2008) recommend treating poker players as low-price buyers, give them the low price they ask for but only by offering a "bare-bones" service and making sure there are strong fences to prevent other services being provided free. They also suggest that, if possible, the seller should try to circumvent the purchasing agent who is trying to commoditise the service and reach the users of the product or service. Poker-players may attempt to contact higher managers in the selling organisation and executives need to be primed on the negotiating position so that they do not over-rule their negotiator.

Nagle and Müller do not refer to "poker-players" but they have this type of customer in mind when they say: "value-driven buyers, and even brand buyers, . . . masquerade as price buyers in an attempt to extract reactive concessions from their preferred supplier" (p. 122). Such buyers may be identified by the effort they expend in time evaluating suppliers in advance, the vagueness of the service specification required and their failure to commit the purchase to the lowest bidder. They recommend that the seller should not submit a bid unless the minimum requirements are explicitly set out and a bid should be accompanied by a clear statement of the low quality/service provided. The seller can indicate a higher price alternative for better service.

Holden (2012) discusses vendors that have a business track-record with the customer and those that do not. The poker-player poses a threat to both. The advantaged player, the preferred supplier, may feel forced to give a discount by the customer's threat to "walk away". To combat this the preferred supplier should take away value if forced to discount and be prepared to bluff back. For example, if the customer calls for a delay, then the supplier should also delay. Poker-players use "rabbits" to provide quotes that can be used to force concessions from the preferred vendor. To avoid the role of "rabbit" a supplier must not be drawn into the process. A customer that asks for a proposal should be "qualified" by questioning the bidding process and whether there is a chance of winning the contract. If the customer evades the questions or refuses access to key decision-makers, it is probably best to walk away. "Red flags" include no previous business with the firm, procurement control the process with no access to the decision-maker, a well-established company already has the business, or the buyer claims that the service is a commodity.

15.10 Policies for customer negotiations

Nagle and Müller (2018) devote a chapter to "Pricing Policy" and Holden (2012) a whole book titled "Pricing with Backbone". Their advice is especially important if customer profitability analysis and/or pocket-price-waterfall analysis reveal inexplicable variations in customer profitability, unacceptable revenue leakages or wide pocket-price bands. These can arise when buyers succeed in negotiating discounts to which they are not entitled, and Nagle and Müller provide examples. An important customer may be entitled to a 25% discount and, when faced with your 6% price increase, argues that, for them, it should be only 4.5%. Conceding such an argument would be disastrous, the customer would not pay the full price increase and would *still* receive the overall 25% discount. A variation is the buyer who argues that the business is yours for just a 2% discount: except the discount applies to all purchases, not just the incremental sales at issue.

Nagle and Müller point out that customers will work out the scope for forcing concessions and will modify their behaviour in response to price policies. If there are likely to be discounts available at the end of a month or quarter, then customers will delay purchases to gain the anticipated discounts. If salespeople respond to a request for a price concession by saying that a more senior manager must be consulted, the customer knows that it is worth pushing for a better deal further up the chain of command.

Nagle and Müller see clear pricing policies as the answer to these and similar problems, and, once established, there must be no exceptions to the policy. Similarly, Holden and Burton (2008) highlight the need for "rules of engagement". For example, that discounts will not be given to small customers, on high-value premium products and services or in some geographical regions. These "rules" must be clear and backed up by willingness to lose the business if necessary.

Holden (2012) reinforces the emphasis on sales policies by recommending that negotiations should be undertaken by mid-level managers and senior executives should, generally, not be involved in price negotiations. Holden argues that senior managers might decide or agree something "at the table" and this will usually be to the detriment of the seller. Instead, the salesperson needs to be well briefed and well-armed before entering negotiations and the key recommendation in negotiations with all types of customers is to avoid giving something for nothing.

For price buyers and poker-players a bare-bones offer, and a tight contract is needed, extras must be paid for. For value and relationship buyers value should be clearly related to price and, if a price concession is granted, the buyer must suffer a penalty of some kind: "The sales rep . . . can be empowered with pre-approved value trade-offs and discount policies" (Nagle and Müller p. 117). The key is to understand the ways in which the product or service adds value for the customer and to "unbundle" the product so that pressure from the buyer can be met by offering reduced quality or by some other concession. For example, service might be excluded, warranty terms tightened, additional payments demanded for rush deliveries or changes to the product, service or contract. The salesperson needs to be well-armed so that an aggressive buyer can be presented with options, rather than simply conceding or sending the request "upstairs" to more senior management.

Keiser's (1988) advice follows similar lines: determine the minimum acceptable deal in advance and be prepared to walk away; listen carefully to customer objections to determine their specific needs and what they value; and shift the negotiation to areas of cooperation if possible. Keiser also mentions the important point of not committing until all issues are agreed. The thread that runs through these suggestions is the need to work co-operatively in as many areas as possible, especially in areas that add value for the customer. However, if the customer insists on a rock-bottom price, then a minimal service must be offered.

15.11 Sales incentives

We discussed the importance of the correct sales incentives in Chapter 4 and noted the importance of avoiding any incentive that simply rewards increased volume or revenue without a link to profitability. The incentive scheme should not reward salespeople for just making sales, it should reward sales that carry at least the standard margin. Nagle and Müller suggest a formula that links sales "credit" given to the profitability of the sale using a formula such as:

"Sales Credit = [Target Price – k(Target Price – Actual Price)] × Units Sold" (p. 278)

A formula such as this will overcome the problem that sales are chased at the expense of profit. However, in some companies the formula could be a blunt instrument, for example, salespeople should be rewarded if a customer is persuaded to trade up to a higher specification product even if this means offering a discount. To encourage this the formula might be tweaked so that, for example, for high contribution products the target price might be set *below* the list or advertised price.

More radically, the salesperson might be rewarded in accordance with the total contribution generated by their sales. However, this implies that salespeople have a good understanding of variable product costs, something that management accountants tend to be wary of.[1] Nevertheless, if a value and contribution-driven culture can be created, together with the right sales incentives, then salespeople can be trusted to deliver. Mohammed (2005) recounts a change in policy at Ford where, in 1995, "Ford took the unprecedented step of distributing its highly guarded yellow card to the sales team. The card detailed the variable profit on each of Ford's vehicles" (p. 41). The result was a change in sales focus as the emphasis switched to selling the most profitable models.

15.12 Implications for management accountants

The main implication here is the need for management accountants to work with marketing and sales managers in developing sales policies. A key recommendation for dealing with all types of customers is to understand the value of the product or service offer and to have a "menu" of service options at a range of prices either to sweeten a deal or to limit the service provided at low-price options. The management accountant needs to provide the analysis that supports these policies. Customer profitability and waterfall analyses provide insights into how the company incurs cost in pursuit of sales and these analyses should be the basis for further analysis of the cost to the company of offering for example:

Access to technical experts	Extended credit terms
Regular service visits	Changes to the service specification
Instant response to problems	Inventory consignments
Priority over other customers	Just-in-time deliveries
Guaranteed next-day delivery	Rush orders

Salespeople need to be alert to identifying the items that customers value and management accountants need to be responsive in identifying the cost of providing the service and the price that might be charged.

Management accountants should be involved in designing incentive schemes and, in the right environment, sharing variable cost information with salespeople. The "right" environment will, of course, include an incentive scheme that ties rewards to the contribution margin generated on orders, contracts or customers.

Note

1 The author made a presentation in one company that included reference to marginal costs. There was consternation round the table because even the mention of marginal cost was banned in that company.

References

Holden R. K. (2012) *Negotiating With Backbone*, FT Press, Upper Saddle River, NJ

Holden R. K. and Burton M. R. (2008) *Pricing With Confidence*, John Wiley and Sons, Hoboken, NJ

Keiser T. C. (1988) Negotiating with a customer you can't afford to lose, *Harvard Business Review*, Nov–Dec, 30–34

Michman R. D. (1991) *Lifestyle Market Segmentation*, Praeger, New York

Mitchell V. W. and Bates L. (1998) UK consumer decision-making styles, *Journal of Marketing Management*, 14(1–3), 199–225

Mohammed R. (2005) *The Art of Pricing: How to Find the Hidden Profits to Grow Your Business*, Crown Business, New York

Nagle T. T. and Müller G. (2018) *The Strategy and Tactics of Pricing*, 6th edition, Routledge, New York and Abingdon, Oxon

Ohmae K. (1988) Getting back to strategy, *Harvard Business Review*, 66(6), 149–156

Sheth J. N. and Mittal B. (2004) *Customer Behavior: A Managerial Perspective*, 2nd edition, Thomson South-Western, Cincinnati, OH

Sproles G. B. (1985) From perfectionism to faddism: measuring consumers' decision making styles, *Proceedings American Council on Consumer Interest Conference*, Columbia, 79–85

Stamer H. H. and Diller H. (2006) Price segment stability in consumer goods categories, *Journal of Product and Brand Management*, 15(1), 62–72

16 Price discrimination in economic theory

16.1 Introduction

Traditional economic theory concentrates on the consequences of assuming that firms can and will adopt profit-maximising policies. Given well-informed, rational, profit-maximising firms, basic economic theory predicts that, in very competitive markets, companies will be price-takers, unable to affect the price they can charge. In the ideal case of a perfect market, the price will be exactly equal to the marginal cost of the product as each firm reaches maximum efficiency and supplies at marginal cost. (Remember that, in economic theory, "cost" includes normal profit, so all the price takers are making normal profit.) On the other hand, if a company has monopoly power, to maximise profit it will restrict output and raise price. If the demand curve happens to be linear then output is restricted to half the perfect market output. Chapter 6 covered the basic ideas of competition and monopoly.

In competitive markets there is a tendency to assume that there is no control over price and the company is a "price-taker". However, a common refrain by price consultants is that this is a sure way to "leave money on the table" as, usually, there are buyers who would pay more than the "market price". The trick is to differentiate the product or service to target these customers.

The aim is to generate monopoly power, and then, following economic theory, the firm would estimate demand for its products at different prices and determine the optimal price where marginal revenue (derived from the demand curve) is equal to the company's marginal cost. Kaplan and Atkinson (1998) point to two problems in applying the "economists' prescriptions": difficulty in estimating the demand curve and difficulty in estimating the cost curve.

Kaplan and Atkinson suggest, "The development of activity-based costing since the 1980s has overcome the second of these problems" (p. 152). However, this seems optimistic. The activity-based hierarchy identifies unit-related, batch-related, product/customer/channel-related and facility-related costs. As volume increases unit-related costs are assumed to vary linearly, batch-related costs become essentially linear at high volumes while product/customer and facility costs are unaffected by volume (at least in theory), consequently cost per unit declines as volume increases. However, crucial to the economic theory of price, is

DOI: 10.4324/9781003272731-16

the assumption that, after falling, marginal cost begins to rise. The optimal price is determined by the intersection of the downward sloping marginal revenue curve and the cost curve *where the cost curve is upward sloping*. It is not clear how activity-based analysis can lead to an upward sloping marginal cost curve, at least not without more sophisticated analysis.

It seems, to the author, that neither demand nor cost curves are easy to estimate and the application of economic theory remains difficult to apply in practice. However, economic analysis certainly has implications for regulators that aim to prevent monopolies arising, control companies that have monopoly power and generally encourage more competitive markets.

The theory of competitive markets, monopoly, duopoly and oligopoly has been outlined in previous chapters, and, in this chapter, two further elements of economic theory are reviewed, price discrimination and Ramsey prices. From a management accounting perspective, whether a practice is discriminatory is irrelevant, what matters is whether it improves profits, fits with long-term strategy and is not illegal. However, in the next section we briefly review price discrimination theory and highlight the difficulties that arise when the niceties of theory are considered.

16.2 Defining price discrimination

Phlips (1983) notes: "the usual answer: There is price discrimination when the same commodity is sold at different prices to different customers" (p. 5). However, he points out that this would restrict price discrimination to sales of (exactly) the same commodity: "say an entrance to Disneyland; on a particular day, senior citizens receive a discount, as do children and military personnel" (p. 5)

The simplest definition, "different prices for different people for the same good," therefore excludes most of the cases where price discrimination appears to be practised. In fact, all the indirect methods based on quantity, product differentiation, time of use and time of purchase would be non-discriminatory. Journeys at different times of day; lunch and evening restaurant meals; matinee and evening performances are all different products. Even purchasing a product in advance at the very least restricts the flexibility of the buyer and, often, an advance purchase comes with restrictions such as non-refundability.

Phlips therefore rejects the simple definition and takes the (common sense) view that significant price differences for similar products with similar cost *is* price discriminatory. On the other hand: "If the price difference fully reflects the difference in the cost of carrying the good from the seller's location to the buyers' location, then nobody would argue, I am sure, that a discriminatory practice is involved" (Phlips, pp. 5–6).

Phlips therefore defined price discrimination as occurring when "two varieties of a commodity are sold (by the same seller) to two buyers at different *net* prices, the net price being the price (paid by the buyer) corrected for the cost associated with the product differentiation" (p. 6). Note that price discrimination occurs when *the same* seller chooses to offer the product at different prices. Observing that the same good is sold at different prices does not imply price discrimination if it is sold by *different* sellers. In that case sellers are simply competing on price. Phlips's definition is adopted by most authorities although, as we saw in Chapter 6, some authors use the term "price differentiation" or even "segmentation" as synonyms for price discrimination.

16.3 Types of price discrimination

Pigou (1932) identified three types of price discrimination.

First-degree discrimination arises if each customer is charged the maximum price they are prepared to pay. This would be perfect price discrimination and the seller would take all consumer surplus from each customer.

Second-degree price discrimination was defined by Pigou as a variation of first-degree discrimination where customers are offered several prices and they choose that price which is below their reservation price (the maximum price they are prepared to pay). To achieve this, they must be distinguished "by some mark".

Third-degree price discrimination involves the identification of different groups of customers and offering them different prices. The more price sensitive customers receive a lower price, and the more price insensitive customers receive a higher price.

16.4 Third-degree price discrimination and welfare

Pigou (1932) quickly dismissed first-degree price discrimination as ". . . of academic interest only . . ." (p. 280) and second-degree price discrimination as also unlikely to be practicable and therefore ". . . practical interest centres upon monopoly *plus* discrimination of the third degree" (p. 282). Note that Pigou's definitions hardly touch on the methods of *indirect* price discrimination.

The early focus, in economic theory, was on the welfare effects of third-degree price discrimination and Pigou notes that output under discriminating monopoly may be greater or less than output under simple monopoly and ". . . if the curves of demand and supply are straight lines, the two outputs will be equal." In this case (assuming that price discrimination does not open a new market) there can be no difference in welfare due to a change in output.

An example:

> Suppose a company produces at marginal cost of £500 per unit supplying two separate markets, A and B.

Demand function in market A:	$\mathbf{Q_A = 1200 - 0.08P_A}$
Therefore:	$P_A = (1200 - Q_A)/0.08$
Then revenue	$R_A = [(1200 - Q_A)Q_A]/0.08$
and:	$R_A = (1200Q_A - Q_A^2)/0.08$
Marginal revenue:	$MR_A = (1200 - 2Q_A)/0.08$

Equate marginal revenue and marginal cost $(1200 - 2Q_A)/0.08 = 500$

Solving $Q_A = 580$ units

$P_A = £7,750$

Contribution: $580 \times (£7,750 - £500) = £4,205,000$

Demand function in market B: $\mathbf{Q_B = 3500 - 0.5P_B}$

Therefore $P_B = (3500 - Q_B)/0.5$

Then revenue $R_B = [(3500 - Q_B)Q_B]/0.5$

and: $R_B = (3500Q_B - Q_B^2)/0.5$

Marginal revenue: $MR_B = (3500 - 2Q_B)/0.5$

Equate marginal revenue and marginal cost $(3500 - 2Q_B)/0.5 = 500$

Solving $Q_B = 1,625$ units

$P_B = £3,750$

Contribution : $1,625 \times (£3,750 - £500) = £5,281,250$

Total contribution = £4,205,000 + £5,281,250 = £9,486,250

If, instead, a single price is offered then:

$Q = 1200–0.08P + 3500–0.5P$

$Q = 4700–0.58P$

and therefore $P = (4700 - Q)/0.58$

Then revenue $R = [(4700 - Q)Q]/0.58$

$= (4700Q - Q^2)/0.58$

And, differentiating, marginal revenue $MR = (4700–2Q)/0.58$

Then, setting MR = MC: $(4700–2Q)/0.58 = 500$

And $Q = 2,205$ units

$P = £4,301.7$

If a single price is charged the total quantity is unchanged but:

Contribution = 2205 × (£4301.7 – £500) = £8,382,748

Setting different prices in the two markets makes a significant difference to the contribution generated. If there are fixed costs of, say, £8 million, charging a single price would generate £382,748 profit but this would be increased to £1,486,250 if different prices could be charged in the two markets. Note that the optimal total volume is unchanged whether a single monopoly price is charged or whether separate prices are charged in the two market segments: there can be no loss of welfare due to a change in total volume if the demand curves are straight lines.

The analysis assumed linear demand curves but, of course, demand curves may be convex or concave and, depending on their shape, output after price discrimination may be greater or lower than output based on a single price. The theory of discriminating monopoly was dealt with at length by Joan Robinson (1969, pp. 179–208) considering various combinations of demand functions in the separate markets.

A key point in the analysis of output with and without price discrimination is the assumption that all markets will be served if a single price is charged. In practice this is not always the case and, if price discrimination means that another market is opened then output will increase. Robinson notes that, without the ability to price discriminate, some activities would not take place, perhaps: ". . . a railway would not be built, or a country doctor would not set up in practice . . ." (p. 203). In considering the "morality" of price discrimination Robinson writes:

> From one point of view, therefore, price discrimination must be held to be superior to simple monopoly in all those cases in which it leads to an increase in output, and as we have seen, these cases are likely to be the more common. But against this advantage must be set the fact that price discrimination leads to a maldistribution of resources as between different uses.
>
> (p. 206)

Robinson refers the reader to Pigou for an explanation of this. The essential point is that output is transferred from the more inelastic to the more elastic market and this means that some customers in the inelastic market are deprived of the product (because the price is higher). Meanwhile, customers in the more elastic market can now purchase the product (because it is cheaper). However, this is "unfair" in the sense that the first group are prepared to pay more than the second group. In the numerical example there is a transfer of 393 units from market A to market B and this causes a loss of welfare because customers in market A have been squeezed out even though they would be prepared to pay more than customers in market B.

Schmalansee (1981) adopts a more mathematical approach to third-degree price discrimination and extends Robinson's analysis. He takes welfare to be the sum of consumer and producer surpluses and, by maximising welfare with respect to the number of market segments, shows that there will always be a loss in welfare unless output increases after price discrimination. He concludes that this might suggest that price discrimination should be illegal but immediately adds that discrimination might allow new markets to be opened and a sufficiently large increase in volume might lead to *an increase* in welfare. Varian (1985) continues the analysis and shows that Schmalansee's analysis holds in more general cases while Layson (1988) provides a neat geometrical analysis of the two-market case with linear demand functions. He shows that the increase in profit from discriminating is twice the loss in welfare that arises because of misallocation.

16.5 Ramsey prices

An important application of third-degree price discrimination arises in "natural" monopolies such as railways and water companies with heavy infrastructure and fixed costs that need to be recovered in pricing. At the same time regulators are likely to limit price increases to restrain the possible abuse of monopoly power. The question the regulator faces is how to restrict prices while recognising that heavy infrastructure costs must be covered. Baumol and Bradford (1970) realised that this problem has the same characteristics as raising taxes while minimising economic damage. There is advantage in taxing products with inelastic demand for, if a product has perfectly inelastic demand, then a tax will make no difference to output, see Figure 16.1a.

However, if a product has relatively elastic demand, then a tax will not only increase the price it will cause output to fall; see Figure 16.1b. This probably explains why governments like to tax items such as alcohol, tobacco and fuel where price increases have limited impact on demand. These considerations led Ramsey (1927) to demonstrate that, to raise a certain amount of tax whilst minimising the impact on economic "efficiency" or welfare, taxes should be increased in proportion to the inverse of elasticity.

Baumol and Bradford (1970) note that the Ramsey "inverse elasticity rule" is equally applicable to the case of a regulated monopolist. Theory leads to the "Ramsey pricing formula":

$$(P - MC)/P = -k/\varepsilon \text{ where k is less than 1.}$$

Essentially the formula indicates that that the markup[1] on marginal cost should be related to the inverse of elasticity. The variable k is always less than 1 and this ensures that the prices charged are always less than the prices that a monopolist would charge if unfettered by regulation. If k is set equal to 1 then the formula leads to the prices that a profit maximising discriminating monopolist would charge (the formula becomes identical with the Amoroso-Robinson equation). The value of k is, in principle, determined by the profit or return on investment permitted by the regulator, obviously, the closer k is to 1 the greater the markup and the more profit. Ramsey prices are designed to allow the monopolist to break-even or make a specified return while maximising social welfare subject to the break-even or profit constraint.

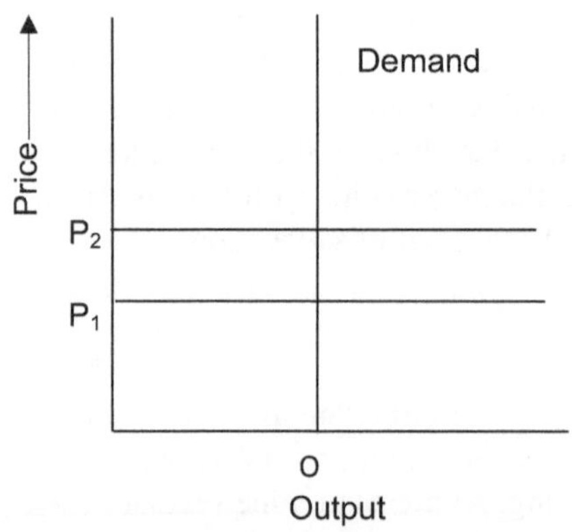

Figure 16.1a Impact of tax on inelastic demand

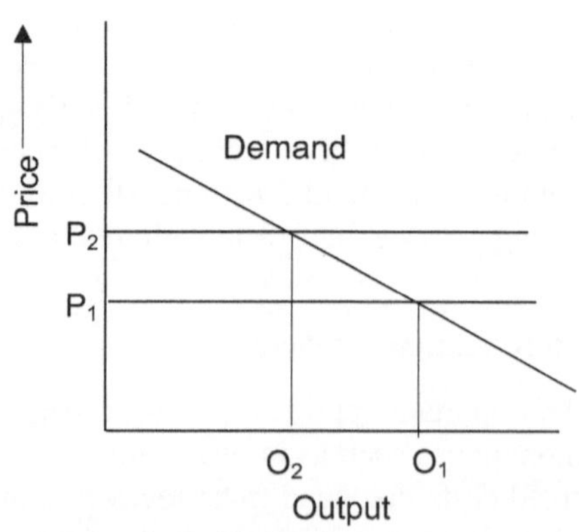

Figure 16.1b Impact of tax on elastic demand

An example

A discriminating monopolist with fixed costs of £100,000 per month identifies two market segments with demand elasticities of -1.5 and -5 at demand per month of 50,000 and 100,000 units, respectively. Variable cost of the product is £2 per unit. The prices for an unregulated monopolist would be $(P - 2)/P = 1/1.5$ and therefore $P = £6$; and $(P - 2)/P = 1/5$ and therefore $P = £2.5$. At these prices contribution would be $(£4 \times 50{,}000) + (£0.5 \times 100{,}000) = £250{,}000$. The monopolist would make an abnormal profit of £150,000 per month.

The mathematical approach to finding Ramsey prices is rather complicated but, observing that, in Ramsey pricing, margins are proportional to the inverse of elasticity, a simple approach can be followed. For two segments we note that:

$$(P_1 - C)/P_1 = k/\varepsilon_1 \text{ and } (P_2 - C)/P_2 = k/\varepsilon_2$$

So, the margins are in proportion to the ratio of their elasticities: $\text{Margin}_1/\text{Margin}_2 = \varepsilon_2/\varepsilon_1$

In this case $\varepsilon_2/\varepsilon_1 = 5/1.5 = 3.33$. The margin for the first segment should be 3.33 times the margin for the second segment.

This observation allows Ramsey prices to be determined by trial and error. In this case setting the margin for the first segment at 41.5% implies that the margin in the second segment should be 41.5%/3.33 = 12.5% and prices can be calculated:

$$(P_1\text{–}2)/P_1 = 0.415 \text{ and } P_1 = £3.42 \qquad (P_2\text{–}2)/P_2 = 0.125 \text{ and } P_2 = £2.29$$

At these prices contribution generated is $£1.42 \times 50{,}000 + £0.29 \times 100{,}000 = £100{,}000$: break-even.

Calculating Ramsey prices is reasonably straightforward if there are good estimates of segmental elasticity and the marginal cost. As we have seen neither is likely to be easy to establish and estimating marginal cost becomes especially difficult if products share resources as in rail transport where passenger and freight traffic share the same track. A similar problem arises in telecommunications where business and domestic users share the same infrastructure.

Shepherd (1992) suggests that Ramsey prices have disadvantages. First, they may be a pretext for raising prices to generate excess profits. Second, "at the very least" there will have to be detailed accounting supervision of the profitability of large and complex organisations. Third, "fairness" and innovation may be just as important as economic efficiency in setting regulated prices. The last point is especially important if Ramsey pricing leads to increased prices for necessities (because they have inelastic demand).

Nevertheless, regulators tend to accept the economic logic of Ramsey prices and, in the UK, a report for the Office of the Rail Regulator noted that the Office of Fair Trading recognised that "it may be more efficient to set higher prices to customers with a higher willingness to pay" (p. 10). Similarly, in the US, the same report noted that the Interstate Commerce Commission accepted the principle of constrained market pricing: "... a proxy for Ramsey pricing as a basis for recovering fixed or common costs" (p. 11) (National Economic Research Associates, 2001). The acceptance of the principle of Ramsey prices by regulators is important because differential pricing across market segments is therefore acceptable and provides some theoretical justification for charging "what the market will bear".

The analysis so far presumes clearly separable market segments, and this implies "third degree" price discrimination where groups can be separated by buyer identity, location or use of the product. For example, a rail company carrying freight can charge different prices for different sorts of freight. The same argument applies to peak and off-peak rail travel, peak users may have no choice but to travel when they do.

16.6 Product differentiation and versioning

Throughout this book the importance of differentiating products has been emphasised. In these cases, the supplier does not offer different prices to different market segments but invites customers to "segment themselves" by their choice of product. In these cases, defining "price discrimination" becomes difficult as it can be argued that travelling business class is a different product from economy class, so price comparisons are meaningless. Economists have typically defined indirect price discrimination as occurring when different prices, not justified by cost differences, are charged for similar products. If we assume that products are "similar" such as, say regular and premium unleaded petrol or flying premium economy versus flying economy there remains the problem of comparing prices and costs. In the literature different authors adopt different approaches to this issue.

Phlips's definition was that "two varieties of a commodity are sold (by the same seller) to two buyers at different *net* prices" (p. 6). This means that there is evidence of price discrimination if $P_A - C_A > P_B - C_B$, or equivalently, $P_A - P_B > C_A - C_B$.

However, Stigler (1966) considered price discrimination to occur if there is a difference in the *ratio* of prices and costs, that is: $P_A/P_B > C_A/C_B$ or $P_A/C_A > P_B/C_B$. Stigler considered this the better definition because it "has the merit of separating a monopolists' behaviour into two parts: (1) the simple restriction of output such that price is greater than marginal cost; and (2) the misallocation of given goods between buyers, which is zero if prices are proportional to marginal costs" (p. 209).

Definitional niceties aside, the choice of price/cost *differences* or price/cost *ratios* has consequences because they can lead to different conclusions about the existence of price discrimination. Most authorities do not seem to concern themselves but, exceptionally, Clerides (2004) considered the issues in some detail. Clerides refers to the two methods as the "margin" (absolute difference) method and the "markup" (percentage differences) method. There is obviously scope for semantic confusion (as usual in discussing price discrimination) and we will stick to the *difference* method and the *ratio* method. Clerides goes to some lengths to show that the two definitions can lead to different outcomes and a simple example will demonstrate this. Suppose that a softback book sells at a price of £10 to the retail market while a hardback version sells at a price of £15. The marginal cost of the softback is £5 and of the hardback is £8. The difference method indicates price discrimination because the price difference of £5 exceeds the cost difference of £3. However, the ratio method yields 2:1 for the softback and 1.875:1 for the hardback. At first sight, also price discrimination *but* now the discrimination is in the other direction, the hardback is "cheaper" on the ratio basis.

Table 16.1 compares the ratio and difference methods. The second case is the one referred to above where the methods both reveal price discrimination *but in opposite directions*. The ratio method implies that the lower priced segment, segment 2, is favoured with a lower margin. However, this would be a strange conclusion in the hardback versus softback example. Common sense suggests that, in this case, it is the buyer of the hardback who is discriminated *against* and it is the difference method that leads to this conclusion.

Unfortunately, there are cases where common sense suggests that the ratio method is superior. If one unit, cost £5, is sold for £10 and two units together are sold for £16 the difference method suggests that there is discrimination *against* the group paying £16 (difference of £6 versus difference of £5 for the group purchasing a single item). This is obviously nonsense and the ratio method, comparing ratios of 2 (first group) and 1.6 (second group), provides the expected answer: discrimination against the group purchasing a single item.

Clerides discusses different cases and suggests that the "correct" method, ratio or difference can be determined by an arbitrage test. The volume discount example does not survive the arbitrage test because the larger pack can be easily broken down and sold as individual items. The book example does survive the test because hard and paperback versions cannot be readily converted. He concludes that the difference method is appropriate when product differences are based on essentially fixed costs and the ratio method is appropriate when essentially based on variable costs. Difficulties arise when differences are based on a combination of both fixed and variable costs.

Pragmatically, Clerides suggests that both methods should be used where possible. If both ratio and difference methods indicate price discrimination in the same direction the researcher can be confident of the conclusion. In the case where the ratio of price/cost in the more expensive market is greater than the ratio in the cheaper

Table 16.1 Comparison of tests for price discrimination

Ratio method	*Difference method*	*Comment*
$P_1/C_1 > P_2/C_2$	$P_1 - C_1 > P_2 - C_2$	Both methods indicate price discrimination. If the ratio method shows price discrimination, then so will the difference method.
$P_1/C_1 < P_2/C_2$	$P_1 - C_1 > P_2 - C_2$	Both methods show price discrimination but in opposite directions.

Note: segment 1 has the higher price, the cost in segment 1 is higher than in segment 2.

market, the ratio test is more powerful: the difference method will also indicate price discrimination. If the two methods indicate price discrimination but in opposite directions, the researcher needs to make the reader aware of this and should not, of course, choose the method that indicates the preferred or expected result.

16.7 Conclusions

This chapter has provided the briefest introduction to the economics of price discrimination. The focus of theory for a long time was on the effects of price discrimination on welfare and output with Schmalansee drawing previous results together and providing a mathematical analysis that provided the foundation for further refinements. Ramsey prices are an important theoretical application of third-degree price discrimination that have guided regulators in determining prices in industries that have not been permitted full exploitation of their monopoly power. Finally, we considered the difficult issues that arise in determining whether indirect price discrimination exists. From a management accounting standpoint this issue is of little importance, but it matters when enforcing anti-discrimination legislation, an important issue in some jurisdictions.

Indirect price discrimination has received increasing attention since the late twentieth century and we have seen how quantity, product and time discrimination can be employed to divide customers into pricing groups. These topics have received extensive analysis in the economics literature and some of the key academic contributions have been referenced in the relevant chapters. For a comprehensive treatment of quantity discounting, the reader should consult Wilson's (1993) *Non-Linear Pricing* and for comprehensive analysis of yield management and dynamic pricing Phillips's (2005) *Pricing and Revenue Optimization* provides examples, historical context and theoretical analysis.

Note

1 An accountant will note that the Ramsey formula relates to margin (the markup as percentage of price).

References

Baumol W. J. and Bradford D. F. (1970) Optimal departures from marginal cost pricing, *American Economic Review*, 60(3), 265–283

Clerides S. K. (2004) Price discrimination with differentiated products: definition and identification, *Economic Enquiry*, 42(3), 402–412

Kaplan R. S. and Atkinson A. A. (1998) *Advanced Management Accounting*, Prentice Hall International, Upper Saddle River, NJ

Layson S. (1988) Third-degree price discrimination, welfare and profits: a geometrical analysis, *American Economic Review*, 78(5), 1131–1132

National Economic Research Associates (2001) *Regulatory Approaches to Cost Allocation*, Report for ORR, prepared by NERA, London. downloaded 24/11/2021 from: www.orr.gov.uk/sites/default/files/om/nera_costalloc.pdf

Phillips R. L. (2005) *Pricing and Revenue Optimization*, Stanford University Press, Stanford, CA

Phlips L. (1983) *The Economics of Price Discrimination*, Cambridge University Press, Cambridge

Pigou A. C. (1932) *The Economics of Welfare*, 4th edition, Macmillan and Co., London

Ramsey F. P. (1927) A contribution to the theory of taxation, *The Economic Journal*, 37(145), 47–61

Robinson J. (1969) *The Economics of Imperfect Competition*, 2nd edition, MacMillan Press Ltd., London and Basingstoke

Schmalansee R. L. (1981) Output and welfare implications of monopolistic third-degree price discrimination, *The American Economic Review*, 71, 242–247

Shepherd W. G. (1992) Ramsey pricing: its uses and limits, *Utilities Policy*, Oct, 296–298

Stigler G. J. (1966) *The Theory of Price*, 3rd edition, Macmillan, New York

Varian H. R. (1985) Price discrimination and social welfare, *The American Economic Review*, 75(4), 870–875

Wilson R. B. (1993) *Nonlinear Pricing*, Oxford University Press, Oxford

17 Conclusions

17.1 Introduction

We began by discussing the limitations of traditional economic and management accounting treatments of pricing. Developments in the theory and practice of pricing have made old debates about the prevalence of marginal or cost-plus pricing methods less relevant. Consumer markets are now dominated by examples of segmented pricing that simply cannot be cost-plus based and, in B2B industries, the extensive advocacy of value-based pricing has surely meant less slavish use of cost-plus methods.

If there is less reliance on cost-plus methods, we can also say that there is little, if any, explicit reliance on economic marginalism. In consumer goods markets behavioural economics has unearthed a long list of customer biases that can be exploited, and price-setting is as much art as science. In B2B markets pricing is likely to be much more in line with traditional economic theory. However, practical advice focuses on the use of break-even analysis; setting minimum and maximum prices based on variable costs and economic value to customer; understanding customer requirements and competitive offerings; preparing for price negotiations with a "menu" of service levels; and setting price policies that avoid unforeseen discounts and revenue leakages. While these suggestions inform better pricing, none formally aim to maximise profits. They do, however, point to the potential contribution that management accountants can make in pricing decisions. The following sections summarise key management accounting applications to pricing.

17.2 Financial break-even analysis

Recognising the difficulties in estimating demand curves pricing authorities suggest relatively simple break-even analyses to estimate the impact of price changes: marketing professionals can assess the likelihood of achieving break-even volume more easily than they can estimate or apply demand elasticity. Break-even calculations can be readily extended to deal with changes in variable costs, sales in multiple markets and the impact of substitutes and complements. Management accountants have an important role to play in guiding sales and

DOI: 10.4324/9781003272731-17

marketing executives through these calculations, and, in determining the relevant contribution: the variable cost needs to take account of timescale and activity-based costing might be employed to estimate batch, channel and customer-related costs relevant to specific decisions.

17.3 Economic value to customer

The importance of customer value is a recurring theme in the pricing literature and there is a clear and obvious role for management accountants when economic value to the customer is estimated in B2B transactions. The quantitative aspects of customer value should be based on the *customer's* incremental cash flows and, if there are long term implications, present value of relevant cash flows *from the customer's point of view* needs to be calculated. A key element in such calculations is the discount rate which should reflect the riskiness of the cash flows (not the cost of capital of the customer). The management accountant should also be involved in communicating the value proposition to the customer and in providing cost data associated with different levels of service offered.

17.4 Product positioning and price-value maps

Understanding "customer value" is a vital step in the whole process of product development and marketing and product features must not be equated with customer benefits: not every customer benefits from a 5G enabled iPhone with an A14 smartphone chip, lowlight photography and a "ceramic shield". For consumer goods there are various techniques to estimate product value such as conjoint and discrete choice analysis although simpler methods can also be informative. A price-value map is especially important if a new product is launched because it helps in predicting competitor reaction. A new product that sits more-or-less on the value equivalence line causes much less disruption than one that is "value advantaged". Such a product can stimulate price cutting by competitors to the detriment of all.

17.5 Volume-related discounting

Larger sizes and quantities are likely to cost less per unit and this, together with stimulation of increased sales, accounts for the prevalence of volume-discounting in both B2B and consumer markets. In theory the customer should be offered a discount for each incremental unit purchased, reflecting the value the customer places on each successive unit. In practice this can be approximated by discounts on incremental units in a series of steps. However, total quantity discounts are often used in both B2B and consumer markets either because of the power of the customer or the simplicity of communicating an offer such as "£6 off when you spend more than £60". Management accountants should be wary of total quantity discounts because of their impact on margins and the potential for customers to game discounts to their advantage. Two-part pricing can be important in some industries and the management accountant can analyse the consequences of different levels of the "entry fee" and unit prices.

17.6 International pricing

International pricing may run into the problem of grey markets where goods are purchased in a low-price territory and resold in a high-price territory. Management accountants can track exchange rates and international prices to identify the "pricing corridor" where the impact of grey markets is minimised. In considering changes in price needed to stay within the corridor the break-even volume should take account of transfer of sales from a low-priced territory where price is increased to higher priced territories (because grey markets become less attractive). If exchange rate movements permit the price to be reduced, then salespeople and management accountants should assess the product's new location on the value map. If the product becomes value-advantaged there may be a risk of competitor retaliation and a price war.

17.7 Product substitutes and complements

The Niehens formula shows how, in principle, the monopoly price for a single product should be adjusted when the supplier also supplies substitutes or complements. The price is reduced if there are complements because increased sales also lead to increases in sales of the complements. On the other hand, the price is increased if there are substitutes. If break-even volumes are estimated, allowance should be made for the presence of substitutes or complements by adjusting the contribution margin of the target product. Following a price reduction contribution margin is increased for complementary products and decreased for substitute products.

17.8 Customer and transaction profitability

The development of activity-based costing has given management accountants the tools to analyse batch, order, channel and customer-related costs in detail and so identify customer profitability. The pocket-price waterfall provides the opportunity to extend this analysis by identifying revenue leakages due to order/volume/competitive discounts, co-operative advertising etc. Identification of the "pocket-price band" or "pocket margin band" to show the range of customer prices and margins can be enlightening, even shocking. Management accountants have an opportunity to demonstrate their value with innovative analysis and reporting. If the pocket-price band can be managed to generate just 1% average price increase, the impact on percentage net margin can be dramatic.

17.9 Customer negotiations

There are different types of customers that require different negotiating approaches and once again, the importance of identifying different levels of product and service is emphasised. If the customer negotiates hard on price, then a reduced service must be offered to make sure that the customer does not receive something for nothing. Conversely, the availability of service options might enable a deal to be closed by offering a relatively inexpensive "sweetener" that is valuable to the customer. Management accountants can contribute to the development of a range of service levels by identifying the costs involved in offering "sweeteners" to close the deal or savings made if service levels are reduced to combat customer pressure for a price reduction.

17.10 Pricing policies and sales incentives

Clear pricing policies and "rules of engagement" with customers are recommended. Management accountants can work with marketing and HR in developing incentive schemes that promote sales behaviour in line with company strategy. "Sales credit" for sales can be linked to contribution rather than sales generated by setting a target price for the product. Flexibility is needed and for a premium, high-priced product the target price might be set below list price. In this case some discounting might be encouraged if it secures the sale of a premium product or service.

17.11 Competition

If costs provide a lower limit for the price and value-to-the-customer a higher limit, it is consideration of competitor strategies and prices that pin down the viable price range. Management accountants can have a key role in analysing the financial statements of key competitors and analysing their pricing strategies. Monitoring competitors and establishing normal industry practice is very important. Price wars are to be avoided and the aim should be to "manage" industry prices. Established companies know their key competitors and there are likely to be well-established traditions in the industry including price-leadership and price-followership. This raises the spectre of possible collusion, and this must be avoided. In many countries there is personal risk to executives if collusion is proved. US law is particularly complex and specialist advice should be taken when doing business in the US if there is any chance that activity might be construed as discriminatory.

17.12 The value-driven company

Although there are obstacles to the implementation of value-based pricing there are companies that have followed this route. SKF, a bearings manufacturer, has demonstrated the extensive use of value analysis to show the value of their products in B2B sales. Ford has made "variable profit" by product available to its sales force. If a company moves to a value-based pricing philosophy, there should be a key role for management accountants as they support economic value to the customer calculations, help in devising product ranges and service options, provide expertise in break-even analysis and discount structures and provide key profitability information to marketing executives and the sales force.

17.13 Final thoughts

Management accountants have long had an important role in supporting production operations and this book is intended to demonstrate that they can be just as important in partnering with marketing and pricing executives to deliver marketing strategies. In new product development they should be part of the multifunctional team evaluating the options for adding value to the customer. In positioning a new product, they can have a role to play in the construction of value maps, evaluating and communicating value to customer and aligning sales incentives with customer strategy. For existing products and customers analysis of price versus quantity taken, pocket-price waterfalls and the pocket-price margin bands can be illuminating if not shocking. Evaluation of volume discounting strategies, target markets, the profitability of product ranges and, in some industries, time-based dynamic pricing may be important as might evaluation of sales incentives.

If the book is primarily intended to help management accountants employ their analytical skills in support of marketing and pricing it should also have a role in alerting marketing and pricing executives to the role that management accountants can play in delivering price and marketing strategy. It is also hoped that the book will serve as an introduction for academics and students interested in price theory, indicating some of the key academic sources and integrating traditional and behavioural economics with recent advances in pricing theory.

Finally, to requote Thomas Nagle:

> One of the missing skills is management accounting, which is usually different from the arbitrary "cost accounting" that companies use to value inventories for tax purpose. People in pricing should be able to do at least rough calculations of costs and how they interact. This is an essential skill to know what trade offs you are making and how they will effect profitability. When costs all get dumped into overhead one cannot see the real consequences of price changes.
>
> (Forth, 2018)

Management accountants can supply the "missing skills" to which Thomas Nagle refers if they become business partners with their colleagues in marketing, pricing and product development. Perhaps this book will help to achieve this.

Reference

Forth S. (2018) *Value-Based Pricing's Senior Statesman Tom Nagle on the Skills Needed for Pricing Expertise*, April 23, 2018, downloaded 29/12/2019 from: www.ibbaka.com/blog/2018/4/15/value-based-pricings-senior-statesman-tom-nagle-on-the-skills-needed-for-pricing-expertise

Index